Eve's *Revenge*

Women
and a
Spirituality
of the
Body

Lilian Calles Barger

Brazos Press

A Division of Baker Book House Co
Grand Rapids, Michigan 49516

Copyright © 2003 by Lilian Calles Barger

Published by Brazos Press
A division of Baker Book House Company
P.O. Box 6287, Grand Rapids, MI 49516–6287
www.brazospress.com

Printed in the United States of America

Library of Congress Cataloging-in-Publication Data

Barger, Lilian Calles, 1955-
    Eve's revenge : women and a spirituality of the body / Lilian Calles Barger.
        p.   cm.
    Includes bibilographical references (p.) and index.
    ISBN 1-58743-040-1 (pbk.)
        1. Women—Religious aspects—Christianity. 2. Body, Human—Religious aspects—
Christianity. 3. Christian women—Religious life. I. Title.

    BT704.B37 2003
    233'.5—dc21   2002034539

Scripture marked NIV is taken from the HOLY BIBLE, NEW INTERNATIONAL VERSION®. NIV®. Copyright © 1973, 1978, 1984 by International Bible Society. Used by permission of Zondervan Publishing House. All rights reserved.

Scripture marked NKJV is taken from the New King James Version. Copyright © 1979, 1980, 1982 by Thomas Nelson, Inc. Used by permission. All rights reserved.

Scripture marked NJB is taken from THE NEW JERUSALEM BIBLE, copyright © 1985 by Darton, Longman & Todd, Ltd. and Doubleday, a division of Bantam Doubleday Dell Publishing Group, Inc. Reprinted by permission.

Eve's *Revenge*

Contents

Acknowledgments   7
Preface   8

1. A Blank Canvas?   11
   Why Our Bodies Get in the Way of Our Search for a "True" Self
2. The Body Is My Altar   33
   How Women Are Trained to Serve the False Idols of Beauty
3. Body Bound   55
   The Inescapability of the Body and the Elusiveness of
   Transcendence
4. Es Una Nena!   81
   How the Current Spirituality Capitalizes on Our Sense of
   Powerlessness
5. Jars of Clay   105
   The Vulnerability of the Body and Its Ultimate Betrayal
6. Daughters of Eve   127
   Our Creation and the Origins of Our Shame
7. The Not-Always-Virgin Mary   143
   Our Bodies as Places of Redemption
8. Made Flesh   163
   How Jesus Takes Our Shame and Renews Our Imagination
9. A Holy Kiss   179
   Creating a Place for the Body

Epilogue   193
Notes   199
Bibliography   209
Index   217

Acknowledgments

Thank you to my extended family, and the women and men of the Damaris Project, including my book agent, Leslie Nunn Reed, for being one of the first to believe in this book, research assistant Joy McCalla for her readiness to think through ideas with me and find the appropriate texts, and first reader Marlee LeDai for her clarifying suggestions and immense support. I am grateful for my editor Rodney Clapp at Brazos Press for his wise and engaged editing and for giving me the opportunity to write this book. All are a continual reminder that none of us are self-made people.

Preface

This is a book about the body, and in particular the concrete and social experiences of woman in and through that body. As such, you might expect it to be a book full of instructions on how to love your body and tips for resisting the unrealistic media images that bombard women every day. It almost seems that this topic demands a self-help approach. Whether your problem is bad skin or bad body image, there are thousands of books that have been written to provide help.

But women don't need another book to help them overcome their perceived shortcomings. This is not a self-help book, and I hope the reader will find that refreshing. I also will not provide a pat prescription for being a woman. I assume that the female reader is already a woman and does not need help from me in continuing to be a woman.

What I am seeking to do is to provide an increased understanding of how our relationship with the body and its social meaning touches upon spirituality, another area of our lives that has gotten widespread attention of late. I address women even though I certainly hope that thoughtful men will read the book; it just might shed light on the body and spirituality for them also. But it is women who have a vested interest in the subject of living in and through a female body. My purpose is not to prescribe an antidote but to contribute to a changed paradigm.

When we begin to look at the body and its associated meanings, it is like looking through a kaleidoscope, getting glimpses of the whole range of human experiences. There are multiple layers both within us and in the social context in which we live. Therefore this is not an exhaustive book about the body, if one could ever be written. I don't cover extensively many areas that are extremely important such as the ethical issues raised by biotechnology, including infertility and life extension treatments. Those who have devoted their lives to these ethical projects are better prepared to take them up. I don't offer a list of dos and don'ts, so you may find yourself frustrated at times if you are seeking concrete answers to specific issues of struggle. I am attempting to get beyond the usual gender split on this issue: women's exploring the pain of being in their bodies through the many books and articles about why they feel fat or hate to look in the mirror; men's seemingly disconnected and often abstracted approach to the body as an instrument of achievement or merely a biological machine in need of repair. Neither provides a desperately needed holistic and integral understanding of how we are to live in our bodies. What I am attempting to do is recover the body from its continually diminishing position in our understanding of the nature of the self, spirituality, and the building of communities.

Of course, my viewpoint is limited, like anyone's, by matters of class, gender, ethnicity, and generation. I can write only from my particular experience. I have chosen those particular bodily experiences and socially derived meanings that from my observation have had the most impact on women in my culture. These experiences affect not only how we understand ourselves but also how we view God and seek meaningful spirituality. I hope to examine some of the ways the world around us has assigned meaning to the body within a multiplicity of cultural exchanges and to provide a new paradigm for thinking about our bodies on a daily basis.

Ultimately, this book is about spirituality, which for many may seem out of place within a consideration of the body. This is precisely why I have written. The splitting of bodily and spiritual issues onto opposite sides of a wide and uncrossable chasm is part of our spiritual problem, though there has been some movement in the culture to address this. To begin to offer one possible set of answers, I will look at the spiritual teachings of Jesus of Nazareth and how his work undergirds the life that we live in the body. But in order to do that we will go the long way around. First, it is necessary that we understand some of the historical and contemporary experiences of women in regard to their bodies. Second, it is necessary to examine how these experiences affect the spiritual outlook we take and the problems they have caused. Last, we'll look at possibilities of seeing ourselves as something other than perennially split between our bodies and souls. What I hope to provide the reader through this process is a clearer understanding of the struggle we experience with the body and a means to begin viewing the entire body-self in a less fractured way. It will require that we face our fundamental disintegrity in relationship to our Creator and ourselves.

The split between our bodies and ourselves can be healed. I believe the paradigm offered through the life and work of Jesus will provide us with deep insight not only into how we ought to live in the world but also, most important, into how to live in our own skin with coherence and meaning.

1

A Blank Canvas?

Why Our Bodies Get in the Way of Our Search for a "True" Self

Women are not in control of their bodies; nature is.

Camille Paglia[1]

I hadn't seen my friend since the spectacular party she had thrown for herself, a milestone birthday. We'd traded so many messages that I was wondering if she was really interested in seeing me at all. I'd picked up vague clues about elective surgery, unexpected absences from work, traces of depression. Of course, we both had tight schedules—very busy in our prime productive years, reaping the rewards of well-executed lives. Always mindful of the passing of our youth, we knew we had to "get it" while we could. But finally we were having breakfast, cups of cappuccino and warm scones. I had wondered what I would encounter, but my friend looked great. In fact, she looked better than ever. I put together the clues and knew I had it right. My friend was parading a new face—those little slits at the ears were still fresh; her hair didn't really hide them.

Did she have to do this? I wondered. It was sad. In fact, it was infuriating. It made me ask myself whether I was ready to die a martyr on the altar of "ugly," wrinkles and all. I felt a sense of shame, but I was not sure whether it was for her or for me.

There were two conversations that afternoon: one about all the exciting things going on in our lives, the other about self-doubt and doubt about each other. Here we were, both of us successful. We had dared to do things our mothers would never have done. We had seized opportunities. We had conquered our worlds. But under the warm glow of career success, I felt betrayed. I'd been left to deal with the visibility of old age and its implications all by myself.

Never mentioning the facelift and practicing a don't-ask-don't-tell policy, my friend was not going with me. She'd found a way to outsmart aging and escape the implications of finding herself unattractive. Her redone face implied that we were not going to gracefully grow old together but would fight it every step of the way in a race against each other. It reminded me of earlier girlhood competitions over who "started" first and whose mother was the first to let her wear a training bra. I'd thought she and I were beyond that. Hadn't we become adult women with a secure sense of identity? Now it was clear, the reality was different: I felt like a schoolgirl eager to be part of the cult of womanhood, and my girlfriend was showing me a new rite of passage.

The uneasiness between my friend and me increased as the morning wore on. I began to imagine a conversation that never happened in which she wouldn't even have to mention men. She would explain how she had to do the face thing for her career. Clients expected her to look as if she was on top of the world, otherwise they wouldn't trust her. She had to show them she still had that youthful edge.

In actuality, we spent a lot of time talking about spiritual things. Really. We talked about God and where we were in our search for a meaningful life. In rediscovering the spiritual search, we discovered we were both learning new things, exploring interior territories, and finding significance in our everyday life. We wanted spirituality to provide us with a sense of purpose and a sure sense of who we were. We wanted more than what material and career success could provide. That was not enough, and we knew it.

Neither my friend nor I wanted to be hollow people, vain and superficial. We took pride in being smart and savvy, not airheads. In the prime of life we were both finding new depths to our spiritual roots, and we longed for more.

What stayed with me, however, was an awareness that this didn't seem to make any difference in what apparently mattered—what we saw everyday when we looked in the mirror. Although we had everything going for us, our bodies were showing signs of wear. In the end I couldn't fault my friend. She just wanted her outside to look the way she hoped to feel inside. I wanted to know why it mattered so much.

Even though we had been engaged in a conversation about spirituality, our dysfunctional relationships with our bodies, as evidenced by her facelift and my emotional response, were not addressed. Our bodies and our souls were not even in the same room. For us, the pursuit of physical beauty was thoroughly disconnected from any notion that the role of beauty may be to point us to God. Our bodies had nothing to say in a spiritual conversation disconnected from our embodiment.

Since this encounter it has become clear to me that women's bodies and their hunger for meaning are on a collision course. In the mist of career success we are still looking for an authentic self. There is no denying it, women are in a body-spirit tension; split to our wits' end. How did we get to this place of uneasiness about our embodiment and its coexistence with an authentic spiritual life? Set up by a cultural history that I will explore in chapter three, we find that our bodies get in the way of transcendence. We find ourselves torn between improving our wardrobes, faces, and figures and looking inward. Designer clothes and eyelifts hide our sense of inadequacy. But getting beyond surface issues requires that we be willing to face our own failures, our aging, and our feelings of lack.

We are on an adventure looking for signs of transcendent life—a place to anchor the soul—and we simply can't say that our bodies don't matter. They matter more than we wish to admit. As Elizabeth Wurtzel says in *Bitch*, "Because I don't like the idea that I'll be getting older and lesser . . . I want to jump out of my skin with my desire for MORE MORE MORE."[2] This need for more in the face of less, this unshakable desire, puts us in a bind. Do we simply forget about our bodies and let ourselves go, accepting the cellulite and sagging breasts, or do we try to mold and control them? We want to move beyond the limi-

tations that the body imposes, but we find ourselves material girls forever riveted by the mirror. Our desire to meet the cultural expectations
of both appearance and career success traps us in a never-ending pursuit to measure up. This increases our sense of having fallen short. We
live with a profound sense of inadequacy. Who are we? What are we
expected to be?

A Long Way, Baby?

Amazingly, this obsession about the state of our bodies is happening at a time when, in the developed world, women are enjoying
unprecedented levels of personal and social freedom. In order to understand how this relates to our spiritual search, we need to take a brief
survey of our social history. Today, not having reached economic and
political parity in the public sphere, we nevertheless are obtaining
increased influence. Politicians can no longer ignore women and their
power. Marketers understand that an "Evolution" is taking place; we're
being catered to by women-only web sites, political networks such as
Emily's List, and our own brand of cereal.[3] When it comes to how the
female body is to be defined and used, there is money to be made, there
are lives to control. The stakes are high. Medical doctors, advertisers,
pornographers, politicians, feminist theorists, and theologians all have
vested interest in how our bodies are viewed and experienced. Advertising slogans encourage us to reach out and touch somebody. Fashion magazines offer tests to see if we are 110 percent desirable, and on
the next page they tell us to love our bodies as they are. Reading our
dissatisfaction, self-help experts coax us to pay for conferences and
books that will tell us why we hate our bodies and what we have
become as women.

Feeding on our desire for an authentic self, public lessons in bodily dissatisfaction are reinforced throughout our lives. One day in my
late teens I was accosted by an overeager cosmetic salesperson whose
mission that day was to "redo" me. Yes, she was right: my nose was
too prominent, and my thin lips needed some definition. Those under-
the-eye circles had to go; they made me look tired. She persuaded me

that to miss what she offered was to miss the essence of femininity. Overwhelmed by her insistence, I complied but left feeling worse about myself. I felt more inadequate than when I had entered the store, and I now had more products than I could afford, was broke, and felt used. Maybe, like every girl, I just wanted to look my best. But the salesperson's attitude was to make certain that with layers of expensive cosmetics, I looked like everybody else.

Another time, around a table set with individual lighted mirrors, a group of my teen friends and I obediently heeded instructions of a cosmetics consultant: "Don't pull! Use upward strokes, ladies." My cousin was picked to be the model—she kind of looked like one—and was turned into an unrecognizable femme fatále, a much less interesting version of herself.

These two events have kept me away from cosmetic counters and parties for the rest of my life. What can be a self-expressive art form has become a means to shame and control us. I now respond to such hijacking of an old art form by buying the cheap stuff at the grocery store. I've learned to be firm about declining anything that celebrates a woman's insecurities.

Since those days the beauty cult has grown into a $25-billion-a-year cosmetic market. It is ready and willing to feed women's insecurity and help us find our "true" selves.[4]

The beauty cult assumes that the body stands in the way of self-actualization and offers means to manipulate it and control its intrusion. In providing prescriptions for our disconnected selves, the beauty cult understands our spiritual need to be who we "really" are and preys on that need.

I currently live in Dallas, which has more retail space per capita than any other city in America. Here women would rather be found dead than be seen without their makeup. Wearing makeup is a duty in Dallas! Mothers teach daughters to cover up personal failures and sooth their feelings with a new lip color. This is done in the name of self-improvement, of course, making a woman's shame strictly *her* problem. New York's Madison Avenue, where beauty is served up at cosmetics counters like a religious ritual, makes perpetual youth mandatory.

It provides hope, packaged in pretty boxes and bottles, constantly confronting us with the cultural ideal.

The current obsession with beauty is part of the body's long history as an instrument of culture. The body has served as a canvas for the art of personal adornment and—from the Sistine Chapel to Calvin Klein ads—is a symbol of what is human. Loaded with nuances of meaning, images of the body are a favorite of artists and the mass media because that meaning can be changed, altered, and controlled. Movies such as *Boys Don't Cry* and *The Crying Game* dared to shock us by challenging our ideas about gender and its performance. As we see a female living out the masculine, or vice versa, gender becomes fluid. The suggestion that definitions written on the body from birth are not static reinforces our desire for an unconstrained self. From the emanuel ungaro fashion spread with its signs of domestic violence under layers of chiffon, to Nike ads portraying an active athletic woman, the body is a site of both oppression and empowerment all in one fashion season. It is increasingly seen as a theater piece to be cut, molded, fashioned, and adapted both literally and symbolically.

By seizing control of the body and manipulating its meaning, a woman can become virgin, vamp, mother, or whore according to culture's trends or demands. The Madonna and Child, a powerful image of our role as life giver and sustainer, is foundational for many, encompassing all of what we think worthy to be called human. To others, this same symbol is the weapon of subordination keeping women in a plush golden cage. Such cultural symbols are part of a larger social ethic that defines woman's place in the world. Black women, in whom issues of race and gender collide, have been subject to an additional layer of controlling images—mammies, hot mommas, hoochies—further objectifying them in marginalizing positions.[5]

Why don't men live under cultural images that have such a strong bodily association? There is no corresponding male virgin or whore with potent social meanings. The image of the warrior places men in the world on different terms. It makes men full agents, changing and adapting the world beyond their bodies. Due to woman's close association with both the body and sexual desire, even things that have nothing to do with sex are sold through use of the form of a seductive

woman. Woman embodies desire. Sunglasses, auto batteries, legal services, and motorcycles are sold by paralleling the desire to consume a
product with the desire to consume the woman. Through metaphor
woman has become an object of consumption forever imprisoned in
her sex, while the physical-based roles of women always threaten to
reduce her to her body.

Regardless of their inadequacy, cultural metaphors like the Madonna
and Child do provide an important function by helping us express the
distinctive relationships between our bodies and the world. As personal
experience changes, however, we must change the definition and content of the many ways women are women. In motherhood, for example, our bodies connect us to the next generation as we conceive, carry
another in our womb, give birth, and nurture an infant at our breast.
But in the twentieth century the concept of mother as always nurturing and sacrificial became for many a suffocating one-dimensional icon,
so we've renegotiated it for the twenty-first century. Still, we can't
absolutely escape the content of the metaphor, because it provides something that we need—the naming of our embodied experiences and the
reality of what we must sacrifice for the needs of our child. Many
women, unable to come to terms with the inherited icons, have forgone
motherhood altogether; the tension between its power as metaphor and
the reality is simply too great. In another twist, pop star Madonna Louise
Veronica Ciccone, popularly known as Madonna, successfully rein-
vented the meaning and content of the virgin through her music video.
Changing what was considered universally a sacred symbol of chastity
into a symbol of seduction, she made the new icon the aspiration of
many young women. But the change replaced one form of bodily containment for women with another.

The female ideal varies, and of course, so does the way women
respond to it. There are Southern belles who have hardly ventured outside the Old South either literally or figuratively. They still wear flow-
ered dresses picked by their husbands and pride themselves on never
having pumped gas. They safeguard their passivity as a virtue. Then
there are young professionals in large cities with upscale careers who
live in a constant state of angst. Warned by physicians that their eggs
are aging, they want to bear children but wonder whether marriage

and motherhood will be their undoing. The Southern belle has absorbed the messages that a certain culture has dictated. The independent city girl cannot escape the limitations of her femaleness.

We all live within a narrow social experience of some kind. We have no control over where we are born and little control over what happens to us along the way; we simply fulfill the cultural scripts, no questions asked. Short of a life-jarring event, most of us never question that script or learn to engage in an actively thoughtful process of living in a way that transcends our cultural experience, whether of the traditional or of the "new" woman.

The Media Ideal

The meanings of our bodily acts and cultural experiences do connect us to the community and ultimately, because we know that we are more than bodies, bring out our hunger for God. But our desire for meaningful life and an authentic self is continually being molded by our environment, which often defines our boundaries and limits our possibilities.

The success women have had in redefining our place in the world has not been enough. Even as we've become more interested in spirituality than we had been in a long time, we currently find ourselves returning to the body for meaning because culture promises that the body is a compelling place to find it. While we've been busy reinventing ourselves, American women of all ages are still being primed by a cultural insistence on a narrowly defined ideal delivered by the mass media: tan, trim, full breasted, with a face to launch a thousand ships. Surrounded by images of airbrushed beauty, as a target market we spend more money, time, and personal anguish every year in the quest to measure up to unattainable standards. We're taught that our duty as women is to show we care about our looks and to demonstrate this virtue by pursuing physical beauty.

The diet industry alone has grown to a $40-billion-a-year business.[6] As media critic Jean Kilbourne has pointed out, overcoming food temptation has replaced sexual chastity as *the* symbol of female virtue. We've been told, "You can never be too rich or too thin,"[7] and some of us are out to prove it—literally. When was the last time you heard a woman talk about dieting for health reasons rather than looks? As a way to use the language of the body, excessive dieting seems to prove a woman's ability to control an otherwise uncontrollable life and to attain social legitimacy.

Besides sex, nothing is more prominent in popular women's magazines, and these contain ten times more diet-promoting articles and advertisements than comparable men's magazines.[8] In addition to the sheer quantity of material, one out of every 3.8 advertisements sends some sort of message encouraging women to acquire a body that is "barely there."[9] The entertainment industry, saturated with gaunt actresses who fear a size 2 dress, considers Jennifer Lopez, secretive about her size, a "big girl."[10] In Atlantic City, the average Miss America contestant works out fourteen hours per week, and some up to thirty-five hours (yes, you read that right!).[11] American beauty, it seems, is a full-time job. Although mothers may be anxious about daughters' chances for upward mobility if they are overweight, the truth is that the average woman is five feet four inches tall and weighs one hundred forty pounds—certainly not obese, yet 50 percent of us pursue a diet on any given day.[12]

Continual exposure to the media ideal skews reality for all of us. Its effect on the average young woman is a body dissatisfaction rate higher than 60 percent in high school and 80 percent in college. The obsession with weight starts early, with 42 percent of girls in first to third grades expressing a desire to be thinner.[13] According to published research, 15 percent of women would sacrifice more than five years of their life to obtain the weight they desire.[14] There are at least eight million sufferers of life-threatening anorexia nervosa (reported in girls as young as eight years old), bulimia, and other associated eating disorders in America; 90 percent of these are women.[15]

In addition to dieting, more American women are resorting to surgically reinventing their bodies. Medical doctors prey on our insecurities, offering costly surgery to obtain or retain "beauty." I noticed no fewer than forty-five ads in one magazine for cosmetic surgery or some other body-enhancing procedure. Cover stories ask the prevailing question: "Should you have plastic surgery?" With the baby-boom generation now in midlife, the answer is increasingly yes. Since 1992, elective cosmetic procedures have risen a dramatic 198 percent.[16] Extreme forms of liposuction, mostly requested by women, can require over ten hours of extensive remolding of the body. Between 1990 and 1999 the number of facelifts in the United States increased sixfold.[17] And as the horror stories of silicon implants in the 1980s faded from our memories, the 1990s brought a sixfold increase in the number of breast augmentations. In 1999 alone there was a 26 percent increase of the procedure (more than 187,000 surgeries) at a cost of $3,000–8,000.[18] Women are willing to risk loss of sensation in the nipples in order to become a more attractive sexual object.

Historically, the breast as a symbol of femininity has been a frequent site of attention. Based on constantly changing fashion, what's vogue has moved from the flat-chested flappers of the 1920s to the current buxom Lara Croft. Even as one group of medical doctors extols the healthful benefits of the breast as a source of nurturing for mother and child, another group is ready to put the knife to them. With breast-feeding socially marginalized and robbed of maternal meaning, breasts have become the premier sexual toy that can be purchased. In many areas, augmentation has become a rite of passage into womanhood and a suitable high school graduation gift as small breasts are increasingly considered a deformity.

With women's bodies seen as a medical "problem," few seem to have sufficient negative reasons to *not* have surgery—except for infection or the possibility of death, of course. Wouldn't you think these would be natural deterrents? With the classic Venus de Milo as mascot, plastic surgeons, emboldened to define the boundaries of beauty, have increased the demand for cosmetic procedures over a relatively brief history. They've redefined what constitutes a deformity, diagnosed lack of self-esteem, and prescribed the cure: surgery, of course.[19] The underlying assumption is that there is an essential "self" apart from the body that is dying to get out and that the surgeon, like a sculptor, will chisel at the flesh until it reveals her. Even in the 1960s it took considerable resolve for Barbra Streisand to keep her nose. Today, Americans have accepted the idea that we should change our bodies simply because we can.

On a daily basis, we can pursue the perfectly sculpted body at our neighborhood health club or a spa, where the majority of customers are women. Spas sell glamour and make millions of dollars a week helping us destress, detoxify, and rejuvenate. To some, the spa has become a necessary ritual to survive a life otherwise disconnected from the body. The question is, where does the health interest stop and the obsession with an unattainable ideal begin? The excessive use of cosmetics, dieting, and surgery imply that the body is largely passive. We see it as pliable, willing to be molded and able to take the abuse. As canvases, our bodies are yielded to receive a multitude of cultural inscriptions. We dare not question the choices available, for, after all, choice is what we've been fighting for all these years. Because our bodies can be understood only in relationship to the larger community, we want our bodies to leave a better impression than who we feel we are. We want our bodies to reflect who we *hope* we are. Today's younger baby boomers are rejoicing at the news that "forty is the new thirty." Older boomers are thankful to Gloria Steinem for letting us know what fifty really looks like. By hanging onto a certain type of youthful beauty, will we find the acceptance that we seek?

Male Backlash and More

Even though we have made great strides in changing the world by entering arenas previously not open to us, we still find ourselves victims of what Naomi Wolf calls the "beauty myth." The idealized female images projected by media dovetail with the fact that men have not changed much; they still respond to "beautiful" women. A survey of two hundred college women found that no matter how these women felt about themselves, their dating activity was directly related to how men saw them. According to the researcher, if you are perceived as "unattractive [according to the female ideal] and overweight, men may have little to do with you when it comes to dating."[20] But haven't women known this all along? Author Dorothy Parker said she had never seen a man forsake a beautiful woman to flock around a brilliant one. Nor a successful one, I would add. I've known plenty of brilliant and fascinating women of all ages with no man in sight. But rarely have I seen a knockout waiting to dance. One woman commented to me, "Inner beauty never gets you picked up at a party." Thank goodness for the older women who consoled me as a teen with the words "There is somebody for everybody," while my prettier cousin attracted all the boyfriends.

The commodification of beauty has become the currency of the relationship market, and men expect women to attempt to meet the standard. Through participation in the beauty cult we hope to acquire not only self-actualization but also love. Is it any wonder that even the most successful among us find ourselves dissatisfied with our body? Excess weight, bad skin, or facial features out of symmetry are too often our enemy, getting in the way of the love we long to have. They remind us of our personal failures and make our career and social successes in a male world appear meaningless. We have not completely taken this lying down, however. Sexually liberated, we seize opportunities to use physical attraction to get the power we still lack. Through consumption of the beauty culture, any daring woman can now attempt to play the part of a man-eating vixen. The problem is that in the end a flesh-and-blood woman cannot compete with the fantasy of the feminine ideal. We always fall short with the messiness of our bodies.

To some, the pressure to meet unattainable levels of beauty looks like a male-instigated backlash against women's social gains—a punishment for competing in their world. Wolf puts it this way: "We are in the midst of a violent backlash against feminism that uses images of female beauty as a political weapon against women's advancement: the beauty myth."[21] The beauty myth implies that we may be allowed to bring home the bacon and fry it up in the pan, but warns: be sure you look good when you do it! Under "power" attitudes we wear a "body by Victoria" in order to feel that we remain desirable to the men we find ourselves intimidating.

The beauty myth, however, does not explain why we buy into the negative comments made by women against women. These include those about Katherine Harris, Florida's secretary of state who presided over the 2000 presidential election recount. To many, her appearance didn't match the appropriate image of a woman in her position. But how she is *supposed* to look to do her job escapes me. Obviously, the beauty myth game is not meant to be won: Harris made it onto Mr. Blackwell's "Worst Dressed Women" list. Not long after, Hillary Clinton took a beating—not for her politics but for her looks in her first few weeks in the Senate. A professional female supporter expressed embarrassment over the newly minted junior senator's appearance. To the media and many others, Clinton's lack of nail polish and lipstick were indications that she was not taking care of herself.[22]

Do women do this to men? I read of no one making remarks about Dick Cheney looking frumpy. In practice, women are more critical of each other than men are of them. Aren't we the first to buy into the beauty myth? Are we hoping that by complying we will finally feel comfortable in our own skin?

Collaborators

The power of the "beauty myth" must be understood in the context of our history, the body's meaning in that history, and the concrete limits of the body itself. In all of these, there is, however, one thing we have not been able to change: our relationship to our own body and how we negotiate that relationship. In our society, what women have attained in terms of social advancement—education, money, power, status, and sexual freedom through contraception and easily available abortion—is meaningless unless we can also be young and beautiful. We've ended up with a need to manipulate our physical images in order to escape reductionistic ideas about our bodies. This despite Betty Friedan's counsel: "The only way for a woman, as for a man, to find herself, to know herself as a person, is by creative work of her own. There is no other way."[23]

Yes, we were good girls and followed the script handed to us by the second wave of the gender revolution in the 1960s and 1970s. We attempted to redefine womanhood on our own terms with a "You go girl!" attitude. But we are still haunted by the question *What is a woman?* In the last forty years women have attempted to unpack this for themselves: Is woman simply a womb? a domestic goddess? eye candy to be consumed by the male gaze? Or are we more than our bodies? Once we spurned inherited images of woman and set out to search for the real thing under layers of nail lacquer and the ten extra pounds, we have redefined, with some success, the feminine ideal by allowing for more individuality. A woman can now be considered a good mother while having her own work. An unmarried woman is no longer an "old maid." Certainly we've redefined many of the terms by which we live, but we have not been able to sever ourselves altogether from the meaning of our bodies, because to do so would be to suffer communal displacement. What we need is to find a subversive act of resistance against cultural dictates strong enough both to tame the mythical beauty beast and to thwart the dysfunctional relationship we have with our bodies.

But because we've been so busy serving the demands of the beauty cult, we've muffled our more profound spiritual need. Even public sphere participation has not camouflaged the sense of inadequacy and longing for more that keeps popping up in our soul. Since economic and social power have not empowered us to deal with cultural dictates, magnified by the media, regarding what it means to be a woman, we find that our bodies and their social meaning are at odds with our search for an authentic self. These exterior relationships affect how we see what is possible for us as we attempt to pursue a spiritual life. Under such hostile conditions, is it any wonder that my friend and I did not want to bring up our bodies in our spiritual conversation?

Thoughtful writers from Naomi Wolf (*The Beauty Myth*) to Joan Brumberg (*The Body Project*) have tried to express exactly what is bugging us about our bodies—and why. Feminism has produced a wide variety of reinterpretations of woman's experience in the world. It has rightfully questioned the meaning, value, and place that women have been assigned. It has attempted to provide political and social solutions. But when we look at what has transpired over the last forty years, we find that the enemy is ourselves. We are collaborators in our own marginalization. We have bought into the male standard as the standard for our lives. Our desire to be accepted in the male world leads us to forget that we are not men. But remembering that we are women causes us to return to the same old gender paradigms, because we don't know how else to live. We have an internal script that keeps playing like a broken record. We ask, how do we resist a gender pattern that is as old as the world? Are we forever trapped in its limits and definitions?

We have heard the feminist writers, but we are no longer willing to settle for economic and social solutions that leave our soul empty or deny our body. We are not willing to give up who we are as women in order to fit a system that has been set up to serve men. Still, it is difficult to escape the marginalization of our gender when many of us rush headlong into our own assault on the female body through practices like cosmetic surgery and excessive dieting. These are joined by contraceptive abuse, abortion, rejecting male sexual correspondence, or engaging in an obscuring of the female body through androgyny,[24] which allow us to become, in a sense, invisible as women and able to navigate the male-defined public world with less notice. So, for instance, like the characters in *Sex and the City*, where women are equal-opportunity exploiters, we hope to have sex as we think men do "and afterwards feel nothing."[25]

But must we subdue the fertility of the female body and truncate our emotional life to function authentically in a male world? Must we surrender to the images and meaning that our bodies have received in culture, embracing their assigned sexual power to further our own ends? As we silence our body or manipulate its meaning, we end up more alienated than ever, live sculptures for the male gaze and caricatures of ourselves.

Listening to the Body

Currently it seems that under layers of cultural meaning, the body is what is keeping us from having the life we wish to have springing from a deep contentment. How we perceive the body's role in our search for a spiritual life is highly influenced by our social context. We find ourselves bound by all its cultural meaning and needing to disassociate the body with all its "issues" from that search.

According to philosopher Charles Taylor, we come to understand ourselves and what is meaningful in life through a dialogue with our world. The world creates for us a "horizon of significance" that helps us determine how to make viable and important choices.[26] We continually reference meanings that are dictated by our environment (at times too much so), and we learn the value of work, relationships, and art from the world we occupy.

The body is also a "horizon of significance" that informs how we are to live, mediating the relationship between the self and the world. Increasingly, however, we are ignoring what it is saying to us. In our current social context the discussion of sex and gender, for example, has become individualized, cut off from relationship. Personal desire has taken preeminence over any constraining social or communal ethic, like fidelity and chastity, leading to a sexuality that seems to erupt out of nowhere as an autonomous drive. Disregarding the body's meaning within the context of community and commitment, the expression of desire becomes a monologue instead of the nuanced dialogue that is needed for relationship with another person. Because we are fundamentally communal beings, we always find that our view of our bodies will reflect our relationship to the world around us, and that we can never completely sever this connection.

The body informs not only our communal life, our dialogue with the world, but also our spiritual life, our dialogue with God. In truth, the body and soul are so completely intertwined that it is often impossible to make a distinction between spiritual needs and bodily needs. This relationship will be explored further in chapter five. Illness and anxiety, for example, have both physical and spiritual dimensions. In the biblical narrative, humans are seen holistically, with longings for God closely associated with thirst and hunger: "For He satisfies the longing soul, and fills the hungry soul with goodness" (Psalm 107:9 NKJV). In Hebrew, *racham*, or "compassion," is the root word for "womb" and "bowels," and is associated with the tender mercies of God. The body itself can be said to "call forth" compassion. The desire for God takes on a concrete bodily expression—the psalmist feels it in his gut. These are more than metaphorical ways of speaking; they point to the wisdom the body provides in directing our attention to God.

As a young mother with a six-week-old baby, I was hospitalized with toxic shock. Running a high fever and vomiting, I had a severe and painful rash that was at first undiagnosed, identified simply as an infectious disease. Because of this I was abruptly cut off from my breast-feeding infant. The feelings of longing and compassion for my son, who was not allowed to visit me, were overwhelming. It was as if he had been torn away, ripped from both my breast and my heart. When my breasts became engorged with milk, the medical solution was to roll in a breast-pumping machine. This added insult to injury. Technology would take care of my problem. No one responsible for my medical care regarded the agony of separation from my son as something to be addressed. The emotional aftermath lasted for many months after I had physically recovered from the disease.

During this hospital stay I also experienced an increased longing for God. My physical weakness, the longing for my son, and my desire to provide him with emotional nourishment paralleled my desire to be embraced in the bosom of God. The experience changed my perceptions of my body and how it could inform my spiritual life. I began to pay attention to its cues, its hunger, its need, and its parallel to spiritual experience. I learned the desire for God is not purely a spiritual exercise but encompasses the needs of our bodies. The sensuality of the body can awaken our desire for God through pleasure in the things that are near to us, but only if we understand that the very nature of pleasure is to leave room for God. Instead of seeing the body as an encumbrance in our drive for meaning, we must learn to listen to the body as a moral space; to recognize its voice and affirm its life.

To understand the body as a moral space that can inform our lives, we may look at how desire presents itself. The senses of touch, smell, taste, sight, and hearing awaken our awareness of need and instigate desire. When need and desire are rightly informed, they will direct us to the things that correspond to human flourishing. We become aware of our needs and desires when we ask ourselves, *What will make me happy? What will bring me pleasure?* But the idea of neediness awakens visions of dependency, of lost autonomy. Need makes us humble. It can make us grovel—and we hate that. Our culture has defined the highest good as freedom from need. We do not want to need anyone or anything, because that is how we have defined freedom. We just want to be able to walk away from people and do our own thing. Painfully aware of our need for things outside ourselves, we are seeking a radical freedom and a form of gratuitous desire that answers to no one but ourselves, free floating, uninformed by any exterior responsibility. Always answering to the body's reminders of our need, we can never have this absolute freedom.

As desire springs from need, not to desire anything is impossible. Desire does not emerge out of nowhere but from a state of lack. Directed by a horizon of significance, my body and a dialogue with the world, my actions become meaningful for the filling of my desire. There is no such thing as pure or "neutral" desire; its object always elicits it. With no compass, desire has no wisdom of its own; it does not know what it lacks, it just lacks. Unable to orient us to what will produce a meaningful life, desire must be informed, oriented, constrained within boundaries in order for it to drive us to those things that will satisfy the lack we experience. I may desire something sweet but not know what will satisfy it, or I may know that I want a chocolate shake. My hunger has been oriented by the particular life experiences that taught me that a chocolate shake would satisfy my hunger for something sweet. My body acting as a moral space has shown me that I need food; my experience in the world has provided me with an understanding of what is useful for food. But desire that is situated in my body can also be misdirected. I can fail to pick up the necessary cues and crave things that will not only fail to provide adequately for my lack but will take me in an entirely wrong direction.

The spiritual role of all human desire is to take us beyond the thing pursued and point us to God. Our desires for social acceptance and beauty reflect our spiritual needs to enter into the divine community. The pursuit of something on earth, like beauty and relationships, can awaken a desire for God because the object pursued can never be fully possessed. Anticipation being greater than realization, there is always a shortfall in our ability to apprehend the object. If I see a beautiful object, I desire it and I pursue it. Once I have acquired it and experience the initial realization and pleasure of its beauty, I immediately sense a lack that prompts a need to pursue more. There is always another pair of Dolce & Gabbana shoes to acquire or a more exotic vacation destination to experience. As a wise person once said, the eye is not full with seeing nor the ear with hearing. But this is not because of a deficiency in the instrument; it is because of mislocated desire. Nothing in this world can be fully apprehended; the lack always remains, for the nature of things on earth is to awaken our desire for something more, ultimately God. Only when we recognize this ever-present lack in ourselves and in the world will we be able to live in freedom from cravings and yearnings. By listening to the lack that is evident in the world, in ourselves, and revealed in our desires, we will be propelled toward true fulfillment, which is found only in God.

In the movie *Babette's Feast,* a small dying parish has lost its vision for God, and its members have turned against each other. Babette, a lowly housekeeper with an exquisite culinary talent, offers to prepare a real French dinner for them. For the parish, living on a daily diet of split cod and ale-bread, the anticipation of Babette's sensual feast threatens to awaken a desire for earthly things. Afraid to need and encounter their own sensual desires, the parishioners vow to keep their minds on higher things and to remember not to taste anything. Each course is elaborately prepared and presented: turtle soup, tender quail, luscious figs, and vintage wine. By the end of the meal, unable to resist its beauty, the parishioners have experienced the dinner as a "love affair where bodily desire and spiritual desire meet."[27] They leave the table with relationships and joy recovered, sensing that the "stars of God have moved closer." Babette's feast, offered in love, has moved them beyond the sensual experience of the meal to a reawakened yearning for God.

The community members' self-sufficiency—evident in their inability to enjoy the physical pleasures of life and accept them as gifts from the Creator—had blocked their spiritual ability to receive and give love. In order to know their need to give and receive love for each other and for God, they must move from rejecting desire to listening to what the desire is telling them, bringing them to a more authentic experience of themselves, of life, of spiritual reality.

My friend who had the facelift and I—in fact, many women all over our country—have been driven by our lack and desire for more into a perpetual and anxious pursuit of feminine beauty. The desire for physical beauty has become disoriented and is failing to fulfill its purpose of leading us to God. But physical beauty is an elusive quest. As we become aware of our failure to meet cultural demands regarding our appearance, we pursue more control of our bodies, an ultimately futile exercise that moves us further from the true significance and meaning we crave.

More Than Symbols

Our personal struggle is over how we will orient the lack and longing for meaning that is a constant in our lives. Desire can be misguided by cultural images that woo us, tyrannizing us as evidenced by our abuse of our bodies through a variety of means, including sex and food. Our desires can be directed toward serving cultural icons that promise significance and control but never really provide either. In our search for meaning we serve these icons relentlessly. But desire can turn in on itself like a rat on a treadmill when the means becomes the end. In the monotonous cycle of desire and pursuit we get nowhere fast. We violate our body's integrity when we place no value on the messages it sends every day, using it merely as a tool to serve our culturally oriented desires. Isn't this the paradigm under which we currently live?

The crux of our problem is that we are caught between the concreteness of our embodiment and the desire to be unimpeded by our physicality, which springs from a divinely given desire to go beyond the limits of our social situation. What seems to stand in the way of our fulfillment is that instead of creating symbols ourselves and setting the terms of our lives, our body becomes the symbol of everything we are not able to attain, including a true sense of self. We cannot be or do what we want. Always reduced to the body by culture, we seek to escape it. But we can never escape our body. Not merely an object of social construction or biological mechanisms, the body is a threat because it is more than the cultural systems that define it.[28] Therefore the current paradigm that silences the meaning of the body will never allow us to find a coherent body-self.

But when all the layers of cultural meaning, analysis, and construction are stripped away, the undeniable reality is that our bodies stay with us like nothing else, the background noise of our life. Don't we experience ourselves as more than a mixed conglomeration of cells, symbol, and context waiting for manipulation? We don't want to be reduced to parts, what they represent, or even what they actually mean. We want to be regarded as a whole human being. We want to live with a certain amount of sureness about our identity, and we want to be women of substance—not cultural props. Most of us find that we are neither a madonna nor Madonna.

Even though our relationship to our bodies is powerfully shaped by the world we live in, what is needed is to recognize that the body has meaning in itself, apart from culture. Its very essence informs the nature of the self. Our body tells us something about who we are. My body is not simply a hunk of flesh. My femaleness and my race are not irrelevant biological accidents; they inform my very being. It is my soul intertwined with my body that deciphers the meaning of my material experience. It is the intertwining of soul with body that allows us as created beings to go from object to subject and to move beyond the complex social context of our lives.

The desires we experience in and through our bodies can point us to the greater hunger we have to enter into a relationship with the divine community. As women seeking change beyond renegotiation of our social position, we have begun searching for a spiritual answer. We need a spirituality that can help us see further than our cultural experience but that takes our body as seriously as we do. Can we find in the Jesus narrative a spirituality that embraces our body instead of one that continually ignores or assaults it? By examining our social experience in the body and by looking at the life and work of Jesus, perhaps we can begin to heal the gulf between our desire for meaning and the disintegrity we experience in our body.

2

The Body Is My Altar

How Women Are Trained to Serve the False Idols of Beauty

If desire begets need, then envy begets desire. The stimulation
of envy or a longing to imitate is the function of the idol.

Marilyn Bender[1]

A girl's adolescence is often occupied with waiting and working
for the beauty that will or will not soon emerge. Upon this her
romantic dreams depend. I remember waiting with my cousin
in anticipation until we could begin to acquire the summer tan-and-
blond look we thought of as the American ideal. Since I was a brunette,
I tanned better. She, a natural blond, benefited magnificently from
many bottles of Sun-In, which only turned my hair a bronzy red. Once
the sunny days arrived, we lay out for hours in the back yard, mari-
nating in Johnson's baby oil, chasing that golden California-girl look.
The guys didn't spend a single hour of the precious summer in self-
inflicted passivity hoping for the "look," of course. Still we lay there
daily, imagining ourselves on the cover of *Seventeen* magazine and talking about the boys. Even today, one of the most anxious weeks in high

school is the week before spring break as girls close themselves in tan-
ning booths and engage in crash dieting, preparing to get into swim-
suits.

Why haven't things changed? Why are we continually obsessed with
our body when physical beauty has shown itself bankrupt as way to
secure meaning in our lives? We have not gotten to this place alone.
Beginning, but not ending, with false cultural ideals, the world initi-
ates us early to prepare to offer lifelong service in compliance with its
demands. Through our growing-up years, a series of messages shape
how we will finally feel about our bodies as grown women. From an
early age we are trained to live as if under a constant gaze. It is not the
gaze of the beloved who ponders us with affection. The gaze we experience studies and evaluates us as women. The weight of this fixed
gaze keeps us ever mindful of the degree to which we measure up.
These are the specific reductionistic terms by which women learn to
live and which we eventually internalize. What we hope to gain is a
feminine identity that will provide us with significance and a sense of
control. The pursuit of beauty begins with our human need to know
who we are and secure our place in the world.

There are two dimensions to beauty, of course. One is transcendent
beauty, virtue, and justice. The other is physical beauty, always culturally negotiated. Because our search for an authentic self takes place
within a cultural dialogue, and in our culture physical beauty is preeminent, the search for transcendent beauty has derailed into a focus
on the body. The pursuit of physical beauty has swallowed up the pursuit of transcendent beauty. This prevents the body from fulfilling its
true spiritual role of pointing us to God. In the process we have lost
our ability to see the lack of justice and virtuous beauty in our life.

This gulf between inner beauty and outer beauty is at the center of
our disintegrity. The need to atone for our body's shortcomings keeps
us kneeling in appeasement before false idols as we seek to extract
transcendent meaning from them. In a culture where physical beauty
is the ground for acceptance, we have no other alternative to pursue.
What pulls us in is the phenomenon of the gaze—the eyes constantly
on us from which we can't hide.

Whether you have it or whether you don't, physical beauty is a constant source of anxiety increased by the pressures of the feminine ideal. Though we are told to cultivate our inner beauty, our sense of virtue and justice, outward beauty always wins the prize. You know beauty matters in a concrete way when your more attractive roommate gets three bouquets of roses on Valentine's Day, all from different men, and you hardly get a hello. For girls who are thought of as plain or lacking physical charm in all the right places, inner virtue is nothing more than the kind of pain Joanna experienced when told by a young man, "You're so beautiful on the inside. Too bad you're so ugly on the outside."

How does one ever get beyond this constant pressure to pursue a particular type of beauty? Is the only alternative rejection? Of course, being too pretty has its own set of problems; it makes women into coquettes, inadvertently toying with the male ego. Some girls are bold and take this on by becoming a tease—or worse. Long before Madonna and Britney Spears showed us how to be virginal and seductive at the same time, there were girls who seemed to know innately how to use female beauty and charm as a weapon. We watched them to see if they could get away with it. Sometimes it backfired on them; they ended up getting married in a hurry or at least worrying over home pregnancy tests, rushed to the offices of discreet doctors by their mothers for an emergency D&C. Sometimes they just ended up with lots of drama and a broken heart. At least they had something going in their life. The rest of us were sitting around waiting for our prince to come.

Under the Gaze

The constant pressure to measure up to the physical ideal makes us ask whether we occupy our body or whether our body occupies us. One counselor whose majority of clients are female told me that women come to see her for a variety of issues—stress, relationships, or work— but that in 95 percent of the cases there is an entangled body issue. Women generally see relationship or even career failure as directly related to their looks. Success in any other area doesn't seem to matter if a woman gets dumped. Male clients have body issues at a much lower frequency. No matter what women achieve or gain, the issue of physical appearance is an issue that emerges again and again. We even refer to an occasional woman as a real "looker."

In an unscientific survey of women and their attitudes toward their bodies, I was looking for experiences that shaped their feelings and views. I received stories of the internalization of the outside viewer's gaze, not the internalization of emotions based on physical experiences like childbirth. Most women I interviewed spoke about the feelings associated with having a nose that is too big, being overweight, or having bad skin. Some expressed fear of dealing with the implications of the questions and refused to attempt an answer. Few women were able to describe what it feels like to dance, float on water, or run— that is, what it actually feels like to live through a body.

Because we *expect* to be looked at, because we have internalized that phenomenon, we have formalized the gaze and created various rituals around it: fashion shows, cheerleading, the Miss America pageant, the elaborate wedding ceremony in which any woman can be Miss America for a day. At an event that should bring together a community to further its future, the bride as an individual becomes the center of attention. She walks down an aisle while the congregation stands and looks not at the groom but solely and wistfully at her. She lives preparing for this moment by dreaming of it and then, once engaged to be married, obsessing over every detail. The expectation that women parade under the fixed gaze of many sets of eyes is as old as the world and often captured in Western art. The female nude painted by such artists as Renoir and Rubens expresses a containment of women under a male gaze that assumes passivity and vulnerability.[2] Queen Vashti in the biblical book of Esther was dethroned for refusing to submit to it. This is never expected of men.

Through the gaze we learn the content of our femaleness. As little girls[3] we fall under its power as our cuteness or our frilly dresses are admired; we are reminded, "Smile! You're prettier when you smile." Because I was a chatterbox, everybody thought I was cute and would give me candy, so I learned early that feminine charm has a payoff. But in emerging adolescence the chatterbox was warned not to turn into a loud woman. Biblical proverbs were quoted to me about loud women who never stayed at home—and these warnings were not always from the lips of men. Nobody mentioned the proverb about the beautiful quality of Wisdom personified as a woman *shouting* in the streets (Prov. 1:20). In real life women didn't have voices that could be heard in the streets. And if you showed a little too much intellectual spunk, it made people nervous about your future. Be attractive, we learned, but not sexually alluring. Don't try to compete with the boys, we learned; instead be demure and coy. Madonna's lyrics express the ambivalence we feel: "When you open up your mouth to speak / Could you be a little weak?"[4] Our experience was often that women were to be seen but not heard.

Emerging Women

At puberty, we become aware that we are being sized up, and this feeds our budding self-consciousness. You are told you can be sporty but must be feminine, and then your mother hands you a padded bra. A series of junior high experiences let you know that even if womanhood can be powerful, it can also be scary. When I was that age, a man told me that being a woman was a privilege—the privilege of bringing life into the world. Was that sort of like carrying the future of the entire human race in my body? To me it seemed like a daunting but noble task. The physical changes necessary for motherhood came soon after, reinforcing his pronouncement upon my body. Further reinforcement came as boys taunted all of us girls for leg hair, modestly budding breasts, and bad skin.

Then there was the big event, the threshold of womanhood, first menstruation, the singular most significant event for realizing that you are a girl, different from boys. Adults' attempts at explaining what was going to happen did not prepare me; neither did the two dismal and fragmented pictures of our internal organs, looking like a Rorschach test, in outdated health books. All I knew was that this was part of the "female problem" my mother and aunts had talked about in the kitchen. I responded with a mixture of thrill and panic—happiness for having accomplished the womanly act, panic that now I was a marked woman. Later worries involved having no period, too many, too heavy, or too few. Late periods made us believers in an immaculate conception. (Maybe you'd kissed a boy for the first time and you were sure a baby was now on the way.) We all have stories of showing, teachers quietly letting us know, humiliation surrounding our periods. These experiences put us in fear of our body under the gaze of the world.

From the moment of its first monthly period our body has to be managed like the perpetual baby-making machine that it threatens to be. There are countless versions of "the talk." This is when your mother, your friend's mother or older sister, or the church lady gives you the news. The talk about men's "needs" starts out sounding more like an apology for the fact that you are a woman and have to put up with sex. What you learn from a series of conversations and slumber-party gossip is that men are wired for lust. They simply cannot help themselves, and it is our responsibility to do the impossible: make sure we do not damage their frail sexual egos, while remaining attractive but not too alluring. A view of skin, shapely legs, and a slight décolletage could simply send a man over the edge of lust. Sex was done "to" you, and at the age of fourteen little about it appeared mutual. Many of us spent early adolescence in ambivalence toward males, both attracted and repulsed.

These experiences of the implications of our bodies may be why Eve Ensler's play *The Vagina Monologues* has touched a disquieting chord with many women. An international hit, it is exactly what its title suggests, a series of monologues exploring the joys, fears, and mystery associated with a seldom-mentioned part of female anatomy. Despite its raunchiness, Ensler's play draws us in instead of repelling us because with great panache the author names the shame many of us have felt for being born with a vagina.

But we are affected in broader ways by the narrow definitions of our gender. At fifteen, an older friend of mine threw a kink into the works and threatened to undo everything I had assumed about sex. I had thought we had no choice in the matter. She confided in me that she had opted to avoid men and was pursuing relationships with women. I realized much later that what we had been told in early adolescence about male sexual aggression and our expected passivity set us up to live unsatisfying sexual lives—accommodating, becoming victims, or rejecting male sexual correspondence altogether. It prepared us to listen carefully to an idea articulated by radical feminist Andrea Dworkin, that under the current gender paradigm, sex is a matter of conquest and possession of the woman.[5]

Passed on through "the talk" was the gender dysfunction of the world. Not seeing men as fully relational beings, and seeing women as less than active agents in those relationships, did a disservice not only to us but also to men. It became a self-fulfilling prophecy and a ready excuse for boys to become boorish men.

Sheila suffered for years before she finally put a name—"sexual harassment"—on what happened to her as the only female in computer classes. All along she had thought the staring and lewd remarks were because she had provoked them in some way, or because the boys couldn't help themselves—they were, after all, male. Ever objects of the male gaze, we, like Sheila, eventually surrender to it helplessly. For those who become aware of the damage, it will take a lifetime to undo what we have learned so well.

All Grown Up

The gaze continues as we explore the world. When I first began working in the late 1970s at a large downtown Dallas firm, I was not ready for the full implications of my gender. I thought that because I had done well in college and shown eagerness to learn and work hard, everything would be fine. Not a ravishing beauty, I was unprepared for sexual come-ons and unwelcome advances in elevators from men twice my age. I had to watch whom I was with and what I said lest it be misinterpreted. I had to watch what I wore, though modesty usually did not seem to make a difference. I complained, but I didn't know what to call what I was feeling; it was just the uncomfortable part of being a woman in a male world.

In an extreme form, the gaze becomes stalking. There was a period when I received anonymous phone calls, flowers on my doorstep, and notes on my car windshield. The message was "I see you, and I know where you are." To some this may appear innocent, suggesting admiration gone overboard, but to me it felt like a threat. The idea of a constant pair of eyes on me was unnerving. Many women have told me of instances of sexual assault and badgering that they've kept secret. We experience the gaze, stalking, and even assault as if we were sleepwalking, emotionally frozen, unable to access our anger. We don't live in a constant state of alarm, because this is our norm. It is only afterward that we realize what happened, and we blame ourselves, what we wore, and how we looked.

After a lifetime of living under the gaze, one day you realize that you are getting older and any beauty that you had or hoped for is fading. Younger men no longer look at you. Older men are too busy gazing at younger women. But instead of feeling relief, many of us experience this as though our security blanket had been taken away. We feel invisible. Our identity was tied up with being constantly gazed at. We are afraid that we will not be able to keep the man we have or get the man we hope for. Every day of our lives, our femaleness has a vast impact on what we experience.

Whether you are unscathed or not, you continue to accept the tyranny of the gaze because you have been trained from childhood to submit to it and dance before it. Gazing or being the object of a gaze is not in itself hurtful. But it is not benign. It becomes hurtful when it does not come from eyes of love attempting to comprehend a beloved but rather arises from contempt for a woman's humanity. Female identity is increasingly sexualized, affecting girls at younger ages. Britney Spears, Christina Aguilera, and Destiny's Child are strutting their stuff and using their sexy girl power. In the 1960s the Beatles sang, "I want to hold your hand"; today Christina dances seductively in her video "Come On Over Baby." Twenty-first-century girls have *Cosmo Girl* instead of the more innocent *Seventeen* that I grew up with. Music videos powerfully reinforce the sexualized image, a succession of images of woman as nymphomaniacs, always ready, always available.

As represented in media, women are only objects, or worse, fragmented parts instead of whole human beings. But the current sexy images are working off the old. What is not new is that underneath demure femininity, women have always been seen as potentially sexually dangerous. Our attempt to exercise our agency in the world has turned on us. We have moved from seeing women's collaboration in the world as passive responsiveness that presupposes no sexual agency on our part to presupposing sexual power as the only power women have. Today's woman has simply been allowed to strip herself of coyness. Our role is still to inspire the valiant warrior or conquer him with our sexuality. We've come full circle: Barbies on steroids. What men feared in female sexually has come upon them, unrestrained. It threatens to engulf the male psyche. But what appears as a new freedom for women, and the opportunity to exercise agency in a sexual way, is the thing that traps her.

Simone de Beauvoir observes that man wants woman to be an object. She makes herself an object, and in this way she exercises her agency.[6] To act out this sexuality requires that she behave out of the old ideas of woman as seductress, but this denies her full humanity. What we end up with is a lie about how a woman should look, what a woman is, and where a woman's power is. Under the domain of the media ideal of "beautiful," she ends up a shadow woman, an illusion; a representation of the cultural image she has been taught to serve.

Beauty and the Ideal

We respond to the cultural demanding images of beauty not only because we seek social acceptance but also because we have a deep human need to pursue beauty. Ultimately beauty touches our sense of justice, the search for what is fitting, the need to have things in their proper order. When moved by great music or by the power of the ocean, we experience a sense that everything is as it should be.

Because we associate beauty with transcendent values like justice and virtue, we tend to see those who are considered physically attractive as more valuable, smarter, and more successful. They seem to be nicer, warmer, more fun to be with. We are drawn to beautiful people. We want to know them and be with them; beautiful people seem to possess the goodness we desire. It is the beautiful heroine that we root for and admire. It is beautiful Cinderella and Snow White who get both the prince and our sympathies, while the wicked stepmothers and step-sisters are described as ugly. To say that a woman is ugly is to say that she is lacking in intangible virtues, which is why *ugly* has been considered the greatest of insults.

But this sense of order in the world is limited, because what we consider beautiful at any point in time is affected by our personal experience of the coherence of the world. Beauty is truly in the eye of the beholder and the result of a cultural conversation. Popular notions of the features of a beautiful woman will always fluctuate, from the small corseted waist of the 1800s to the current full and, often, augmented breast. Regardless, the reigning cultural ideal of womanly beauty is the image we are taught to emulate.

But beauty has a dark side too. It can tempt us to pursue it too earnestly; it can incite envy or unruly desire in those of us who lack it and can make us resentful. Beauty creates tension for both those who seem to lack it and those who seem to posses it in abundance. If you are considered beautiful you know that others may envy you, and you wonder whether you are truly loved or serve only as a man's trophy. You wonder where your value lies.

How the ideal woman comes to be the ideal is an ongoing process of gender negotiation that is continually changing. Throughout great classic works of literature the beautiful woman inspires, but this beauty remains largely undefined. It has no particularity. Its content is not fixed, and its attributes are of a transcendent quality. In the *Iliad*, Helen of Troy is never described except as beautiful. There is no image of her except what our imagination brings to the text. In William Wordsworth's poem "She Was a Phantom of Delight" the beloved is described as "a moment's ornament, / Her eyes as stars of Twilight fair; / Like Twilight's, too, her dusky hair."[7] Likewise in the biblical Song of Songs the beloved is described through metaphors: "Behold, you are fair! You have dove's eyes" (Song 1:15). To those accustomed to highly concrete images, these descriptions appear ambiguous and quaint. What we fail to appreciate is that these highly nonspecific descriptions invite us to create an imaginative vision that could apply to any woman aspiring to be the beloved. For the most part, beauty was in the imagination, and before the advent of the visual mass media any young woman could dream of cultivating it, even develop it over time.

At different times there has always been a negotiated feminine ideal. In the print-based culture of nineteenth-century America, the content of ideal femininity was accessible mostly to the racially and economic elite, through the cult of "true womanhood."[8] Nineteenth-century femininity included the belief that by nature women were more virtuous than men, reflecting spiritual piety and sexual purity. For this reason and due to their fragile nature, "good" women needed to be protected from the world and helped into carriages. Woman's delicacy and virtue were part of the argument for keeping women in the domestic sphere and out of contact with public vice. Only upper-middle-class white women, and not their household servants, could attempt to be models of softness and delicacy. At the other end of the class spectrum, farm women, immigrant women in factories, and slave women who served as the "mules of the world"[9] could not presume to even attempt to model fragile femininity under the harsh conditions of their everyday life.

Black women in America have had a particularly difficult time living up to cultural images of ideal womanhood. In 1851, against this feminine ideal, a black former slave named Sojourner Truth railed against ideas that denied her the vote and legitimacy as a woman. Standing tall at six feet, with muscular arms and a strong face, she recounted her life story: she had worked as hard as any man, having plowed, planted, and gathered into barns. She had borne children and seen them sold into slavery. She had taken cruel lashes. Her ringing call "Ain't I a woman?" comes from this famous speech. The strong and determined Sojourner Truth was certainly a woman, but nothing about her met the cultural expectations of her time. Womanhood is more radical than cultural ideals embodied in white middle-class values. Yet today the cultural negotiation of femininity still excludes many women.

The introduction of photographic images and the rapid dissemination of their use had a profound effect on how we view beauty literally and what we consider an attainable ideal. In *The Body Project* Joan Jacobs Brumberg uses diaries of nineteenth-century girls to illustrate how much of girls' self-concept was directed toward inner character like service to others, self-control, and charity compared to journals of contemporary girls, which almost exclusively concentrate on outward appearance. Current diaries of girls who are exposed to an infinite number of images are catalogs of desires for improved body features and plans centered on their pursuit. It was not that young girls of the nineteenth century did not care about physical features—they did; but looks were not treated as a source of self-esteem to the degree they are today.[10] Victorian girls sought to cultivate the inner virtues associated with good character. Today, surrounded by concrete images of the ideal focused on the physical, young women who in reality come in a great variety of shapes and sizes must strive to become dangerously slim, emulating airbrushed models. They are left with no imaginative place to go.

At a time when women of many classes and races have greater economic, political, and social access, the camera that ought to reflect the multiplicity of ways women are women has instead narrowed the concept of beauty and made it more demanding. The move from print to an image-driven mass-media culture, along with the corresponding consumerism, means we are constantly bombarded by concrete and codified images of beauty that assault the senses. It is estimated that Americans are exposed to three thousand commercial images per day.[11] There is not only an almost universally prescribed beauty ideal but also a universal belief that any woman can attain it through consumption. By paying the price and buying the right clothes, haircut, hair and skin care products, and makeup, girls as young as eleven can be transformed—or so says the myth.

As documented by Jill Kilbourne, current images that flood mass media show women as sexual objects, passive and always available, a narrow definition of woman as forever young and slim, with doll-like European features, porcelain skin, and lustrous hair. Less frequently women of color are accepted—as long as they have the preferred "white" features, or to fill the desire for exotica or Asian submissiveness. The influence of pornography on the mainstream media is evidenced by the fact that female beauty is inevitably sexualized, with women portrayed as little girls, sexually vulnerable and seductive at the same time.[12]

In reality the mass media beauty ideal is unrealistic and unattainable in real life except by extraordinary means—even by the models and actresses themselves. The images on the covers of fashion magazines start with an average model who is five feet eleven inches and weights 117 pounds. With these measurements, she represents only 2 percent of American women.[13] In real life, fashion models must deal with puffy eyes, skin breakouts, chapped lips, and bloating. But an entire industry exists to deliver airbrushed, computer-manipulated and -enhanced faces, re-created through a succession of body modification practices. Well-known models such as Cindy Crawford, Naomi Campbell, and Gisele Bundchen are rumored to have improved their market value through cosmetic surgery; it is part of the job. A Los Angeles plastic surgeon reports that he has even removed a rib from a model in order to help her appear thinner. In this new millennium, surgery performs the role of the corset[14]—the containment of woman to a prescribed ideal. For a career that ends at a relatively young age, top models spend tens of thousands of dollars on their smiles, cheeks, breasts, and skin, purchasing the exaggeration of feminine features. Cosmetic surgery is seen as the extension of an art form that has always been with us—the fabrication of female beauty through performance.

The Death of Beauty

In a culture saturated by mass-produced and mass-disseminated images, the content of the beauty ideal is distorted particulars[15] out of context of relationship, place, and time. Though these images are not people we can know and comprehend, they contain what is legitimated in the culture and as such shut down an imaginative vision. Because the image is concrete and detailed, it fails to inspire the mind's eye. No room is left for the imagination or for a variety of conceptions of female beauty.

Although the role of our desire for beauty is to move us toward the good, in a culture saturated by photography, video, and digitized images, this function of beauty is lost. Even superstar Julia Roberts could not meet the false expectations of perfection and used a body double in the film *Pretty Woman*. Routinely body-parts models provide the perfect hands, feet, or derriere, creating a fragmented false image increasing our dissatisfaction with our real bodies. The particularity of the image created actually denies beauty its transcendent quality. This further colors the social conversation and affects how we all compare ourselves to false ideals.

Psychologists have found that men's perception of attractiveness is relative and can change. Fabricated images of ideal femininity have destructive implications. The "*Vogue* factor" can make an average and real woman appear less attractive next to a manipulated image of a highly attractive woman.[16] Constantly bombarded by images of extraordinary beauty, men may find that the false ideal gets in the way of appreciating a real flesh-and-blood woman. She can never measure up. He can never find relational satisfaction. What does this unobtainable beauty do to the romantic aspirations of men who must settle for the ordinary? What happens when what it means to be "the beloved" is no longer articulated with words but communicated by explicit *images*? Unlike the past, when the plainest woman could see herself in love poetry and romantic novels, an image-laden culture leaves little room for the romantic imagination. By emptying beauty of its ability to point us toward the good and its role in opening us to the transcendent, mass-media culture ironically manages to be antibeauty.

While the mass-media image is a codification of who we are to be, the body is seen as an extension of the image, an instrument to be manipulated in order to carry the cultural script. The image is not about what is there but about what is not there. It oppresses through exclusion. The image demands that we meet its expectations, so we find ourselves bound to try to negotiate our human imperfection with its perfection. An unattainable but seductive illusion, the image works by setting up the criteria for legitimation and producing in us self-conscious shame. We find ourselves in a narcissistic and infinite house of mirrors, buying the false promises of advertisers in order to make up for our lack. The pursuit of beauty is no longer about seeking what is just and true but about oppression, the message that we are never good enough. Beauty cut off from the transcendent virtues of justice and truth serves as a counterfeit.

Given that we operate from lack, what might it look like to be defined by what is *included?* In order to get a glimpse of what is possible in answering this question, I asked a massage therapist how she managed over twenty-eight years to deal with the wide variety of bodies she works on: bodies that are maimed, skeletal, obese, scarred, hairy, ravaged by disease. Her answer was that as a student she attended a training session in which she observed a couple who changed her paradigm. The woman, she told me, was quite large and round, while her partner was a handsome man with a Greek athletic build. She observed how this man lovingly gave his sweetheart a massage with a gaze full of love. He touched every curve and every fold of her skin with complete care, never rushing. My friend understood that this was how she was to view every body that came to her and to see the beauty that was there—not what was lacking.

If we desire to be embraced for what we are, why do we continue to submit to the gaze that excludes? With no alternative place on which to fix our own gaze, the cultural images of beauty become for us an idol and begin to fulfill a spiritual role.

Idols and Illusions

The media images that rivet us are extensions of communal values, and as they live off our social nature they begin working in us as a transcendent power. In their role as the idol, they fill the space of the rejected Creator in which we try to anchor our rootless selves. Idols are agents of control. As self-created false gods, they provide order in the midst of cultural chaos. They provide meaning and make a claim of allegiance on our whole being. They give us clarity. They tell us how to live and who we are. The claim they have on us is extremely difficult, if not impossible, to escape, and we are driven to serve them. The alternative is to be excluded, and that is to find ourselves socially adrift.

What the idol promises in exchange for our devotion is an illusion of power over our life, illusory agency to become what we wish, and a fraudulent identity from which to speak. It promises the possibility of escaping the mundane aspects of our life and finding coherence.

But even if we manage to move toward meeting its demands, we exclude those who fail to meet them. We view those who fall short with disdain, as "other." The biblical prophets warned against idolatry at the same time they warned against injustice, because the worship of idols was linked to the oppression of those who were marginal, the poor, the stranger. Injustice and false idols that are not worthy of our service are implicitly tied together. By serving the idols of femininity and beauty, we become like them—made of wood or celluloid— and we begin to lose our humanity.

Cultural idols demand service by bringing all subjects into the realm of their gaze. Even those who transgress against the image in order to find an authentic self find their protest is defined by it. Youth culture is notable for these types of acts. Transgressions are at first socially marginalized, but over time they are co-opted by the image and fashion industries. Bod-mod is an example of this progression. What began as extra ear piercings, acts against cultural norms, over time became accepted in the mainstream. To continue transgressing against the image required that piercing move to other parts of the body. The sight of nose or brow piercing, which initially shocked, no longer fazes most people. In the late 1990s, "heroin chic" fashion spreads used gaunt models with zombielike postures and hollow eyes in an attempted transgression of the ideal. The heroin addict became an inspiring cultural hero living on the margins against mainstream values. In creating "heroin chic," fashion stylists and editors attempt to access the middle-class hunger for an authentic self and their buying power. The consumer adopts alternative fashion while still being dictated to by the changing image. So for most, service to the cultural idols is not a form of rebellion but of conformity.

Place of Atonement

Our need for meaning, identity, and allegiance is so great that we are willing to serve the idol by participating in enhancing and manipulating practices wherein the body is simply a passive object. Beyond this, when our service to the idol fails we resort to extreme practices of atonement.

It was the desire to offer one's body in the service of something bigger than oneself that required prohibition of human sacrifice in the Old Testament, along with cutting and tattooing of the flesh in ancestor worship (Lev. 19:28). Human history is replete with ancient civilizations that in times of distress and out of a need to pacify angry gods engaged in offering their children on bloody altars. That horrifies us, but have we been offering up our own daughters to the false idols of femininity? Across cultures, when an event was considered sacred, marking the body through tattooing and scarring was the ultimate expression of devotion. Even though ancient human sacrifice resulted in the death of an individual and cutting had a different meaning, the difference in our practice today is a matter only of degree and context, not of substance. We find in ourselves a need to offer our body in service or mark our body for something outside of ourselves. For some this involves all-consuming work, sports, or the pursuit of beauty. Before the idol, the body becomes not only a bearer of the cultural script but also, as in ancient civilizations, the location of meaningful spiritual ritual. Under the idol, all the practices in which we engage our bodies, such as the use of cosmetics, dieting, exercise, and cosmetic surgery, become spiritual service.

In such a spiritual role, the body is the place of redemption. It is the altar on which we atone for failing to meet the expectations of the idols of beauty or of the world. We have a deep desire to be acceptable, to pay for our shortcomings in ways that affect many areas of our lives beyond the realm of the feminine ideal. Self-injury is an instructive example of the extremes to which we will go in our need for atonement. This year, more than two million Americans—most of these young women in their teens and twenties—will intentionally cut or burn themselves. The most famous exemplar of such practices was Princess Diana, a woman whose public persona was an international idol of fairytale femininity. Apparently she could not meet the expectations of her own persona.

When I first started looking at this issue of self-injury, I was unaware that I knew anyone who had practiced it. Within days after I had begun the research, several persons in my circle told me of their experience as cutters or having friends who were cutters. It is easy for us to dismiss self-injurers as sick people dealing with personal demons. But by looking at what we think of as extreme, we can learn something about the social meaning and spiritual implications of the body as well as shed light on our problematic relationship to our own body.

Self-injury does not happen in a meaningless vacuum. Like anorexia and bulimia, self-injury not only is an individual problem but contains a strong social and spiritual component. Studied extensively by psychiatrist Armando Favazza, it was brought to popular public consciousness by Marilee Strong in *A Bright Red Scream*. According to Favazza, "self-mutilation is the deliberate, direct, nonsuicidal destruction or alteration of one's body tissue."[17] The sufferers of self-injury may engage in a variety of body-harming acts including head banging, plucking hairs, burning, and bone breaking. Self-injurers are atoning not only for their own sins but, through pain, for the sins of a world that has become hostile for them. It is a form of obscure social protest, rebellion, of escaping the world's confinement and their sense of powerlessness.

Attracted to blood, self-injurers experience cutting as a highly ritualized and meaningful experience. The motivation that drives this behavior is the desire to control one's body, which is particularly important to victims of sexual abuse. For these persons, controlling one's body is a desperate and available means to control one's life. They feel disassociated from their body, and mutilation provides a way to reconnect with it and feel alive. Self-injurers are desperate to relieve intense emotional pain and feelings of anger, shame, guilt, and loneliness, along with disassociation. Physical pain provides temporary emotional relief and often produces a state of euphoria. In the movie *Girl, Interrupted,* the main character, Susanna says, "I know what it is like . . . you hurt yourself on the outside to try to kill the thing on the inside." The scars of cutting serve as historical markers and provide certainty about their existence. Strong states, "The body is, indeed, the temple of the soul. Cutters are living proof that when the body is ravaged, the soul cries out. And when the soul is trampled upon, the body bleeds."[18]

Body and soul are so profoundly linked that to think of ourselves as other than a psychosomatic unity makes little sense.

Self-mutilation is one way we bring the body into the search for an unobstructed "true" and reconciled self. Aided by consumerism with its promise of self-actualization, it becomes cosmetic surgery. It joins a continuum of which an extreme version is the phenomenon of apotemnophilia. In this practice a person seeks the amputation of a perfectly good limb in order to align her body with her internal concept of the self, a self that has only one leg or a hook for an arm.[19] As ghastly as this sounds to most of us, it is the progressive extension of the search for "the real me." Phrases like "the way I really am" and "becoming myself" litter our social landscape. We talk of loving others for who they are inside, not understanding that to really love we must love the whole person, including the body. This view should lead us to honor what the body tells us about each other. Because so many of us have suffered due to our physical differences, we long to be loved in spite of them.

A more prevalent and recognizable form of mutilation is the popularity of body piercing, tattooing, and branding, promoted not by seedy tattoo parlors but by Hollywood celebrities and rock stars. In an industry where identity and the remaking of identity makes the difference between failure and success, body modification allows one to write a new, more authentic self. To many devotees of this art form in which the body is the canvas, the practice has nothing to do with seeking pain. It is about expressing oneself as an individual. People who pierce their bodies give reasons such as sexiness, self-expression, and spirituality. Ads for tattoos and piercing often include religious and ritualistic language such as "making the world a holier place."

Those who practice body modification often resent being put in the same category as self-injurers, but the lines between bod-mod and self-injury are often blurred. The pain associated with piercing seems to have some meaning to those who pursue it persistently, but bod-mod devotees would rather place themselves over against the mainstream that uses cosmetic surgery to conform to social images. By transgressing social boundaries, they hope to make a self-identifying statement and recapture the self on their own terms. Due to a continually changing social environment, however, the effect is short-lived. The transgression soon becomes the new boundary and the new stasis. Bod-mod is an additional example of how the body serves as both a place to locate the self and a place of deep spiritual significance.

Sensing our lacks, through a variety of body manipulating practices we women hope to gain a surer sense of who we are and carve out a clearer identity. What begins as a search to find ourselves ends up as the spiritual means to atone for our failure. It is an expression of our search to repair our disintegrity and atone for the breach between our outer and inner selves. By molding the body in a multitude of ways, we are attempting to use the body as ballast for an unanchored self, lest it float away and never return. But in the process, we violate the body. We silence its voice, furthering the disintegrity we experience.

When I asked a number of women, "Does your body have any meaning?" I was generally told, "No, it only has the meaning I give to it," or "Only what I do with my body has meaning." We have come to believe that the body has no value except what we give it. We refuse to acknowledge any claim that the body may have on the self. Maybe hidden in Old Testament admonitions against cutting our bodies in cultic rituals is an understanding that the body can be used to serve what is not worthy of it. But we have no regard for the integrity of the body because ultimately in death it will betray us, so a disconnected and frightened self strives to subdue it. We are in an irreconcilable position; our bodies trap us in concrete limits and cultural meaning. Without them we lose the grounding we seek. In a constant war between the body and the self, we are caught between two unsuitable options. We find ourselves always negotiating and renegotiating our identity, which is continually changing even as the image changes.

In the contemporary culture of medical technology with its promise of unlimited possibilities, a multitude of disembodied communications and free-floating identities, we operate under the assumption that the body has no say, does not initially assert itself, and only lives out the collective imagination. Is the body only a sacrifice to be offered on an altar for a wandering cultural "soul"? We need to find a final atonement for the pervasive sense of failure we experience. Can we do this in a way that dismantles the demands of the beauty image and provides an identity that is grounded in something beyond ourselves? For women, this may make the difference between living in freedom and living under the domination of cultural images. We must find a place of permanence in which to anchor our wandering selves and a way to fulfill our need for beauty. We need a fresh paradigm for thinking about our bodies that renews the imagination for viewing beauty and ourselves.

3

Body Bound

The Inescapability of the Body and the Elusiveness of Transcendence

I opened my eyes on the world with enmity
between myself and my nature.

Nawal al-Saʿdawi[1]

It was a cup of cappuccino that provided an opportunity for me to discuss the meaning of the body with a young black lesbian. At a Midwest feminist conference, we had just listened to a panel discussion in which three speakers spoke of their sexual identities and orientations. All female, one was a straight-vanilla lesbian who seemed rather old-fashioned in comparison to the other two. One was a transsexual female-to-male, the other a bisexual whose gender identity seemed to change with the direction of the wind. The bisexual described how some days she felt butch and slicked back her short hair and wore boy-cut jeans and T-shirts, while other days she felt femme and wore sexy dresses, high heels, and full makeup. I could see that it was all in the attitude. Her gender performance—and it truly was theater—changed based on whom she happened to be involved with at the time. It appeared that some people brought out the butch while others brought out the femme. I wondered whether there was a real person under all this and whether relating to her would be like having a relationship with a phantom.

The woman I was having coffee with had come out as a lesbian at fourteen. She was wearing a feminine outfit that was quite different from her attire the day before, a pin-striped suit. Our discussion centered on why she had rejected womanism (incorporating black women's experience) as a distinct feminist perspective and on the nature of lesbianism as a philosophy. It was a pretty heavy conversation, I must admit. But the simplest question was the one that seemed to confound us the most. What I asked, and am still asking, was "Do our physical actually existing bodies matter in all this?"

I hope it is becoming clear by now that in our search for meaning and a more authentic identity, our bodies have become obstacles to be overcome. But as we seek transcendence, can we radically sever who we are from the body? It appeared that in the panel discussion about gender identity and sexual orientation, sex itself was wholly disembodied. No references to the body were made except as an appendage to the discussion. There was no questioning whether our sexed bodies provide any information regarding the nature of our sexual identity.

I asked the young lesbian whether she had ever considered her body as informing her identity. I wondered whether it said anything about her and how she was to live. She was ready to affirm that her race was important in informing her identity, but she hadn't thought about her sexed body in quite the same way. She wasn't sure she wanted to go there.

Like most people, I have trouble thinking about the body without thinking about the mess of it. It is a complex set of needs, yearnings, and assumptions, overlapping in physical and cultural space, that continually limit our possibilities. In our attempts to transcend our social situation, we do not want our body to define the content of our life whether by race, age, sex, or disability. But to talk about sexual orientation and desire without talking about the bodily field in which they are expressed is to engage in dualistic thinking that will forever keep us from having a coherent understanding of ourselves. As unfashionable as it may be, the reality is that my body informs me every day not only about my place in the world but about what is needful for my life to flourish. How we view the body and our own body ends up directly affecting what type of spirituality we will embrace and how we see our relationship to the Divine. The current formulation of how the body, specifically a woman's body, is related to spirituality has set us up for *disembodied* spirituality.

Before launching into any discussion of the nature of desire and of sexual identity, orientation, and practices, ask yourself: *What do I believe about the body?* Once you have clarified this, your viewpoints regarding all other issues will follow. If you hold that the body is purely a biological accident with no meaning of its own, it will drive you to a different end than if you believe the body has innate or given significance. Because currently we generally regard the authentic self to be the inner self, we often see the body as only a material stage on which self is actualized.

The movie *Boys Don't Cry*, about a young woman with a gender identity conflict, puts this in graphic terms. As we find ourselves sympathizing with Brandon's pain of living in a hated female body, do we ask where the tragedy really is? Is it that Brandon is trapped in the wrong body that impedes her actualization, or is it Brandon's estrangement from her body? We come to believe that for Brandon the body is the source of her problem and this must be fixed, instead of that Brandon needs emotional healing to breach the gulf she experiences between herself and her body.

We must not underestimate the pain depicted here, but the conversation needs to begin with the nature of body and how it informs sex and gender identity. From this starting point we can begin to examine desire lived in and through the body. We begin to see that the body is the bridge, an active agent, between our needs and the world in which they are actualized, connecting the self to the world and mediating that relationship.

In light of feminism's aggressive critique of the radical separation of mind and matter, spirit and body, our wholehearted disregard for the self-knowledge the body provides is amazingly disturbing. The last time I checked there was virtually nothing about my life that has not been affected by my body, from the fact that I am a mother to the clothes I wear and the healthcare I receive. Feminism is, in fact, a response to the devaluing that women have received due to their bodies, and "body studies" is the topic of the moment. However, in most formulations the body is either the site of oppression and protest or a historical and physiological object. What we hesitate to do is to talk about the body as an active agent informing and forming our lives.

With a long philosophical history that continually identifies a woman with her body, it appears that sometimes women do not want to bring up the subject because it may remind us of who we are and therefore undo all the social advances we have gained. In the midst of the politics of difference and the fear of essentialism, bodily difference is still a taboo. But as women we may be in a better position than men to understand the futility of attempts to transcend the body, as well as the need for its spiritual recovery. When we look at the assigned social meanings we have been trying to escape and the price we have paid, the inescapability of the body becomes most evident. This is why we need to explore the philosophical history of the nature of transcendence and woman's embodiment.

A Natural Woman

As a philosophical corrective to essentialism, it has become fashionable to completely separate the biological body from the social interpretation of that body. "Woman" is how the word *female* becomes interpreted in culture. I assume that woman as a social category is rooted in femaleness; that is, when I am looking at a physical female form I can be sure I am looking at a woman.[2] But its not quite that simple. There has been so much cultural layering that I would say none of us really know what a "natural" woman is. We identify with the soulful lyrics of Carole King's, *You Make Me Feel Like a Natural Woman*, "I didn't know just what was wrong with me,"[3] because we feel like mockups of a "possible" woman or a woman in drag. Most of us don't fit the ideal.

I have a vagina, ovaries, and yes, even a womb; this tells me something about the sexual relationship that can fully embrace this reality. Female physiology is such that sexual response is not solely a pleasure response. It also has a function that is instructive. Research has
shown that female orgasm opens up the cervix and propels semen
into the uterus.[4] The body itself seems to assume that there is sexual
correspondence between the sexes. But in pursuit of unrestrained sexual pleasure and an "authentic" self, we have cut off the role of the
body in informing the nature of personal authenticity. It no longer
tells us anything about how to live as women (and men) because it
has been silenced.

In the social conversation on sex and gender on countless web sites
and tell-all television shows and in magazine articles, the sexually differentiated body appears cut off as a signifier of value that makes
claims and informs our life. Popular discussion of sex often resorts
to a medical and mechanistic model with diagrams and descriptions
of sexual techniques. We are inundated with sexually laden articles
such as "10 Ways to Turn Him on in 5 Minutes" and "The Magic Fin-
gertip Trick." Has the body become nothing more than a machine or
a stage for sexual performance? Does the body say nothing of its own?
Does it simply respond to the desires of the self? In our need to oppose
biological determinism, which reduces us to wombs, we often act as
though the body's function had no voice in informing our sexuality.
But gender and sexuality cannot be spoken of only in terms of disembodied desire or social context, because beyond it all, we live in
sexually differentiated bodies.

According to Yale theologian Miroslav Volf, "The sexed body is the
root of gender differences that are themselves always socially interpreted, negotiated and re-negotiated."[5] Grounding gender differences
anywhere other than at the *fluctuating* intersection of biology and culture is an exercise in futility. Many of us resist reductionist definitions
based on our physicality, because to define a unique human being in
advance of knowing the individual is to do violence to the reality of
who that person is. Many of us have suffered personally from cate-
gorical disregard of our uniqueness. Both women and men are human
beings who are vastly more than definitions of femininity or mas-

culinity. To try to pin down gender by saying all men are initiators or all women are responders is practically useless, even though it may sound comforting. You will find more than one man who is less aggressive than more than one woman; but does this make any of them less of a woman or man? I don't think so. Part of the beauty of being created beings is that there is a mystery to gender beyond what we can neatly identify.

Still, the fact that there is mystery in gender doesn't mean we can't say anything at all about it. We can begin by saying that the biological body acts as a signifier in society. It notifies us that we are dealing with a man or a woman upon whom culture layers meaning. As we attempt to uncover woman as she has been distinctively created, we must engage in a continual process of pulling back cultural layers, uncovering her relationship with her Creator.

Woman as Body

A look at the historical dialogue reveals that woman's close philosophical link to the body and the human quest for transcendence have parallel roots that appear to be at odds. In the history of Western culture, woman—more than man—has been associated with physical and sexual desire. As a philosophical problem that needed to be solved, she has been closely associated with the body, the mundane, and the immanent.

Plato's *Timaeus* states that God "made the soul in origin and excellence prior to and older than the body, to be the ruler and mistress, of whom the body was to be subject."[6] This sexless and preeminent soul provided the basis for identity, and the body was associated with matter, which was the source of ignorance. Plato's sexual asceticism—his idea that sexual intercourse is the result of the dominance of lower instincts over the higher functions of reason and therefore to be regulated for procreation alone—"reinforced the philosophic point that the body and mind, desire and action could be severed."[7] In Plato's sex unity model there was no difference between the souls of men and women. The problem for Plato was not women's souls but women's bodies and their role in mothering. The female body was seen as inferior to the male's and suggested punishment for the soul that occupied it.[8]

Plato provided women with an opportunity to escape identification with their bodies in the world, but at the cost of their concrete bodily experiences. In *The Republic* women are deemed capable of becoming guardians, ruling with elite men, but according to political philosopher Jean Bethke Elshtain, only by being stripped of psychosexual and social identity. This identity is grounded in the particularities of embodiment situated in time and space and thus fastened to "biological imperatives." By attempting to abstract these, in effect, Plato silenced a woman's body and her physical experience in order to allow her to transcend it.[9]

Aristotle continued to build on some of Plato's ideas, but to solve this problem of women he proposed a sexual polarity. His overarching question for Plato's social vision was, who would look after the home if women joined the men as guardians? Aristotle associated woman with passive and lower matter and considered that she needed to be awakened by the active superior male, who would shape her identity. He described woman as deformed and imperfect. It was her association with man through obedience that would shape her life, he claimed,[10] because woman does not contribute the essential "seed" for procreation but provides only the bodily stuff; man provides the truly important soul. Aristotle's distinction between the female passive body and the male active soul, full of potential, had enormous influence, and we have lived with its legacy ever since. To this day men are seen as more active and engaged in the world, while women are seen as passive by nature and more closely tied to the home.

In the fourth century, Augustine continued this line of thinking to identify woman with the temporal and man with the spiritual. Augustine tried to maintain equality in the spiritual ream while maintaining sexual polarity in the world. The result was a fragmented and often contradictory view of the relationship of woman to man. Man needs woman for her procreative capacity, Augustine argued, but woman's sexual allure and her connection to the flesh keeps her forever tied to the body. He claimed that marriage and its sensuality draw a man away from his spiritual pursuit. Augustine's most disturbing statement reverberates throughout history: "the woman herself alone, then she is not the image of God."[11] Both a necessity and a hindrance to man, woman unaccompanied is incomplete, Augustine claimed; only in her role as "helpmate" to the man can she participate in the image of God. No wonder so many women have seen marriage as the beginning of life.

Historically, women have bridged the gap between spirituality and body in different ways. In the medieval period, a time when women were especially associated with the body, some women with no formal ecclesiastical power developed a concept of service to God that involved harm to their bodies. Through control of their bodies they were able to exercise power within a social hierarchy that otherwise limited it severely. Propelled by spiritual curiosity, a desire to give transcendent meaning to their social placement, and a narrow definition of female piety and embodiment, they forged a particular expression of spirituality. They would provide the church with a visible demonstration of the sufferings of Christ, frequently embracing a "holy anorexia," celibacy, loneliness, self-inflicted pain, and their own marginalization. Subjugation of the body and suppression of its sexual meaning were seen as critical to touching God and identifying with the suffering humanity of Christ.

These women were known for their extreme acts of penance; they rejected material beauty, comfort, and human intimacy for what they believed to be the beatific vision. Mary of Oignies cut off pieces of her own flesh. Beatrice of Ornacieux pierced her hands with nails. Catherine of Siena engaged in self-flagellation and slept on a bed of thorny substances.[12]

As shocking as some of their practices may be to us, we may have something in common with these religious women—the assault on the body that they were willing to endure in order to control its meaning. They also rightly understood that a spiritual life must deal with the body, not ignore it. They understood that the body's needs, experiences, and meaning have to be dealt with in the spiritual search.

But the legacy of the women of the medieval period has reinforced the popular misunderstanding of Christianity as an anti-body/antiwoman religion. If the way of Jesus excludes women and assaults our bodies, I, for one, wouldn't find the path appealing. Yet many of us still believe that being spiritual will condemn us to ugliness and fleshly renunciations, opposing life in a material world. It leaves little room for those of us who love the gathering of friends, enjoy the sensuality of our body, and generally find the world's material beauty a good thing. Essentially we are asking, *Can I be spiritual and have a social life?* For some the life of the body and the spirit remain in irreconcilable opposition. Many have forfeited a spiritual life altogether.

Transcendence

Early Western thinkers, along with many others since then, constructed a script that today is highly problematic. When women are seen as pure matter, pure sex, and pure body, they find it difficult to view themselves outside their body, yet remaining in the body becomes confining. The traditional views acknowledge that this unfortunate state hinders a woman's spiritual growth. The attainment of virtue and wisdom by women is either slowed down or impeded altogether when, as in Plato's philosophy, the cosmic female remains a passive recipient of male seed with no identity of her own.[13] By nature, then, women are at a disadvantage in the search for transcendence.

Enmeshed in this Western philosophical history is racial and cultural elitism, the legacy of privilege, which excludes those considered "other" whether they are men or women. For black women, who are further identified with the body and who have been seen as essentially tied to the earth, aspiration to culturally defined transcendence alongside elite men is an impossibility. They must overcome not only gender but also race. In the search for transcendence it appears some women are more equal than others.

The problem increases when we come to believe that transcendence requires that we escape our bodies altogether. It was the seventeenth-century French philosopher René Descartes who took the necessary steps for us to see the self as pure mind, distanced from the body. The body and everything outside the mind becomes only the mind's extension. A search for what is *real* requires that we escape the world that we inhabit. In order to do this Charles Taylor observes "we have to objectify the world, including our own body, and that means to come to see them mechanistically and functionally, in the same way that an uninvolved external observer would."[14] According to Susan Bordo, the result has been a "supermasculinized model of knowledge in which detachment, clarity and transcendence of the body are all key elements."[15] The Cartesian "knower" is actually "nowhere" and experiences the self as "absolute detachment." The human person becomes all mind, and the body is only a machine to be regulated.

Cartesian dualism has had a profound effect on how we talk about the self and how we view woman in her body. Under this legacy, we are still continually looking for the self that is beyond our body and supposedly more real than our body; we seek means for escaping the limitations of the body.

According to philosophical reasoning like that of Descartes, in the search for transcendence the body becomes a prison from which the soul must escape.[16] For women who see themselves as trapped in an uncooperative body, both concretely and due to its social meaning, this escape is an imperative. In *Unbearable Weight* Bordo states, "What remains the constant element throughout historical variation is the construction of the body as something apart from the true self . . . and as undermining the best efforts of the self."[17] For women this undermining is at the root of embodiment; always betraying us and always tying us to the mess of it. The Cartesian proposal is that to transcend our everyday experiences and to see the things as they really are requires that we achieve a disembodied view from "nowhere." This, alongside the philosophical legacy we've inherited from the Greeks, places women in an altogether impossible position, increasing our desire to escape our body or at least whittle it down to occupy the smallest space so we can be free. According to Bordo, philosophical history has bequeathed us the idea "that which is not body is the highest, the best, the noblest, the closest to God; that which is body is the albatross, the heavy drag on self-realization."[18]

My clearest experience of the impossibility of this was when I was eight months pregnant. On an extremely hot Texas afternoon—in the time before cell phones—I found myself with a flat tire, a three-year-old child in a car seat, and no water, stranded on the side of a busy freeway. I got out of the car while traffic flew past me. I felt immensely vulnerable, in a situation beyond my control, hoping to rely on the kindness of a stranger. I was experiencing a view from "somewhere"— in a particular place, in a particular body. A spirituality that required me to transcend the reality of my bodily limitations would have been useless to me.

If spiritual transcendence requires a flight from our body, then our spiritual journey is unstable, if not altogether impossible, because our body keeps crashing in on us. Short of the literal escape from our body that is not yet possible; we have committed ourselves to subduing them and bringing them into compliance with whatever instrument is at hand.

Tied Down

Many, but not all, feminist thinkers have built their theories on the assumption that woman's body is the problem that must be overcome. Camille Paglia says, "My code of modern Amazonism says that nature's fascist scheme of menstruation and procreation *should* be defied, as a gross infringement on woman's free will."[19] In this environment woman has no choice but to begin to look for a "real me" beyond her body if she is going to in any way escape its containment. Her desire for radical freedom and autonomy is at odds with the body that keeps her grounded.

While men are able to transcend the mundane through their work of building structures and institutions in the public sphere, women are tied not only biologically to reproduction but also philosophically to the home. The reproductive role of women, according to Simone de Beauvoir, traps her in the realm of the mundane; the day-in-and-day-out reality of maintaining life, washing dishes, doing laundry, and wiping children's noses. It is women who have been left to nurse the sick and the young, to cooking, and to reducing household odors.

Beauvoir describes man as regarding woman as hindered and "weighted down" by her body while he has a "direct and normal connection with the world which he believes he apprehends objectively."[20] Through the woman, man secures his grounding to the earth and to the immanent while remaining pure mind. As opposed to women, men have escaped the reductionist and relational meaning of their body through world-engaging work. As they are in their "mind" they are alienated from their body. Even though the male body has a strong presence in the world and man appears to be in ownership of his body, he is not present in it. As he gains transcendence in the world he remains cut off from the relationships that are mediated through his body as son, husband, and father.

While woman is seen as needing in a concrete bodily sense, man supposedly wants and desires in abstraction and without needing.[21] Man sees his body primarily as an instrument of achievement and conquest of the material world; a ready sacrifice on the battlefield. As man has sought transcendence and escape from the mundane association with woman, he is alienated from his bodily experiences and his own humanity. His mental and world-engaging work detaches him from human relationships, yielding distant husbands and absent fathers. He has settled for the manhood of conquest over experiencing a full humanity.

Man must recover from this severing in order to live as an integrated body-self—a whole human being. Women, seen as immanent and grounded to the earth, provide the connection men need. The situation in which we see men as having only one thing on their mind is the result of being so absent from their body that the phallus serves as a tether to keep them grounded. Sexual actualization gives men certainty of their existence and a way to overcome their own disintegrity. Instead of a healthy sexual desire, there is obsession with sexuality, a sign that the self has vacated the body and is seeking to recover its grounding.

Men's recovery of their bodily connection would lead them into their full humanity and release women from playing out their immanent role alone. The sex-obsessed model of maleness that we have been trained to accept would fade away; more men would develop into integrated human beings, fully engaged in communal life.

How women are seen often is different from the day-to-day reality of women's life. While it's true that historically women have taken major responsibility for the private sphere, they have also been involved in a great number of activities beyond the home. Around the world, women have never simply stayed in the house day after day rocking the cradle. We have all seen television images of African women working in the fields with their babies on their backs. Before the Industrial Revolution in the United States, women were involved in a variety of economically significant activities for the household, especially making candles, butter, cloth, and soap, all of which could be traded or sold to provide for other needs of the family. Women often served as the only medical practitioners, educators, and social organizers in their communities. For black women in the United States, the split between men's paid work in the public sphere and women's unpaid work in the private sphere never existed. Because black women and new immigrants have always worked outside the home as sources of slave or cheap labor, they have continually fallen short of the feminine ideal.

A review of women's history shows that the idea of woman as culturally passive and inactive has never held up in real life.[22] Globally, in times of devastation women have been the maintainers of the social fabric, yet their contributions have consistently been devalued and overlooked simply because they are women. During the Industrial Revolution, the center of economic life began to shift away from the family farm. The private sphere began to be severely reduced as what had been produced in the home came to be produced in factories or turned over to experts. The twentieth century brought a huge number of labor-saving devices, and home economics experts heralded the housewife's freedom to become a full-fledged consumer, uninvolved in meaningful production. Childcare professionals in the public sphere increasingly directed childrearing, which remained in the home. Thus the private sphere was entirely emptied of its productive contributions. By the 1950s, for many middle-class women, it was simply too small.

Public versus Private

Before Betty Friedan had written *The Feminine Mystique* about middle-class white women's "problem that had no name," women already felt significantly devalued. We were ready for a new script. Second-wave feminism encouraged women to leave the private sphere and enter the more significant and productive public sphere.

It needs to be understood that second-wave feminism's discussion of the tension between private and public sphere described life for those who lived in a particular position of racial and class privilege. In the public sphere, elite women as well as men came to achieve transcendence through productive work and be involved in universal pursuits. But this reinforced the belief that the work occurring in the public sphere and associated with men was ultimately more important and took priority. By entering the public sphere at the expense of the private, woman legitimated the male world and rejected her own. The new "elite" women soon found out that the public world of work, as currently arranged, marginalizes human emotion and vulnerability, especially female reproductive life.

What is needed is for those in the public sphere to embrace the difference and particularity of the private sphere and to recognize that there is no "natural" division between private and public. Life is organic; there is constant flux between public and private spaces and blurring of their boundaries. Poor women have continually lived in this flux.

The blurring of public and private spaces for me occurred when I was eight months pregnant and, as a CPA, received a business call requesting my services on behalf of three young men who were on the verge of becoming technology moguls. As I drove to their offices I wrestled with feelings of doubt and questions regarding my competence. Would my pregnancy, which could not be hidden, affect their opinion of me? Would I lose these potential clients over biology? I realized then and there that the private was now public and that I could assert my presence and expertise by navigating the overlap. I had to be willing to overcome feelings of shame and to see myself as more than a womb. I was not hysterical, unbalanced, or overly emotional. My mind was good. Pregnancy was merely the beginning of an overlap between two things I had never put in the same category—financial statements and breastfeeding.

Divided thinking regarding these kinds of realities is what has kept men away from their children and kept women from using all their abilities. Today the significance of the private sphere is hanging by a thread, reduced to the particulars of personal conversations and needs. The public sphere and its concerns are of utmost importance, leaving the women who remain in the largely invisible private world to do the culture's emotional heavy work. In a relentlessly profit-driven society, things that are not measurable, economically profitable, or quantifiable are devalued along with what women have always actively contributed to life.

Under the current terms of our society, for woman to fully participate in the privileged dimension of the public sphere as it has been defined by males requires that she abandon her difference and embrace sameness with men. The alternative is for her to redefine the public-private overlap on her own terms, with the risk of diminished public-sphere influence.

In the mid-1980s I sought a way to both care for my infant son and continue my professional work. My aspiration for both public influence and private responsibility had been shaped by racial dynamics that had allowed me to assimilate into the dominant culture. This made certain things possible, like practicing a profession out of a home office. But living in such an overlap also created a stigma, the suspicion that I was less than a serious participant in the world. As my child grew older, I moved to an office outside the home and noticed a corresponding increase in the respect I was awarded. The lesson: mothering/breastfeeding and serious work are at odds with each other, not because they are inherently so but because when women do what women need to do, it is devalued.

To go along with sameness and establish public-sphere viability, a woman must escape the difference inherent in the female body and engage in a whole gamut of body-denying acts. She must suppress her fertility, abort untimely pregnancies, and deny her child the breast.

The transcendence offered by the public sphere requires that she take on a pseudo-male persona.

The Remedy

In our society, the problem of transcendence for woman is ultimately a problem of her biology. Carrying the bigger part of the reproductive burden, the female body comes loaded with many more complexities than the male. We have a monthly reminder that we are women because of what our body will and will not do—a point so obvious that it's uninteresting. Of course, technology is rushing to help us out of the jam of "incessant ovulation." The birth control pill has been wildly successful because women are intuitively, if not consciously, aware of the public-sphere implications of their bodies. The acknowledgment that the female body has been the site of woman's oppression has motivated radical feminists such as Shulamite Firestone to propose that women must overcome their biological burden by seeking technological solutions to procreation and the "tyranny of pregnancy."[23]

In 1960 the U.S. Food and Drug Administration approved the use of the birth control pill. Across the ensuing decades, the pill has had a profound effect on work, marriage, and maternity patterns. It has allowed women to pursue educational and career opportunities without the interruption of unplanned pregnancies.[24] Women have thus entered the professions en masse, and educational institutions and employers have opened up to investing in women because now there is much less worry that they will drop out due to pregnancy.

With the public sphere rejecting woman's reproductive capacities, is it any wonder that many young women fear motherhood? Pregnancy and motherhood can appear to threaten your survival as a legitimate person even as they legitimate you as a woman. *Woman* and *person* not being the same thing, the woman needs the pill in order to safeguard her personhood.

Now we are being advised that we can use the birth control pill to suppress menstrual periods altogether. While writing this chapter I found www.noperiod.com, a web site dedicated to exploring the suppression of periods with birth control pills. In a recent article on PBS Online, *Healthweek,* one female doctor portrayed menstruation as an unnecessary health hazard.[25] While one is taking oral contraceptives, monthly periods are medically unnecessary; we were allowed to keep them only to reassure us that the pill is "natural."[26] This is an example of the expansion of hormonal therapies, reproductive technologies, and high-tech medicine available to tame the female body from puberty through menopause. As medical science labors to lighten our reproductive burden, shouldn't we question whether it is operating under a pervasive misogyny in regard to women's bodies?[27]

The pill has also changed the way we view sex and our relationships. For the average woman, the pill has provided a way to divorce sex from procreation, so she can make herself available to any sexual partner she chooses at the moment. Woman is now considered to be available 24/7/365. Widely used even among the most socially conservative groups in America, the pill has changed how we view sex, the availability of women's bodies to male desire, and woman's willingness to ignore her reproductive uniqueness in the name of sexual pleasure.

Since sex and reproduction do not occur in the world with no other mitigating circumstances, and since most couples do not have unlimited social, emotional, or economic resources, it is a matter of personal responsibility that they seek to limit the number of children they bring into the world. Managing our fertility is part of our stewardship of life. It is also extremely important that women understand their own reproductive body instead of leaving it shrouded in mystery, in the hands of medical doctors. Nevertheless, the separation of sex from procreation does not happen without affecting the wider social dialogue regarding the place and role of sex, and particularly the marginalization of childbearing and the female body in its reproductive capacity.

The change in the social dialogue begun first as a disconnection of sex from procreation moved quickly to disconnect sex and marriage. Unmarried couples can freely engage in sexual intercourse without fear of an unwanted pregnancy. Men can expect full access to a woman's body with the confidence that any "problem" will be taken care of by her. The shame of pregnancy out of wedlock is a thing of the past; the days of a "shotgun wedding" are over. But the disconnection process has continued, and now we are seeing the complete severing of the sexed body from gender. We no longer need the commitment of marriage or the complementary gender to have "sex." Reliable contraception and abortion on demand have provided women and men safety valves to let them engage in sex without bringing their whole selves into the relationship.

Without contraception, trust is the greatest issue. A woman will think twice about engaging in sex with a man who is not trustworthy; the risk to her is not equal. The interjection of contraception changes the sexual dialogue by diminishing partners' sense of the importance of trust needed for intimacy.

Contraception has also had an impact on marital sex, because men now tend to make the assumption that no matter what time of the month it is, their wife's body is available to them. They automatically assume she will comply, because she does not have to worry about pregnancy. (Natural family planning methods tend to work against this dynamic, since they involve both partners in managing their fertility.) Contraceptive technology makes it easier for both the man and the woman to ignore the emotional backdrop to the sexual act. A man can have access to his wife's body, demanding that she continue using contraceptives, when her desire may be to bear a child. The converse may occur as well, with the wife eager for sex with contraceptives while the husband desires children. They can both fail to acknowledge mutuality in the procreative stewardship of their relationship. The use of contraceptive technology can quickly become contraceptive abuse when men and women ignore the spiritual and emotional aspects of the sexual relationship.

Beyond the Erotic

As in every area, in regard to our bodies we need to live and love with intentionality. Because our bodies connect us to others at deep levels, our attempts to escape our biological body become escapes from the community and all the relationships it mediates. Because the act of sex is an act with the body—both a biologically concrete and a culturally porous space—driven by a need to fully disclose oneself to another, it cannot be freed from its communal role. The spiritual and emotional aspects of sexuality do not remain solely with the couple. Sexuality cannot yield only to individual desires, tastes, and inclinations. What we do to and in our bodies affects the entire community. It is simply not a private, individual matter.

Abortion, like all sexually related issues, is not simply a woman's personal option. It erodes the interconnectedness of the community by attacking a powerful symbol of woman's compassion, the womb, rendering it fruitless. The widely practiced violence of abortion is not a sign of progress but a sign that women's reproductive ability needs to be exterminated in order for society to go "forward." In an environment hostile to women's bodies and through abortion, women participate in a war against their own bodies, objectifying them. The feminist slogan "our bodies, ourselves" becomes "our bodies, not ourselves." Even those vocally opposed to Cartesian dualism, including some radical feminists and ecofeminists who usually extol the value of the female body and the need to recover its meaning from masculinist assumptions, will yield to abortion under a paradigm of "control" over one's own body. At the same time that emancipation of women and the earth from male domination is promoted, women become agents of an internalized subordination; acted out in and against their own bodies. We have become the most recent colonizers of our own bodies.

As women give birth to the community through their bodies, we are attempting to build a community with increasingly frayed edges. Serial marriage, same-sex relationships, and the acceptance of chosen single parenting are continuing to have strong effects on the meaning of kinship. The severing of sex, gender, and procreation from the body is changing the meaning of relationships at a fundamental level, making all relationships purely voluntary and without any binding biological connection. One expert has estimated that over seventy thousand children are born each year from donor sperm. These are

children engendered absent a loving and communal relationship manifested in the bodies of the parents. Many, now in their twenties, are
looking for their biological fathers.[28] We are producing children who
grow up without a profound sense of bodily connection, the grounding soil for personal identity. In this scenario, the prospects are for a
continuation of the disintegrity that we all experience and a lessen-
ing of our humanity.

In pursuit of radical freedom and transcendence, are we rushing
too quickly to sever kinship ties through sexual and relational options?
Maybe we need to reconsider how our bodies give us profound connections with those who have gone before us. Increased longevity is
making it possible for kinship ties to extend to five living generations.
Throughout our lives we create a common history through the meals,
tears, and beds that are shared.

I remember all the childhood sleepovers when I shared a twin bed
with my aunt Marta, sleeping with her feet near my face. She had put
a lot of miles on those hardworking feet, and they never saw the inside
of an Elizabeth Arden salon. My cousin often had the same experience, and we laughed about it for years. Still smelling Aunt Marta's
feet, we realized those were bonding times that let us know who we
were and where we had come from. From our birth to our death, the
human experience and its history are tied to our bodies.

The increasingly disconnected ways we are choosing to bring children into the world reflect wholehearted disregard of the importance
of communal relationships to a person's sense of identity. At the same
time that we long to be more connected to the community, it appears
that communal ties place a greater burden on women, not only biologically but also socially. This is most intensely seen in our ambiva-
lent attitude toward motherhood. Childbearing and motherhood have
consistently provided legitimization in cultures where the barren
woman is a cursed woman. Women speak of infertility as the worst
experience of their life, the cutting out of the heart. Leslie Brown,
mother of the first "test tube baby," had said to her husband, "You'll
have to find yourself a proper woman. I've nothing to give our marriage now that I can't have a child."[29] As a means to transcend our

mortality, the drive for children in both men and women is strong, but for women legitimacy depends on it.

The legacy of Betty Friedan and second-wave feminism has been a severing of the tie between white femininity and the responsibility and privilege of domesticity. The split of private domestic life assigned to women and the public life assigned to men has been, in this culture, a feature of white middle-class gender dynamics. Unlike black women, who have always been expected to be mothers *and* workers, white women find themselves spending half their lives trying to navigate the male world and avoid detection as women. This requires that they remain child-free. But they spend the other half trying to recover their womanhood by pursuing motherhood. In this tension between having children and not, having biology at the beck and call of convenience has intensified women's ambivalence toward motherhood.

In my survey on the body, many women who put off childbearing by tricking their body with contraceptives noted that when they experienced infertility later, their fear of their body intensified. When they were ready for children, their older and less fertile body simply did not cooperate. Prepared to assert themselves in every other sphere, they found that their bodies seemed to have independent lives.

Those of us who become used to efficient, well-planned lives will have trouble with pregnancy until we learn to see it as a creative process instead of an engineering project. Pregnancy requires a woman to be totally present in the now of the body, making her keenly aware of her femaleness. It is a period of intensified vulnerability and sensing her interconnectedness with humanity—literally. Everybody is interested; even a perfect stranger in a grocery store aisle won't refrain from commenting on her swollen belly.

Certainly, pregnancy has significant communal implications. But although the childbirth experience holds profound meaning for the community, it has been increasingly medicalized and is now often treated like a disease or a traffic accident. It is true that medical science has saved the lives of many mothers. But the argument is about who has the lion's share of control. Clearly, natural birth has been marginalized both by the medical establishment and by women themselves, who relinquished it out of fear or a desire for convenience. The current U.S. rate of nearly 25 percent of births being by cesarean, a medically unjustifiable level, demonstrates that women are increasingly disconnected from their own birthing process.[30]

Neither are we encouraged to nourish children at our breast, for society is more shocked by the sight of a breastfeeding mother than by a plunging neckline. Nursing mothers are forced into bathrooms to sit in stalls while they feed their children away from public view, or worse, they are hooked up to breast-pumping machines so they can continue working in an environment that excludes their babies. The entire female reproductive life cycle has been marginalized.

And the trend continues with promises of more extreme measures in the future. The same medical science that freed woman from unwanted and untimely pregnancies is now attempting to turn her into a manufacturing site with infertility treatments and surrogacy. In a society that values production more than reproduction, it is natural that women's reproductive capacity should be turned into a tool for capitalistic exploitation. Reproduction continues to be severed from the body through technologies such as donor insemination, in vitro fertilization, and surrogacy. These make women and men into a means of production and children into products. Reproductive technologies have created a class of "brood mare" women who bear children for the more affluent. We all know of others besides model Cheryl Tiegs, who used a surrogate to carry her twins when she was fifty-two years old.[31] In the name of reproductive freedom, the elite new woman no longer needs to bear her own child.

Manufactured human embryos can now be made available for any end—a logical outcome of contraceptive abuse, abortion, and a general philosophy of reproductive liberalism. The trend assumes procreative autonomy and the right to procreate by any means possible. It continues to see women as breeders and their bodies as predicable problems to be tamed and controlled by medical technology.[32] The social pressure to be a mother is so strong for some women that they are willing to risk their own health in order to conceive under aggressive and invasive infertility treatments that cost hundreds of thousands of dollars.[33] The emotional toll of failures, miscarriages, and incidents of multiple births equals or exceeds the physical toll, with babies at risk for serious complications and neurological problems. The human cost of reproductive technology is extremely high. Under expensive reproductive treatments, who would not feel cheated if they received less than their ideal offspring?

The $100 million infertility industry is growing and promises to deliver a better and improved child. There are more than three hundred in vitro fertilization centers in North America, and in 1995, 9.3 million women in the United States were using some kind of infertility service. In 1996 alone, 21,198 babies were born through technology-assisted reproduction. This is double the previous year's total. Still, with the highly experimental methods only 20 percent of couples take home a baby.[34] Technology is also available to create families with two mothers and an anonymous sperm donor. At California Cryobank, a sperm bank, 40 percent of the customers are single women who are no longer willing to wait for a suitable husband or have chosen to make their home with another woman. As children are increasingly produced for their ornamental effect, human eggs can be purchased from the young, intelligent, and beautiful for three to five thousand dollars, and up to fifty thousand dollars has been offered for one exceptional human egg.[35] In vitro fertilization can be produced with any of four possible parents: husband, wife, sperm donor, and egg donor. Embryos conceived outside the womb change the question from one of relationship to one of ownership, and individuals are asserting rights over them as property. The possibility of a cloned child in the near future further increases the distance between our bodies and our offspring.

In the United States today, a child can have a genetic mother, a gestational mother, and a social mother—each a different woman. At the same time the country can easily be mistaken for a child-free zone. Today it appears we are seeking children very much like David in the movie A.I.—perfect, always good, always loves you, and doesn't use up any resources.

When I was growing up in Argentina—and this carried over to our immigration to the United States—children were present everywhere. We went to weddings, funerals, and other people's houses for dinner. We were nearly always included in adult activities. There was a lot of noise, but nobody complained. Okay, they complained, but it just added to the rambunctious atmosphere. We were fully part of the community, whereas today's American child has become a status symbol and a disposable fashion accessory. In the end, a society that excludes children devalues women and ultimately all human life. This communal breakdown steals our humanity.

As we have sought transcendence by overcoming biological barriers, we need to consider what we have lost. As women, we have experienced firsthand the effects of contraceptive and technological reproductive abuse along with abortion, anorexia, bulimia, cosmetic surgery, and other body manipulating practices. Under the duress of the social meaning of women's bodies in advanced societies, freedom of choice has become an illusion. When issues of race are intersected, possibilities of escaping the terms of our embodiment are even more limited. Promises of more tools to enhance our reproductive "freedom" should make us ask, *What exactly are we being offered?* We have seen how what are presented as "remedies" for our embodiment in the end steal our humanity and begin to break down our communal relationships. Breakdown in community makes all relationships tentative.

In our attempt to transcend the social meaning of our bodies, we wage a spiritual war in our bodies. What we are seeking turns out to be a form transcendence that betrays the entire body-self. Under disempowering terms that marginalize our bodies, we find ourselves operating under the assumption that our body is a prison for the soul—the true self.

I believe the body is instead imprisoned by a disoriented soul that holds it under siege. This incarceration of the body by the soul has produced a spirituality that is hostile to the life we live in the body. It seems to require that we ignore the place and cultural meaning of our bodies in order to reach the divine. The wrongful assumption of an inner "higher" self drives the popular spirituality that we are being offered in our culture. Such a spirituality can't address the everyday issues arising from the relationships and creative endeavors that the body mediates.

Given both the futility and the perils of attempting to escape the body, we must refuse any spirituality that is *disembodied*. We need to recover our relationship to a God who is near and a spirituality that addresses our social experience as women. This is the only way we will be able to regain our full humanity and find a path that embraces the life we live in the body yet does not reduce us to the body.

4

Es Una Nena!

How the Current Spirituality Capitalizes on Our Sense of Powerlessness

Yet our narratives, or ways of thinking, are *grounded*
in our bodily experiences in nature and society.[1]

Charlene Spretnak

I was born in a small private clinic in Buenos Aires. The clinic allowed Protestants to avoid the Hail Marys and other rituals required in public hospitals by stern-looking nurses—that is, if you wanted your medicine! I can imagine the small room where I was born resounding with the proclamation in a hearty male voice, "Es una nena!" Had the doctor announced, "It is human!" it just would not have had the same ring. This simple proclamation was one of the most important things that has ever been said about me.

"It's a girl!" That first phrase uttered at our birth comes loaded with possibilities and anticipation. It also comes with complexities and questions about our nature and what we are to become. "One is not born, rather one becomes, a woman,"[2] Simone de Beauvoir says. We are future mothers, wives, sisters, girlfriends, and always daughters. The various relationships grounded in our bodies need definitions and parameters.

81

For better or worse, it is the work of parents, extended communities, and mediating institutions to teach us how to negotiate these. The difference of being born female follows us throughout life. It starts early, with a set of assumptions about our nature and a social experience that creates a sense of lack of control.

This chapter will look at how in learning to navigate the male-defined public world we have experienced a continual alienation from ourselves, producing feelings of powerlessness. As our secular dreams for social, economic, and political power began running out of steam and our obsession with our body has grown, we are now rediscovering spirituality. As we attempt to face our failure to become all we could be, we find that the difference that has identified us since birth is to blame. Our search for a spiritual solution starts with self-help, treating our failures as personal problems that have developed in isolation from a cultural dialogue. Yet a cultural history in which the nature of transcendence and our bodies are at odds has major effects on the spirituality we embrace. The polarizing view of our spiritual nature, body against self, shapes the spirituality we are being offered and how it is packaged to us as women. It is a spirituality that capitalizes on our sense of powerlessness and ignores the sociocultural limits we experience due to our embodiment. It is a spirituality that seeks to break us away from the body-bound experience while still acknowledging our "difference." Since this difference is situated in our body, can a spirituality that ignores our bodies be effective in giving our everyday acts meaning and coherence? In previous chapters we have seen how the body performs a spiritual role in not only pointing us to the transcendent but also keeping us connected to the community. Can a disembodied spirituality provide the connection to the divine and human community that we crave?

The Difference

Before most of us were received in a pink blanket, scientist and psychologists had spent decades studying sex differences. So far they haven't decided, and probably they never will, how much of our femininity is learned or imposed by our environment. The research studies provide a list of gender-specific characteristics: women listen, pay attention, and respond more to a speaker, smile more, and change their behavior based on cues from those around them. An easy conclusion is that women are more relationally dependent.[3] Men, on the other hand, interrupt more often and are more likely to state their opinion and stick with it, which suggests the conclusion that men are more assertive. But these findings fail to answer the question: Is this biological or simply the result of reinforcing gender expectations? For the average person these well-studied gender differences sounds like common sense that ends up packaged in countless relationship books. Given the wide-scale pursuit of gender equality over the last forty years, it is surprising that popular talk of difference has made a significant comeback. Have we finally realized that equality has always been practically problematic even though the idea of equal value has been given near-universal lip service?

Equality generally gets implemented as sameness rather than equal value of genuine difference. Structural equality with men has often made women subject to male life cycles, expected to compete on the same terms as men in institutions that have been set up by men for men. Being late or leaving to attend to a sick child prove that we are not as committed to our work, too distracted by family matters. In the pursuit of practical equality, sometimes inadvertently and sometimes quite deliberately, men are set up as the standard by which we measure our lives. We find ourselves exasperated by the need to work a double shift to prove our worthiness. This may be why women have been leaving corporate America at twice the rate of men to build their own companies and home-based businesses.[4] Maybe some women are finally catching on. As Germaine Greer noted, "we have settled for equality but what we need is assertive difference."[5] I believe we are witnessing the beginning of difference without shame.

Two assumptions undergirding much of today's gender research need to be examined and questioned: first, that we can link findings of "sex difference" to all males and all females and therefore ignore great individual variation; second, that all behavioral difference is biologically based and therefore unchangeable—a biological deterministic approach.[6] Because difference is based on averages, any two individuals of opposite sexes may be statistically similar in characteristics such as verbal ability and aggressiveness.[7] When all men and all women are considered together, the bell-shaped overlap is greater than Mars and Venus are willing to admit. For example, a University of North Carolina at Chapel Hill study of the difference in math ability between the sexes shows a mere 1.5 percent difference, with males having a slight advantage.[8] Is this biological or is this due to math's being deemphasized for girls as they get older? It would be irresponsible to conclude from this study that any one girl is less competent in math that any one boy. In all likelihood from person to person the difference is not present.

It's important to be aware of assumptions, since in the past sex difference conclusions were likely to be used against women, to justify keeping us in a certain social position. Hormones, still often invoked as the reason for sex difference, are often interpreted as causing deficiencies in women. The same hormones that are supposed to make women want babies and take care of other people also supposedly make us irrational and prone to hysteria. Women's hormones require medical intervention, while male hormones are often used to excuse bad behavior—the "wired for lust and violence" argument. Biochemistry is going beyond hormones to research at the cellular level in an attempt to pin down gender difference. How much of the difference between men and women is accounted for by nature, however, and how much is due to nurture is still a topic of debate. What we can say is that any actual difference between biological male and female bodies is accentuated by nurture in a culturally defined space. Difference rooted in how males and females physically experience our bodies is real. Plainly, women carry the reproductive burden. But how the culture interprets the meaning of this difference is what often creates our troubles.

"The fundamental thing is that women are more like men than anything else in the world," wrote Dorothy Sayers.[9] Even though it has become fashionable to speak of men and women as though they were from different planets, we are more alike than we are different. Men and women together bring life into the world, creating bodily ties and communities. Together we are subject to a whole list of limitations that are simply human. Together we also share a huge range of human attributes, such as the desire to protect and provide for those we love and the need to be respected. Nevertheless, in the need for social order, we are continually motivated to define what makes us different and to draw the line between femininity and masculinity. But an enumerated list of gender differences, in the end, doesn't really tell us anything. What matters is what we do with the differences—how we interpret them and what their implications are for how we construct our lives.

According to gender researcher Sandra Bem, no other human experience has as extensive and intensive effect on every domain of life as the dichotomy of male and female. "Toys, clothing, occupations, hobbies, the domestic division of labor—even pronouns—all vary as a function of sex."[10] In this way society assures order for itself. One is taught the appropriate behaviors and attitudes and how to move about in the world as a woman or a man. Many of us lose our way. Many women learn the lessons too well, forgetting our originality and individuality and merely playing the script handed to us. Or we fail to learn the lessons adequately, thereby causing ourselves pain because we never measure up. A woman who complies with the cultural lessons has it easier.

The worst-case scenario is that one simply cannot comply because one's body won't cooperate by meeting the ideal. For Melinda it was difficult to project demure femininity. As a girl of eleven years she had grown to the unfeminine height of five feet ten inches and a full 36DD breast size. She took up space and towered over the rest of the class. Her consolation prize was to cultivate inner beauty, but she was still being judged in the world by outer beauty.

An overly boisterous girl also finds herself at odds with a system that values quiet influence over direct engagement on the part of women. Her world is ready to silence her through subtle but clear messages.

To doubt the social process of woman-making and reject the gender script that is handed to you at birth is to reject the offer of womanhood—as if womanhood could actually be granted to you, as if someone could decide to *let* you be a woman. Thus we reach conclusions early in life about the nature of masculinity and femininity and what is to be valued in each.

I concluded early that the male mind was much more complex and interesting. Men thought about grand things, adventure, and the meaning of the universe. From my dad and his friends I learned about Nietzsche, the evils of communism, and Armageddon. They expanded my imagination and taught me to think about what might be possible. No matter what their actual lot in life was, the men I knew always thought big and talked big. In a faith-based community with a strong sense of justice, never would I be told that I could not do something. It was my father and two uncles who dared to live a dream by immigrating to the United States.

The women in my family followed along with simpler visions. For them, coming to the United States offered the possibility of emulating the American housewife and acquiring a matching washer and dryer. They taught me about the material world: how to make a good pasta sauce, sew a dress with no pattern, collect S&H Green Stamps for toasters, and the value of having a safe place to return to—a place called home.

It was an unspoken expectation that I would simply continue in the way of all female flesh. But I knew early that I wanted *both* the adventure provided by the world of men *and* the safety of women's cozy niche. It was my task to figure out how to bring these two worlds together.

Reemergence of Difference

The struggle between the two worlds followed me into the turbulence of the 1970s, when women began a massive crossover in a series of women's firsts. We were attempting to escape the limiting definitions of our gender and shake our sense of powerlessness. I came of age as limitations on women's participation in the privileged sectors of the public sphere come down one by one. It seemed as if every day on the evening news Walter Cronkite was announcing how another woman had crashed through a gender barrier. In 1971 Billie Jean King became the first woman athlete to earn over $100,000 in a single year. In 1973 Emily Howell became the first female commercial pilot. One after another, smoked-filled, walnut-paneled men's clubs and executive suites opened their doors.

Armed with the pill, women seemed to have freedom for endless opportunities, and gender differences were now of no consequence. The secular promise of earthly power wooed us. Women, we believed, could do anything if given equal access. We took this to mean that if something could be done, it should be done—especially if it had only been done by men before. We could play as well as the boys, and in stiff dress-for-success suits we could emulate their attitudes. We rushed to divorce court or postponed marriage and developed a stiff upper lip. Some of us had our babies and were back at the office full-throttle in six weeks flat—no problem. We thought of ourselves as men in skirts and called ourselves "Ms." To be segregated as women and be addressed as "the girls" was perceived as demeaning. To question our own limits was not allowed.

By the mid-1980s we had proved that indeed a woman could accomplish a great deal in the upper levels of the public sphere if she was willing to pay the price. And there *was* a hefty price for participation in these male-dominated arenas, places that had been closed off not only by gender but by race. In the decade that followed, however, we were reminded that we only had a few childbearing years remaining. Threatened by a shortage of men, boomer women began to reevaluate. When we stopped long enough to consider what we had accomplished, we began to look at the kind of woman we had left behind. We wanted to recover the potential mother, wife, aunt, sister, and daughter that had been sidetracked by new opportunities and was now missing in action. We wanted more, and we gave birth to a boomlet. But the identity of this new mother was no longer tied to the home. The privilege of domesticity gave way to the privilege of sameness. Daycare became a growth industry.

As women became established in the ranks of middle management and the professions, the world felt the impact of our presence. Though often it was only lip service, companies that had previously ignored the working mother trumpeted their family-friendly policies. Flextime, parental leave, on-site daycare, and job sharing became hot topics in public conversation. We wanted it all. Companies starved for educated and trained labor gave us the mommy track. To some this looked like a way to use our talents and pay us less. To others it allowed the possibility of obtaining the elusive balance we were seeking. For me, and a growing minority, this was not enough. When my husband and I were ready to have children, I left corporate America to start my own business.

But was the corporate accommodation to the new professional working mother proof that we were merely bringing our "personal" issues and all the implications of our difference into the office? Carol Gilligan's *In a Different Voice* showed that women are indeed more relational and have their own "ethic of care" to guide them. Other writers took up these themes. A variety of studies told us that women's social and team-building skills make them particularly well suited for the new work environment.

But it was also this cooperative approach that was keeping women in middle management.[11] Experts were telling us that we were trapped by an inherent "need" to nurture that led to putting other people's dreams ahead of our own. Desperate to make sense of the parts of our lives that didn't, we read Mars and Venus books, nodding in agreement. We didn't even complain about the narrow gender definitions. "Difference" was in again. We knew it all along; guys just didn't get it. Years of feigned sameness and solidarity with men were replaced by the politics of difference. And frustration with attempts at sameness and the reality of difference had set us up for a distinct spiritual awakening.

Fading Secular Dreams

By the mid-1990s, with women securely trapped in middle management by an unyielding system, feminism was declared dead.[12] Its political power had been neutralized by its gains. But when statistics about women's advancement are thrown around in the early years of the new millennium, we often don't know whom to believe. We are now being told that women can have any job or life we choose and that the glass ceiling is in our own heads. Carly Fiorina, CEO of Hewlett-Packard and one of the few women who have made it to the top, was quoted in the press: "I hope we're at the point that everybody has figured out that there is no glass ceiling."[13] At least not for her, so what is holding back the rest of us? I was about to find out.

After over twenty years in business, I was in a hotel ballroom one day with over one thousand professional women to hear the likes of "Dr. Phil" and Suze Orman talk to us about getting control of our lives. We were there to find out what was holding us all back. Among the spiritually laden encouragements to create our own reality through positive thinking, a lesser-known black speaker was making us laugh. I was wiggling in my seat, waiting for the punch line, as she encouraged us to be as loyal to each other as we are to the men who leave us. The crowd roared. The message was that women are different and must stick together in order to make it to the next level and smash the glass ceiling once and for all. To reach the next level of success, we were told, we must tap our undeveloped spiritual side.

This was a long way from my early career days, when I attended stodgy, sterile business gatherings where we talked about time management and budgetary controls. Long gone are the days where a conference exclusively for women would be rejected as marginalizing. We have now been introduced to a spirituality whose main feature is to provide us with super-charged self-esteem ready to overcome any remaining barriers. This power spirituality combined with a new enthusiasm for gender difference promises to take women to the next level and secure our dreams.

There is no doubt: previously secular women have been rediscovering the power of spirituality. We are no longer willing to settle for only economic and social advancement, no matter how expansive. As male-defined secular power gave way to feminine-defined spiritual power, we have learned that what our mind can conceive we can achieve. Women have begun a movement to harness our spiritual potential and break the internal glass ceiling, calling it self-help. We had fought for choice in all areas of our lives, and now choice needs to be taken to a metaphysical level. The message is simple: We need to tackle our interior world the way we handled the outer world. We can pull ourselves up by our metaphysical bootstraps and confront all those fears and insecurities that keep getting in our way. If only we felt good about ourselves, we could enjoy the fruits of our labor and run our lives instead of our lives running us. Self-help experts advise us to do some emotional archaeology and recover the inner child. It is low self-esteem, not believing in ourselves, and fear of success that have kept us from true happiness. We need the "courage" to be rich.[14] The interior voices of abusive fathers and impotent mothers need to be silenced. We are encouraged to look within, listen to our own inner voice, and imagine a new world for ourselves.

Iyanla Vanzant tells us to "use the power of choice to create optimum conditions; a choice is a mental magnet that attracts everything like it unto it."[15] Through a meta-choice, a choice that affects the universe at a cosmic level, we can create our life regardless of the outer obstacles we face. Through the gateway of self-improvement we can become whole people by uncovering and valuing the powerful inner woman who is waiting to come out. Our task is to simply unleash her.

But the spirituality that is currently being offered is cut off from the body's implications. It is a continuation of viewing ourselves as having an autonomous "true self." This spirituality proposes a Cartesian dualism in which the self is not only beyond but also more real than our body. We have become accustomed to think of "the real me" as the portion of ourselves that is not limited by physical boundaries or constrained by social demands. In some way this dislocated self seeks to touch something bigger than the immediate. "The real you" is the stuff that advertising campaigns and motivational speakers trade in. It is all tied up with talk of self-discovery and self-invention, and it is the substance of daytime television shows about those who leave unsatisfying jobs and marriages to go find themselves.

It is difficult to reconcile this unencumbered self with women's social reality, so we blame ourselves. We look at perplexingly low numbers of women at the top and begin naming the self-limiting attitudes that have kept us underrepresented in many fields. At times it appears that we have been victims of systematic exclusion. At other times we look like amazons fully in control of our destiny. The reality is that while we have made great strides in fields like law and business, where women have come to dominate many mid-management positions, in Fortune 500 companies women are still represent only a dismal 4.1 percent of top earners and 12.5 percent of corporate officers.[16] Women still earn only 20 percent of engineering degrees and remain a small minority of those in the engineering profession.[17] Even these numbers come at a price. Where you do find women in these ranks you also find fewer children, fewer marriages, and more divorce. You also see more unconventional marriages. Four out of the five top women in the Fortune Power 50 list have husbands who don't work.[18] The explanations for the shortfall, which we have heard before, have a familiar ring. Women are opting out for domestic life. They are not risk takers. They are too concerned about everybody else to exercise the ruthlessness needed to gain access to the top. Basically we are being told that we are wimps and we are the reason our success has been limited.

Then there is the perennial internal reason articulated by Helen Grieco, president of California's chapter of the National Organization for Women, in reference to women in the high-tech industry: "Women have to be encouraged to be smart and technologically powerful and that will not impact their sense of being feminine and attractive."[19] Clearly, self-limiting behavior and self-talk are getting in our way. Gender dichotomies still play in our heads; we see ourselves as powerless, intuitive beings largely defined by our sexual attractiveness.

Our femaleness and what it symbolizes clearly point to the need to redefine power and success for ourselves. But the secular dream will require a stronger solution than economic and social answers have provided. As we are assured that our new place in the world will not be taken from us, the questioning begins. Is this all? Is this the limit of what women can become? Why do we still feel powerless? We begin to search for a kinder and gentler life—a spiritual call that will allow us to succeed on our own terms.

"You! Got! The Power!"

At the dawn of the new millennium, Americans are spending over 2.5 billion dollars a year on self-improvement, trying to unleash their true self[20]

This is a very different scenario from the late 1970s, when I started my business career. As women were busy making their initial entrance into the male bastions of power, I watched those going before me. They demanded entry into the exclusive male business clubs, networking lunches, and boardrooms. We wanted access to the same level of political and economic power that men enjoyed. To do this we emphasized our sameness and solidarity with men, and we tried to ignore their sexual boorishness.

Now, along with tea and a fashion show, we are encouraged to "turn our dreams into reality" and be "catapulted into our destiny."[21] This type of marketing attracts sell-out audiences because it is women who have self-esteem problems, appearance anxiety, and depression. We followed the rules given to us by life coaches, we color-coded our wardrobes, yet we still agonize over missed periods and yeast infections. The self-improvement industry makes money off our self-loathing; why else would it need to keep reminding us to love ourselves?

Of course, spiritual gurus and marketers understand the existential fix women are in. They understand our need to escape the female experience and all its limiting implications, and they use spiritual language as a borrowed marketing tool. This is why audiences of Deepak Chopra, author of *Ageless Body, Timeless Mind,* are mostly female and mostly professional—they're the ones who have hit the wall.[22] (By the way, you can buy his book at your local aromatherapy bar.) As Chopra puts it, "women are more open," and by being so, women have made spirituality the fastest-growing segment of book publishing.[23] This also must be why the no-nonsense, practical, middle-America Lands End catalog began featuring a column called "Her Turn" where we are told to unfold our soul and seek inner silence and moments of illumination.[24] Huh? What this actually means in real-life terms escapes me.

Women in the first decade of the twenty-first century are being propelled into spirituality against a broader cultural backdrop. The emphasis is on a mix-and-match, nonexclusive spirituality of the moment, not the old-time religion inherited from your grandmother. "Religion" is now associated with self-perpetuating institutions and old rules and rituals that are disconnected from everyday experience. "Religion" brings to mind dull and irrelevant sermons, guilt-producing admonitions, and a total lack of humor. Many people in our culture believe that religion produces hung-up people unable to live fully, people much like the parents portrayed in the film *The Virgin Suicides*—so rigid that they're unable to deal with the emerging sexuality of their daughters.

Yet with 96 percent of Americans claiming a belief in God, the question of whether God exists can be left to academic ivory towers. The rest of us want something user-friendly that provides an explanation of who we are and where we are going and gives us a sense of power. But a society that has made the self-made person its hero is now finding itself at the end of its emotional rope. We don't care what you call God, just as long as the concept makes you feel better. What women care about is, can God or something close to the idea of God rescue us from an endless cycle of pursuing more but ending up with less?

Our secular disillusionment is making way for a spiritual awakening that promises to give us more than what we have obtained through renegotiating our social placement. It will provide a way to address our more elemental needs. But will it be able to take us out of our own skin and help us smash through interior barriers, to break through both the limits of our femaleness and our limiting self-talk? We have not negotiated all the terms by which this spirituality will overhaul our lives, but it seems that spiritual fads and old-time religion have gotten mixed up with consumerism. American commercialism has finally met Maslow's need for self-actualization. The result is exemplified by model Christy Turlington, a practicing Catholic and hardcore yoga devotee, promoting a line of clothing for "mind/body sports."[25] The mixture of timely marketing and profession of faith makes one wonder where the money stops and genuine spirituality begins. This extends to corporations across the board.

Businesses are not only marketing to the public demand for the spiritual but realizing that their own employees want work and career to be more than economically rewarding. Previously, due to fear of exclusion and causing offense, business had avoided any language smacking of the religious. Staunchly secular American business was busy delivering the bottom line, not saving our souls. But no more. In order for business to attract and retain highly skilled workers, they must provide more than good benefits and working conditions. They must offer employees a more powerful intangible, provide means for people to realize their full potential. Like the women's conference I attended, which was sponsored by a major business organization, many individual companies are tapping the power of in-house spirituality in order to increase the bottom line. While exclusionary "religion" is out, spirituality, defined as "interconnectedness," is big.[26] Companies hope to transform their environments by increasing the feeling of meaningful "interconnectedness" among employees and customers. This in turn will yield larger consumer spending and more economically productive employees.

Spirituality driven by economics—and vice versa—is everywhere. A scan of business news includes a parade of prayer breakfasts, books the likes of *Jesus CEO, The Tao of Leadership,* and the Dalai Lama's *Ethics for the New Millennium*. Muslims are rolling out prayer rugs. Shamans are being called in. Office décor is following feng shui principles. Companies like Ford hire ecumenical chaplains to make the hospital visits and attend to crises previously handled by local church clergy. Xerox looks to revolutionize product development by inviting employees to a "vision quest," where at a retreat in a natural environment they seek inspiration from the muses on how to build a better product.[27] Refusing to be left behind, through the Alliance of Holistic Lawyers even divorce attorneys are seeking to become healers and peacemakers, soothing painful emotions.[28] Clearly the genie is out of the bottle and into the executive suites.

As business has seen spirituality as a potential source of profits, the medical profession is looking to spiritual practices for new ways of healing. Not leaving the scientific mind behind, the new field of "neurotheology" seeks a biological basis for our spiritual quest.[29] Research has concluded that religious people are less depressed, have healthier immune systems, and deal better with addictions.[30] Spiritual belief is seen as way of coping with a stressful world. The effectiveness of prayer, therapeutic touch, and a vast array of Eastern and alternative medical practice is being researched by a previously hostile medical establishment. In her popular *Women's Bodies, Women's Wisdom* Christiana Waldrop offers a mix of traditional and alternative medicine with a dose of spirituality: her chapter "The Female Energy System" includes an explanation of the chakras, or centers of energy, defined and originating in the Vedas, a sacred Hindu text.[31] Apparently there is enough sickness and pain to go around, and traditional Western medicine needs all the help it can get.

Paracletes

As women, how we view our bodies will affect what type of spirituality we will embrace. Media, technology, and a broader social history of ambivalence about the body contribute to how we ultimately view the relationship between soul and body. Matter and spirit are being further disassociated. For women with their philosophical tie to the body this can be a relief. Americans are turning more and more to the Internet for their faith experience; on various sites you can communicate with a channeler who claims to speak for Jesus himself, participate in a coven, or request healing from a distance. Capitalizing on the 78 percent of Americans who express a need for spiritual growth,[32] Belief.net, a super-charged inclusive spirituality and religion site, serves up a wide assortment of beliefs and practices. Here you can experience "the Way of the Cross," join a prayer circle, and try a variety of meditation methods as well purchase an array of "spiritual" products. Cofounder Bob Nylen says of Belief.net, "We want to be the America Online for the soul, the Yahoo for the internal life."[33] To be sure, interest in spiritual practices has always been part of American culture. Now more of us are interested in extending the boundaries of traditional religion with its ties to a local community to the virtual faith of a bodiless self.

For escape of the spirit from the body, technology is promising more than the Paraclete coming alongside to assist us; it is promising to become the spiritual experience itself. Miniaturization has created the future possibility of nanobots, blood-cell-sized scanning machines that when injected into our body will enhance our brain capacity. Some predict that by 2029, through the injection of billions of nanobots into our veins, we will be able "to enter a three dimensional cyberspace—a virtual reality environment" without ever leaving our chair. Technology will also seek to open up the limits of the body by allowing the possibility of downloading our entire consciousness into a computer so we can live forever as a disembodied being. Ray Kurzweil, inventor and high-tech entrepreneur, announces, "I regard the freeing of the human mind from its severe physical limitations a necessary next step in evolution. . . . Technological evolution, therefore, moves us inexorably closer to become like God. And the freeing of our thinking from the severe limitations of our biological form may be regarded as an essential spiritual quest."[34] Thus technology is promising spiritual immortality and deliverance from the mess of the body.

The technological disconnection between transcendence and history, place, and embodied community began with early radio and television preachers, who saw the electronic medium as a way to spread God's Word to the masses. They inadvertently contributed to the increasing assumption that the spiritual quest is a solitary activity that can be pursued in the comfort of your own home.[35] Mediating institutions appear less and less necessary for spiritual practice. Though we claim to want community, we are increasingly reluctant to make the physical and emotional commitment necessary to actually create and participate in it. It is easier to join a cyberspace community of believers or follow an online teacher, because the medium does not require much of us. We can bypass bodily presence, which demands response to a multiplicity of physically mediated communications. Eyes, body language, and smell give me clues to who you are and what your life means. In cyberspace you can bypass dealing directly with my physical presence and communicate in a narrow and confined space.

In cyberspace accountability is practically nonexistent. We can ask, "Who is my neighbor?" and there is no answer. In cyberspace we can remain anonymous and disconnected while retaining an illusion that we "know" one another. In cyberspace we become a people without a history. We experience the dispersion and perhaps the dissolution of community.[36] This dislocated spirituality places a premium on inner space and ignores the concreteness of the outer space we occupy, blurring the diversity of individuals for an illusionary unity. We can ignore race, gender, and disability, which inform how each of us experiences the world. The world that is seen through the computer monitor is a flattened, homogenized world sanitized of all bodily markers. It produces a spirituality that rejects matter and expresses a profound hatred for the limits of the body and its social placement.

A means to escape the body in some way is an old message that new pharmaceutical gurus are preaching also. In the 1960s the counter-culture prophet Timothy Leary popularized the idea of mind expansion through tricking one's brain with psychedelic drugs. Psychedelics were presented as a possible way to God, providing "liberation from ego and space-time limits."[37] Altering our consciousness through chemical means provides relief for the pain of being in our body. Today mood-altering drugs are a mainstream way to cope, maintain our sanity, or simply handle being female. Medical doctors such as Andrew Weil promote "integrative medicine" and appear to have no qualms about the use of mind-altering drugs.[38] Worldwide, Prozac, a psychiatric drug commonly prescribed for depression, is a $597 million business for Eli Lilly and Company. It is the third best-selling prescription drug in the United States.[39] Repackaged for women, it becomes Serafem, to relieve the quintessential female issue, PMS, and promises to make you "more like the woman you are." Instead of questioning the sociocultural factors that drive a woman's depression, physicians and pharmaceutical companies associate her symptoms with her embodiment. The identification of PMS as a psychiatric disorder, still inconclusive, furthers the idea that women are irrational and trapped in uncooperative bodies. It seems that while men may be set up by culture to use drugs to get in touch with God and experience transcendence, women are set up by biology to need drugs in order to cope with being in their bodies.

New Matriarchs

But against the grain of technology that expresses hostility toward the body, an opposing theme has recently emerged. The matriarchs of feminist spirituality are offering a spirituality that is resident *in* women's bodies. In the words of this counter-movement's most vocal antitechnology theorist, Mary Daly, "the demonic forces of technomadness are armed not merely to kill off but also to *hideously and irreversibly mutate and mutilate all Elemental Life.*"[40] According to radical spiritual feminists, "Elemental Life" is grounded in women's bodies. They are challenging "necrotechnologist" or death-loving men who seek to subdue nature and women's bodies through all forms of body-hating technology. They rightly question biotechnology with its promise of artificial wombs, cloning, and genetically designed human beings. They charge that both women and the earth are under assault, that technology is seeking to destroy not only women and their life-giving power but the earth that provides life for all of us.

These spiritual feminists oppose not only patriarchal technology but any and all spirituality that emphasizes transcending body and nature. Because women are associated with the body, at the root of all these systems, according to Charlene Spretnak, "the objective of patriarchy was and is to prevent women from achieving, or even supposing, our potential: that we are powerful in both mind *and* body and that the totality of those is a potent force."[41] The cycles of menstruation, in step with the waxing and waning of the moon, as well as pregnancy and lactation, give women an elemental power to give life. In feminist spirituality these processes are the source of a spiritual power that men fear. In response men seek to control women through "invented" cultural power. The spiritual feminist paradigm calls women to free themselves from the dictates of the cultural power men control and assert their elemental spiritual power.

According to researcher Cynthia Eller, the new feminist matriarchs are calling us to recapture the ancient matriarchy that reigned under the purview of the goddess.[42] Although its existence is rejected as unlikely by leading anthropologists, the idea is capturing the imaginations of many women. It is a call to envision an Eden when "power was greatly respected for what it is, the production of interlocking life, and it was given *worth-ship*."[43] According to the myth, in this ancient society women were recognized for the life-giving power they possessed and their bodies where held in high regard, while men had little sexual and cultural power.

By embracing the difference manifested in the female body and its associated spiritual power, the new matriarchs hope to overcome the social limits enforced by patriarchy. It is women's psychological dependence that continues to legitimate male political and social power, they claim, hoping we become woman-identified to soothe the negative experiences of our lives. According to Carol Christ, "the simplest and most basic meaning of the symbol of the Goddess is the acknowledgement of the legitimacy of female power as a beneficent and independent power."[44] No longer looking for male saviors, women will find the goddess within themselves.

Feminist spirituality may bring to mind earth mothers sitting around a circle tasting their own menstrual blood, or the Amazon warrior portrayed in the popular television series *Xena*. But mentions of the goddess and the ancient matriarchy are being made in speeches by previously secular feminist leaders. The goddess as a symbol of spiritual female empowerment has emerged because it makes sense at the moment, driven by three things: the resurgence of difference as a place from which women speak, the need for women to go from secular accomplishments to more encompassing spirituality, and the sense of powerlessness that women feel. The convergence of these social-cultural factors has allowed feminist spirituality to go mainstream. You can catch the goddess on ivillage.com during the weekly webcast *Goddess Power Hour.* Through a weekly lesson you can learn about the pantheon of goddesses and find the one the suits you best. But ultimately the goddess is about "seeing our basic womanliness in a new light," developing a more valued and powerful version of our self. As proponents of this movement would say, there is a goddess in every woman.

By playing off woman's difference, women's desire to find meaning in existence, and the powerlessness that women feel, feminist spirituality has taken the politics of difference to a new level. It assumes women's greater spiritual sensitivity springing from their biology and proposes that this essential difference requires that they create spiritual symbols, rituals, and language that express their elemental place in the world.

But will recovery of the goddess as a religious symbol break women's psychological dependence on men and male authority? After economics and politics, is this the logical next step in the advancement of women? Have we no other place to go? Such a move from the transcendence of virtual reality to immanence can trap us in an essentialist view that limits us to our experience and inherited ideas about what it means to be a woman, not only in body but in soul. This spirituality relates our worth and power exclusively to the functions of our body and the maternal attributes that are seen to flow from it. It reinforces the idea that due to our bodily nature women are interconnected, nurturing, and intuitive as opposed to rational, courageous, and self-reliant.

This approach is problematic on many levels. For those who are mothers but who wish to see their lives in a broader scope, it is suffocating to be limited to the experience of motherhood. For women who do not or cannot bear children, it creates feelings of somehow having missed one's vital life purpose. Others will find these female images limiting in a vast number of ways, such as the consignation of women to largely relational roles as opposed to the action orientation ascribed to men. Such images also limit men, since in this view men are unable to overcome their separateness and aggressiveness toward nature. They are excluded from spiritual transformation by virtue of their inability to bear a child and thus cannot fully participate in the hope for the human community.

Feminist spirituality illustrates that whatever we do *with* or *to* our bodies will be motivated by a host of social meanings we have inherited. Feminist spirituality works off the existing gender paradigm with its ideas about women as naturally intuitive. Whatever meaning we wish to extract from our bodies is dependent on what has been layered on them by the larger culture; we do not simply create meaning out of nothing. We must take into account the way we wish to live our lives, and we must negotiate how we will live in the body we have while seeking a spiritual life.

Feminist spirituality does understand well that a spirituality disregarding the embodied life will not take us far, because our physicality is the locus of spirituality; the place in which spirituality occurs. It is fundamental that in seeking to embrace humanity in all its nuances, we deal with the reality of our life in the body, because we are embodied souls.[45]

Renegotiating the Body

Since the body is the location in which spirituality is lived out, the richness of our spiritual life depends on how we view life cycles, aging, beauty, intimacy, illness, and finally our own death. Spirituality must provide potential ways for us to operate freely within a complex web of gender relationships, images, expectations, and assumptions. It must provide freedom—not from the body, but to imagine what is possible even within the body's limitations. Both disbelief and faith create practice and are made flesh in the body. My actions and work in the world are done through and in my body; the truest test of what I profess to be. What we need is a spirituality that honors the body we have and comprehends its social meaning but does not reduce us to it. We need a spirituality that allows us to remain in the body as we reach for something greater and outside ourselves, along with a social vision that redeems the whole person in community and in place.

A woman's spirituality must deal not only with the concreteness of the body but also with the symbolic life that is lived through the female body. The question is, how are we to live in the body when the female body has become a painful place to reside? Faith that truly matters must answer this, because without it there is no real faith or spiritual life. Being in our bodies is so painful that it has become normative for us not to question the absence of the body from our search for mean-ing. What makes us nervous about bringing the body into our spiri-tual search is that on every quarter our bodies have been used against us and we hoped that spirituality would release us from their limita-tions. When the meaning of the body is mentioned, we become skit-tish, fearful that we will be reduced to our bodies. Will it be used against us because it doesn't measure up? Are our thighs too thick? Is our skin too sallow?

At this point women are looking for the power not only to trans-form oppressive systems but to transform who they are. The spiritu-ality we need must be able to illuminate this change. It must inform the ordinary life we live as women, not only or primarily sacred spaces and times. What is needed is a protest of faith more radical, at the root, than social or political solutions can deliver alone. Ultimately the spiri-tual is political, and a protest of faith implies that faith is a political act—it divests the cultural paradigms of their power and speaks for justice. Protest is not only about being in opposition to something but about affirming what is true about ourselves and the world. We can bring into question cultural paradigms through faith in a Creator who defines our boundaries as created beings. We can be in the culture but not ultimately defined by it through participating in God's invisible kingdom. Out of the powerlessness that we experience, faith in God's creative and redemptive acts becomes the locus of our new paradigm of power. And we're going to need this kind of faith, because from every corner, regardless of all our efforts, our embodiment continues to threaten to reduce us.

The fact is, our bodies do imply limitations, sometimes messy lim-itations. And for even the boldest among us, cultural images of beauty and the symbolic role of the body are only part of those limitations. Camille Paglia got it right: "Incarnation, the limitation of mind by mat-ter, is an outrage to imagination."[46] The body keeps us nailed down and connected to the material world. Jesus confirmed this priority of the immediate that is manifested in the body when he taught us to pray, "Give us this day our daily bread." The prayer for daily bread serves as a reminder of the needs of the present moment and that today has enough claims of its own. The certainty of the body's need for daily bread directs us toward a spiritual wisdom made manifest in the body. According to Jesus, we do not have to ignore the body in order to be spiritual; even in its frailty it provides an indication of how we should live and how we are to carry on a spiritual life.

The spirituality of Jesus provides a paradigm for thinking about the body as a place of redemption, not as something to be escaped or ignored. It is a paradigm based on who he is and how he related to those he encountered firmly grounded in space and time. Because of Jesus' redemptive action in and through his body, he can provide us with clear understanding of the body in the divine plan. This requires that the spirituality of Jesus deal with the sense of shame that keeps us from embracing the life of the body. It is the shame of both being born with the difference—the female body—and our own disintegrity.

Before we look directly at Jesus of Nazareth and his redemptive work regarding our bodies, we need to look at the essential origins of the fractured body-self that we experience. This disintegrity discloses itself most readily in how we deal with the suffering and death that is ever present in our lives. The next chapter considers how we experience our suffering flesh and its fundamental, inescapable powerlessness

5

Jars of Clay

The Vulnerability of the Body and Its Ultimate Betrayal

Frailty, thy name is woman!

Hamlet

Penniless and with little prospect for the future, Marsha, a twenty-four-year-old woman from southern Russia, boarded a bus for Germany. She was anticipating work as a housemaid. Unknown to Marsha, the kind woman who had arranged the job placement was a member of a sex trafficking ring. The job was a lure into an international web of exploitation. When Marsha arrived in Berlin, she was taken to a small apartment where she met twenty other young women from Eastern Europe. After a few days her passport was taken; she was told that there was no work for her as a domestic and she would be required to pay the thousand dollars for her trip by providing sexual services for men. In the small storefront bar Marsha was expected to sell her body multiple times in the course of a day. She saw that girls who didn't cooperate were beaten across the back or drugged into submission. With no money, passport, or knowledge of the German language, she had no way out. It was only through a police raid in which she was charged with prostitution that Marsha was able to make her way to freedom.

Like Marsha, each year millions of women and children are lured or forced into prostitution under the threat of beating and emotional intimidation. Over fifty thousand women are trafficked into the United States every year—many from Mexico, smuggled in under false promises of work as nannies and domestics. Close to 200,000 Nepali girls, many under the age of fourteen, are sex slaves in India. Trafficking includes recruitment under false pretense, transportation, and sale of women for sexual services, domestic servitude, debt bondage, and other slaverylike practices.[1] The stories of beatings, disease, and forced abortions are endless. Most are left not only with physical ailments but with devastating emotional and spiritual damage accompanying feelings of brokenness and disassociation. After sexually exploitive experiences it is impossible for many of these women to return to their home countries due to social taboos that would subject them to additional humiliation, discrimination, and ostracism. Driven from their communities and their own bodies, they become women without a home.

Having a female body is the source of these victims' vulnerability. It is this distinctively female vulnerability that drives our sense of powerlessness. But to embrace the life of the body each of us must face the *human* vulnerability we share with men. The fact that we have a body both connects us to the world in profound ways and betrays us. The pain and joy of the body provide us with a certain degree of knowledge about the world and ourselves. The body draws us close in intimacy and locates us in a community. But having a body means that we are continually faced with its limitations; it exposes us to suffering and forces us to deal with death. While our motivation is for life, the reality of death is at our heels—this is at the root of our spiritual conflict. How we deal with it as a society and individuals will affect how we live. The spirituality we embrace must be at peace with terms of our embodiment, our suffering, our joys, and our death.

Physical vulnerability has been associated with woman's reproductive work of pregnancy and lactation and her usually smaller size. It has engendered a host of implications about the meaning and boundaries of her life. Women are often seen to be by nature not only physically weak but, by implication, emotionally and mentally weak as well. An intellectually strong woman is said to "think like a man," implying that women as women are not capable of rational thinking. There is no debate: the world has a long and consistent history of female subordination and victimization due to her generally smaller size and more sexually penetrable body.

The Symbolic Load

In the last twenty-five years rape has been brought out of the closet of silence to be addressed in the public conversation. It is, however, not new, and its history touches on the crux of the gender problem: the rule of man over the more vulnerable woman. Susan Brownmiller's classic *Against Our Wills* chronicles the use of rape throughout history as a tool of control, keeping women in a state of fear and vigilance. We think twice about walking alone in a dark parking lot. In war the female body has been used consistently as a battle site, with women viewed as part of the booty, spoils for the victor. In World War II General Patton realistically assumed that despite his most diligent efforts, generally and "unquestionably" in war there would be raping.[2] It has been at the core of colonization, westward expansion, and black slavery in the American South.[3] But unlike other forms of brutality, such as pillaging of cities and massacre of civilians, rape is located and engaged in women's bodies and associated with their meaning.

The symbolic role of a woman's vulnerable body is seen in the incidence of man-on-man rape in prisons. When women are not available, stronger men turn on physically weaker men in a game of domination and control through rape. In this way weaker men are layered with the meaning of women's bodies, "womanized" through a display of dominance by men seeking to secure their manhood.[4] The symbolic womanizing of weaker men through rape is an extension of the belief that woman's subordination is situated in her body. It is her body and its meaning that justifies her subordination.

Though rape has been used routinely in war, it was not until 2000 that the first case of wartime sex crimes was brought to the International War Crimes Tribunal. More than ten thousand Bosnian women, some as young as twelve, had been rounded up in rape camps in the early 1990s. The rapes were part of a systematic attempt by Serbs to destroy the Muslim and Croat people.[5] In a separate U.S. federal trial, Croatian psychiatrist Mladen Loncar testified that the rape camps were an effort to destroy the individual identity of women and the men and children related to them. Historically, raped women have been damaged goods. They have little credibility in the courts, leaving fathers and husbands in need of compensation. Subsequent to brutalizing rape, Bosnian women continued to be victimized through rejection by their own Muslim people, who prize virginity and monogamy in marriage. Many men rejected wives and daughters who had been raped. Women pregnant with the offspring of their tormentors were driven to despair and suicide.[6]

Serbian defendants claimed that Bosnian women were willing participants, a defense that has been used in every culture throughout history. This defense requires effort to dispute because of a universal definition of woman as a hysterical witness or a seductress.

Thus the multiple effects of rape make it one the most hideous tools of war and crimes against society. It attacks not only a woman's body but all her communal relationships that are mediated through her body, thereby creating spiritual and social havoc. The bodies of mothers and wives serve as social-relational symbols of the community, shaping the female experience. In cultural chaos, attacking them is a means of spiritual genocide, along with the conquest of land. It breaks down the cohesiveness of the relationships that are grounded in women's bodies. For women the embodied symbolic load becomes intolerable.

In our world, the burden of reporting rape lies with the woman, but in order for her to do so she must have a voice in the community. It is difficult if not impossible for women to have such a voice when they are little valued. Women's devaluation can be seen globally, as pregnant and nursing women, along with children, bear the brunt of personal physical assault. In cultures that value boys more than girls, violence begins in utero with sex-selective abortions and female infanticide. In other cultures, under shortages of food, young girls are limited in their food intake so that the more esteemed males can receive adequate portions. Access to precious educational resources is denied due to the belief that girls are in less need of the knowledge that would open up the world to them. These are among many limitations placed on girls simply because of their female bodies.[7] It is not physical vulnerability alone that makes females more open to abuse, but a universal deep-seated belief that girls and women are less valuable and that their life is meaningful only in the context of the male life.

More often than not, women do not even value themselves but instead blame themselves, internalizing their subordination and passing it on the next generation. This internalized subordination yields more violence, whether it is in the form of domestic abuse perpetuated by men or female genital mutilation, of which women are the chief practitioners. Explaining why this is so has been the project of countless thinkers. Regardless of what explanation is formulated, it remains the reality for many of the women of the world. How to solve it still eludes us.

Worldwide, pornography and porn-inspired advertising, female genital mutilation, international sex trafficking of women, epidemic domestic violence, forced abortions, honor killings, and an endless number of abusive cultural practices make the female body a site of dysfunction and assault.[8] In the biblical narrative, a story from one of the lowest periods of Israel's history, marked by injustice, illustrates what happens to women's bodies in cultural chaos. A concubine, already marginalized by social status, is given up and offered for a gang rape that lasts an entire night. In the morning her husband, who had allowed this brutality, finds her dead on the doorstep. He then dismembers her body limb by limb, cuts it into twelve pieces, and sends the pieces across the land as a declaration of war (Judg. 19). Just like this, cultural disintegration readily shows up in or through women's bodies. It appears that, universally, the physical vulnerability of women and deep-seated ideas about the meaning of womanhood incite domination in men and self-loathing in women.

Vital Energy

But female vulnerability is not situated simply in woman's smaller muscles and lighter bones. It is also created through cultural expectation of female passivity. In Victorian America, women's bodies were believed to be more fragile than men's due to menstruation and pregnancy. Edward Clark, a Harvard Medical School professor in the late nineteenth century, argued that middle-class parents should not send their girls to college if they hoped for them to marry and bear children. Clark claimed that intellectual challenges would draw to the brain vital energy from the reproductive organs and threaten female fertility. Another popular idea of the time was that physical exertion would damage woman's reproductive capacity (her reproductive organs could fall out or atrophy) and masculinize her.[9] In spite of the immense physical contributions of women in colonization and western expansion, and of African-American women on plantations, such ideas prevailed. Yet none of these women actually had the luxury of frailty.

Even baby-boomer women can remember sitting out of physical education classes because we had our periods. Teachers who thought they were doing us a favor instead were perpetuating self-limiting behavior. The less you do, the less you can do. In an environment of enforced mental and physical passivity, white middle-class women avoided strength-developing activity for decades in order to preserve their femininity. Through social constraints, female vulnerability is reinforced and feminine frailty learned. In *The Frailty Myth* Colette Dowling chronicles how assumptions about the extent of woman's frailty die hard. As late as 1985, the American College of Obstetricians and Gynecologists issued guidelines restricting physical activity in pregnant women. Instead of individually focused advice limiting heart rate and increased bodily temperature associated with aerobic exercise for the pregnant, the guidelines became an across-the-board standard for all women, accepted without clinical study. By 1994 these guidelines were challenged, however, and the American College of Obstetricians and Gynecologists rescinded it, allowing for individual variation.[10]

In spite of holdover fears of masculinization, women are gaining in terms of physical strength. What women are physically accomplishing today would have been unthinkable fifty years ago. Throughout the last several decades we've seen women's increased participation in formerly male sports. In 1984 women were finally allowed to compete in the Olympic marathon. The common understanding up to then had been that women should not and could not compete in such a physically arduous race. Women are still breaking gender barriers in new Olympic sports such as the pole vault and bobsled races.[11] In 1999 the U.S. women's World Cup-winning soccer team included two mothers who continued a rigorous workout schedule in order to prepare for world-level competition. Joy Fawcett, the highest-scoring defender in U.S. women's national team history, was, at the top of her athletic career, active throughout three pregnancies and breastfeeding.[12] After her second pregnancy and in top physical shape, she was back on the soccer field in forty days, traveling with a nursing baby. Increased opportunities for girls and women to compete in sports is allowing the acceleration of performance results and the breaking of new records. The new women athletes are redefining the nature and extent of female vulnerability. Assumptions of women's frailty must be examined in light of constantly changing cultural expectations about what women can do and should do.

Pain and Certainty

Woman's vulnerability must be understood within the larger context of human weakness we share with men. Human vulnerability is both the beauty and the futility of our bodily experience. Even those who are not sports fans are spellbound by the graceful performance of Olympic athletes who push their bodies to new limits. We tune in to the evening news when another adventurer has overcome the odds and met the challenges of a perilous mountain. The human body, strong and resourceful, can endure extreme pain and embrace brutal hardship. It is amazingly resilient to assault. War-zone stories portray human courage under unbelievably harsh cir-

cumstances. Famine-afflicted people produce horror as they seem
to call out to us from television screens with hollow eyes and bloated
stomachs, but we are also amazed that they survive. Stories of human
endurance captivate us—but why? Is it because our flesh is under
normal circumstances so fragile, like fired clay easily shattered?

Our own everyday frailty becomes most real to us when we experience bodily pain. The memory of physical trauma can last a lifetime. I had an encounter with intense physical pain early in my
childhood. A victim of a fire in our small two-room house, I found
myself in a hospital emergency room with serious burns, stripped
naked, on a gurney. Cold, in pain, and defenseless, I could not control my sense of shame and vulnerability. I have never forgotten it.

Many years later, again gripped by pain, I felt out of sorts and
tense when I first entered Marci's womblike massage room. It took
me in gently, warm, dim, with the sound of flowing water in the
background. Like a midwife assisting in a rebirth of my body, she
coached me with encouragement, and I followed her instructions.
I feared the pain but managed not to fight it. For this one hour I
would try to follow her instructions to be in the present and let my
anxieties go.

I'd been to a massage therapist before, once on a lark in Hot
Springs, where I landed on the massage table of an old guy whose
previous experience was working on Las Vegas showgirls. The second time was at a snooty salon, part of a "day of beauty" given to
me as a Christmas gift. Both of these times I'd rather forget. Was it
bad lighting that kept me from relaxing, or a therapist who wouldn't
stop talking? Yet here I was on a third therapist's table under a much
different set of circumstances, a result of badgering my doctor for a
little more attention after being told to take two ibuprofen and call
him in the morning.

I had injured my back in a rear-end auto collision, and intermit-
tent pain would shoot up from my hip to the middle of my back at
the slightest provocation. Any movement proved to be unbearable.
At one point I was hanging on to walls just to move around at all,
going from heat pad to ice bag, losing time from work and feeling
useless to my family. Feeling cut off and with my thinking fuzzy, I

fell into depression. Days blurred together. Pain was having a profound effect on my emotional and mental state. At the moment of extreme pain I didn't care what was happening around me.

The experience of pain truncates every other concern, and according to Simone Weil, it alone has the power to "chain down our thoughts."[13] As you retreat into the body, hearing becomes muffled and sight opaque; your world crashes in around you. In the words of Elaine Scarry, "intense pain is world-destroying."[14] You are fully in the screaming immediacy of the body. Through the reduction of the world around you, pain brings you into the present, where the body lives. Though the body has a history, it does not live in the past or the future, for unless pain has left a physical marker, when it is gone the body has no memory of it.

According to Scarry, "to have great pain is to have *certainty*."[15] Don't we live most of our lives outside the certain nowness of the body? Anxiety and regrets continually project us into the future or cause us to regress into the past. As we escape the present, the body becomes in a sense entrapped by the soul in a tug-of-war to claim the self. If we avoid pain and meet our basic survival needs, we are free to live the life of the mind, considering what could have been and what may yet be. In the mind we can avoid the present too. But people who have experienced sudden catastrophic illness such as cancer often speak of how the illness taught them what was important and how to live in the moment, grateful for each day as it comes.

Both men's and women's bodies are subject to moment-by-moment weariness, disease, injury, decay. Our bodies mark the passing of time with inevitable aging, no matter how much we try to delay it. We bring the world closer to us through our work, pour ourselves emotionally and mentally into some kind of creation— and then our bones drive us to rest. Disease torments the strongest among us. A sudden injury opens our body to the world and makes us bleed. Our bodies make us the vulnerable humans that we are, reminding us of the immediate. It is the present moment that bodies live in that we must deal with if we are to have a spirituality that embraces our entire humanity. In order for it to matter, spirituality must understand the instructive role of the nowness of the body.

A Delicate Balance

But the suffering of the body is not isolated. It is in constant dialogue with our emotional and spiritual self as we seek meaning to the suffering we experience. The greatest affliction, as Weil describes, is not bodily suffering alone but what we experience in "the absence or death of someone we love, the irreducible part of the sorrow . . . akin to physical pain, a difficulty in breathing, a constriction of the heart, an unsatisfied need, hunger."[16] The interconnection between our bodies and our souls is delicately balanced. Medical science has made it clear that depression, grief, and anxiety make us at least somewhat more susceptible to physical ill-health. We also understand the reverse: physical maladies can drive our emotional life. Sorrow is said to bruise the heart, causing it to ache. Anxiety takes our sleep and makes our stomach churn. Our knees tremble with fear. There are many daily situations in which we experience an active case of nerves or a full-blown panic attack with sweating and heart palpitations.

The sickness and dying of others remind us that our lives are fleeting. At the news that someone has been diagnosed with an incurable disease, many people find it hard to resist the thought that somehow the individual failed. We find it hard to believe that disease and suffering are not caused by individual sin, bad karma, or negative emotions that boomerang. We want to find meaning in the suffering. The body brings up an existential angst that continually haunts us. It creates a cosmic necessity for answers to the questions of identity, meaning, and control that the body makes manifest. But the body can't answer the questions, because the body dies, and this is the crux of the human dilemma. The dignity of humanity includes our ability to dream, think outside of ourselves, inspire, and create, but our weakness is readily seen in our sick, aging, and dying bodies. Nothing reminds us more of our humanity, our finiteness, and our unstable existence than our flesh. After dreaming big dreams, the body seems to expose our human limitations and the brokenness of the world in need of redemption.

Presence and Touch

It is not only our own brokenness but the brokenness of other people that is continually before us. It is through looking at the need of redemption in others that we see our own need and begin to find a way toward healing. Driven by her faith, Michelle is a young woman devoting part of her otherwise comfortable life to alleviating pain in the grit of the inner city. She understands that suffering has a face. It is the swollen face of Josie, a heroin-addicted prostitute with full-blown AIDS and, most likely, hepatitis. The sight of Josie is repulsive. Her entire face is covered with open sores, various wounds, and scars that serve as historical markers of her tragic life's journey. Not merely the product of her own folly, Josie is among the castoffs, the marginal, those who visibly bear the dysfunction of the world in their bodies. Michelle has chosen to simply lend her presence to this woman and others like her who exist between life and death in a seemly unredeemable situation. By looking into their eyes and through small gestures of affirmation, Michelle participates in the recovery of these women's dignity and affirms their humanity. But she does more in this act; she is recovering her own humanity.

Mother Teresa also understood the power of presence and touch on the streets of Calcutta. Picking up a woman who was near death from malnutrition and disease, she carried her to a safe place. The woman took hold of her hand with a smile and said "Thank you" as she died. Those words gave Mother Teresa the motivation to continue, one broken human being at a time. She was only one of many who have devoted their lives to the intersection of the greatest of human virtues, love, and the greatest of human vulnerability, suffering. The alleviation of suffering requires that we be willing not only to be present but to touch the untouchable. Through the body of the healer to the sufferer, love does its greatest work in both.

Those doing healing work understand that physical presence and the human touch have the power to profoundly affect people. According to the Touch Research Institute of Miami, physical touch through massage has been shown to reduce stress levels, aggression, loneliness, anxiety, and reduce the symptoms of many diseases including asthma, cystic fibrosis, and diabetes. Physical touch has been shown to decrease symptoms associated with socially situated disorders such as anorexia, bulimia, and depression.[17] For both children and adults whose health is compromised, touch is vital to recovery and healing.

Physical presence and touch are also necessary components of intimacy. As mutual and naked self-disclosure with another, intimacy, in the words of songwriter Natalie Merchant, asks that you "trouble me, disturb me with all your cares and your worries."[18] The abandoned disclosure of intimacy requires both emotional and bodily trust that what I place in your hands will not be refused but will be cared for, cherished, and valued. Intimacy requires both physical and emotional presence. We feel alienated when a friend who is depressed is present in body but emotionally absent. We also feel hurt when a friend doesn't make time to be with us, because a friend who is never physically available is a friend no more. Friendship and the cohesiveness of communities require both physical and emotional presence.

Our profound sense of brokenness as human beings comes from the betrayal of this basic human need for intimacy that the body mediates. In a society where more people live alone and touch is increasingly eroticized, is it any wonder many of us are suffering from skin hunger? My early years in an Argentine community exposed me to continual hugs and kisses even when I didn't want them. It was not unusual for visitors, even those who were not part of the family, to greet and be greeted with plenty of physical affection from both men and women. To be in someone's home was to be embraced in a literal sense. But in today's American society it is not unusual for a unmarried person to go two weeks or longer without being touched at all by another person. We are in need of the reminder of bumper stickers that say "Hugs not drugs." With no nonerotic way to receive the necessary human touch, we are set up for indiscriminate sexual activity. Up to 40 percent of young people newly arrived on college campuses, lonely and starving for physical contact, engage in the hookup, a casual sexual relationship without commitments.[19] The desire for touch and intimacy, along with other social factors, is so great that women often delude themselves into thinking sex will motivate a man to "be there for her." The problem is that this type of encounter does not bring the whole person as a unity but a disjointed and fragmented presence with no intentionally. Body and soul must be brought *together* for true intimacy to occur, meaning we will "be there" for each other. The body mediates intimacy, but it does not produce it alone.

Betrayals

The immediacy of the body allows us to access the world and to relate to others in the present moment. It provides a certain degree of knowledge. Through pain and pleasure our bodies assure us that we exist. Self-injurers use pain to get into the nowness of their bodies. The rest of us do the same thing through pleasure. That's why sex and roller-coaster rides are such great sellers—they make us feel alive. The body's concreteness and the senses are ready to provide knowledge about the world and ourselves as well as connectedness with others. Through the body we draw near. The body mediates our relationships and the creative spirit. Through our body we gain a sense of place and belonging; and this is its wonder.

But the body also brings a built-in betrayal. Promising life and the means by which we participate in the world, in the end it delivers the blow of death.

Because the body dies and is subject to decay, even as the body provides us knowledge about the world and our relationship to it, this knowledge is uncertain, unstable, continually in flux. It is a wasting and porous space, subject to both cultural interpretation and physiological limits. As much as we seek to treat the body like an object, it does not behave like an object. It is not easily controlled, and we quickly learn that the body is not ordered. Social meanings change; controlling images demand different things on different days. In one context we are expected to show vulnerability and in another strength. The senses can deceive, and the knowledge that they provide doesn't have the degree of certainty that we desire. We seek a degree of knowledge about the self that is impossible to obtain from the body; we see ourselves in the mirror and wonder if this is all we are. The body alone is limited, full of contradictions, unable to provide adequate knowledge about the nature of the self and its relationship to the world.

In light of this reality it is interesting that radical spiritual feminists seek to see the body as a *source* of spiritual knowledge and power. It is also interesting that this type of spirituality is a phenomenon of the well-fed and affluent who have the luxury of good medical care, fitness centers, and carryout meals. The arrogance of affluence is blind to the uncomfortable physical state of most of humanity. Does it make sense to tell a Bosnian woman who has endured incredible suffering and is on the brink of death that her body is spiritually powerful? The body of a woman who has survived rape and abuse experiences disintegrity and loss of control. Her powerlessness is situated in her invaded body; it demands a rescue from without. So why is it that we have become so obsessed with an ambiguous body that will ultimately betray us? Why has the frail body become a place to which we look to provide a sense of identity, meaning, and control?

Part of this is that we have lost any sufficient anchoring for the self and we are seeking to find a permanent location in which to take root. The contemporary self has no stable source from which to emerge and has become a dislocated wanderer. For thousands of years personal identity was a matter of commitments and identifications to and with the land and one's clan. The narratives of place and kinship provided a framework with which to determine who we were. Century to century, things remained essentially the same, people did not venture far from the particularities that gave them an orientation. In the old days you could know a great deal about someone simply by knowing where they were from and who their kin were. A strong sense of community provided a workable, if otherwise limiting, identity. Today, with much more freedom to choose our own way in the world, we are more likely to lose ourselves in the process. Industrialization and radical individualism have aided in this uprooting. The increased anonymity offered by the Internet and urban sprawl decrease our sense of belonging. With increased mobility and the breakdown of marriage, urban children grow up with disjointed sets of friends and fewer permanent ties. Their lives are a conglomeration of school friends, club friends, friends at

Dad's house and friends at Mom's house, stepparents, stepsiblings, and grandparents across the country.

In addition, specialization of work has placed emphasis on what you do rather than where you're from. I can know more about you by knowing you are a stockbroker than by knowing you are from Chicago. I know that as a stockbroker you care about the bottom line and are willing to take calculated risks. Due to increased geographical mobility and the "Wal-Mart effect" that drives out local distinctions, Chicago, like all places, has begun to lose its unique flavor. If you travel at all, you have readily seen that every place begins to look like every other place, with the same chain stores and slogans. Today our identification is primarily related to our work because we are more likely to stay with a profession than to stay in a place for a great deal of our lives. For many the workplace has become the new identifying family.

Another sign of a wandering self is the cult of individualism that puts a premium on personal taste and freedom. It has yielded opportunities to reinvent ourselves. Instead of kinship and place, our identity is based on "lifestyle" choices, from soccer moms to the childfree. The move toward identities of choice, instead of those based on relationship and place, is threatening to turn even previously unthinkable practices into a lifestyle. ABC News reports that web sites have sprung up that teach young women how to become anorexic, with tips and advice on drastic weight loss through pills, purging, and starvation diets. The proponents of the sites claim that anorexia can be a freely chosen lifestyle. They simply want to band together with other like-minded people.[20] Such identities based on associations can be easily dropped and others adopted. With no grounding perspective and no transcendent source, the self is in constant flux and in continual need of a makeover.

With more help than ever for finding our true selves, more books to read, and more seminars to attend, it appears that we are in fact further from having a strong sense of self. Even as we have more and more possible identities from which to choose, *we do not know who we are,* except through fleeting and easily broken associations. Economically rich, we are communally poor.

In this scenario the body becomes the location in which we can create a surer sense of identity and recapture a sense of place. We want control over our piece of real estate; the body becomes the new land to be conquered. As previous chapters have shown, by marking the body both literally and figuratively we gain a degree of assurance about who we are and the meaning of our life.

Harsher Realities

Even though the body informs the self, the body as a source of identity is ultimately futile. Ellen's friend was dying of ovarian cancer. Weakened by the heavy load of the disease and subsequent treatments, down to ninety-two pounds, she was unable to care for herself. Ellen sat with her through the days and nights that stretched as an endless wake, waiting for death to arrive. They hoped against hope when some days seemed better than others.

In the midst of this bodily suffering, two orblike objects were clearly visible in the dying woman's body. Like invaders that projected from her decimated torso, the C-cup breast implants had been acquired in better days. Perhaps she had hoped to hold on to youth and capture a particular type of beauty that had eluded her. What remained at the end of life was this juxtaposition of the cultural tokens of femininity and death's knocking at the door. The cultural female ideal had arrived at its final betrayal.

In the end, the ravages of disease and death cannot be adverted. Even as we attempt to control the body's meaning in increasingly aggressive ways, it delivers the final blow.

Humanity has always had to deal with death and reconcile itself to this ever-present reality. It isn't natural. We are born to think of life and youth as eternal. We are wired for the unending optimism of a life that keeps on giving. The reality is that death has invaded this pristine vision of life and the meaning of death must be learned. We all remember those moments in our childhood when it dawned on us that death is real and that pets, grandmothers, and even children die. Communities must deal with the pervasiveness and motivating power of death and give it meaning. How we speak about death, prepare for it, and acknowledge it as a culture reflects our spiritual viewpoint.

Death is a tragedy to the body-self, but we have learned to make it "natural." To make death acceptable we must make it either invisible, by denying it, or more attractive, by couching it in the language of freedom, cleaned up by the funeral industry. We often promote it as another choice in a series, thereby trivializing it.[21] Our culture is in the process of seemingly defanging death through a slow metamorphosis of the language and communal rituals associated with it. In the process we deny each other a public space in which to mourn. We silence the cries of the grieving.

Those who grieve visibly are harder to find. In the last three years I have attended five or six memorial services and only two funerals. The tone of each of these two events is very different. A traditional funeral seeks to comfort the living and acknowledge the dead. Sorrow and hope are juxtaposed. A contemporary memorial service feels different. There is no corpse; death is little mentioned; and the point is to have an upbeat celebration of the dead person's life. You get lively music, humor, and a nice spread of food. A cultural outsider could mistake it for a wedding. I can't remember ever attending a corpseless memorial service when I was young. Someone's death meant seeing a body at the dreaded obligatory viewing. People mourned in their homes; friends brought food to help those left behind through the sorrowful time. In a death-sanitizing culture and with the increased practice of cremation, funerals as we knew them in the past may be going the way of Victorian tear bottles, black armbands, and widows' veils. When it comes to death and dying, out of sight and out of mind is how we prefer it.

How we are expected to grieve has changed also. In 1927, Emily Post recommended that a widow's formal mourning period be three years. Current etiquette books address mourning in the most cursory of ways; some skip the topic entirely. The current social climate enforces a brief period of days considered appropriate for visible mourning. Corporate America usually allows three days off for the death of a close relative. Visible grief beyond these few days is considered morbid, a sign that you are emotionally "stuck" and need help. Meanwhile, when we're moved to comfort people who are grieving, our gestures of sympathy feel intrusive. The surrounding culture makes us feel pressured to pretend that nothing significant has happened. We are given little time or place to mourn and to acknowledge death as the enemy of the flourishing of life.

As a culture, we entered the millennium distanced from death more than any previous generation. With no major wars on American soil, we had managed to assign death a marginal place in our consciousness. In the decade of the 1990s we had lulled ourselves into believing that we were immortal, untouched by pain and tragedy. We lived as though there were no dying, no final day of reckoning, no accounting. Detached from the vulnerability of our bodies, feasting on cultural froth, we were living to look good. This was our path until September 11, 2001, when two hijacked commercial planes flew into the World Trade Center towers and one flew into the Pentagon. A fourth, intended for the White House, smashed into the earth, killing all aboard. The devastation took the lives of thousands and touched millions. In a matter of hours the realities of death came literally crashing down on our monuments to transcendence. The emotional and spiritual impact reverberated across the nation and the world.

Muslim extremists attacked the World Trade Center towers because they were symbols of U.S. economic, political, and cultural power. To them the towers represented our arrogance, the West's attempts to overcome human limits by reaching toward the heavens. To us they represented our freedom and autonomy. We were shocked to learn of Muslims willing to throw themselves headlong into death for their vision of transcendence and heavenly virgins. We were perplexed by that willingness to die for idealism and a long list of grievances, among them a hatred of the legal, economic, and social freedoms of women in Western society.

Many Americans who believed women's new social position was settled suffered a rude awakening upon learning that in the name of dignity many women in the world are still hidden behind veils. The position and meaning of women continue to have global significance, inciting hostility and assuring continual domination of women in various societies.

In the aftermath of the World Trade Center attack we Americans faced a full awareness of our human vulnerability. We quickly turned to those physically near for assurance. In the face of devastation, uncertainty, and death, we desired to be with those we loved. We called and rushed home to hug a neighbor or kiss a child. Even hard-core competitive professionals who had occupied the plush offices of the WTC were suddenly willing to sit with each other and reveal their most private tears. Life—and physical closeness—became precious.

As the human drama unfolded in the following week, news anchors lost their slick veneers and stumbled over the words, choking on their emotions. Individual stories of pain, suffering, and the corresponding heroism in the face of death moved our hearts. A previously self-declared "objective journalist" cried on national television. Late-night comedians seemed irrelevant. Overnight, reality shows and the cult of celebrity looked foolishly trivial. Dating services were busy with those who found themselves alone.[22] It was as if someone had pushed the reset button, rebooting our spiritual sensitivities and returning us to ground zero. Nobody was arguing about the appropriateness of prayer. Briefly, even staunch religious anti-institutionalists found themselves in houses of worship, no longer willing to settle for an absent spirituality.

But for most of us the tragedy was mediated by the television, which gave it a certain amount of distance. Even those of us who rarely watch found ourselves glued to the TV in the days after the attacks. The images looked like a bad made-for-TV movie in a continual rerun. A relative few experienced personal loss. For the rest of us, the mass mourning was over the destruction of the world as we knew it. Numbed by the unreality of television pictures, some found themselves compelled to drive across the country to look with their own eyes into the abyss. After smelling the smoke, we took pictures as a means to contain the tragedy's significance. "Being there," whether at the site of terror or with those we loved, gave us the degree of security we needed when everything else was shaking. We buried this neediness as soon as possible, but at least for a season we felt vulnerable again, our bodies and dreams exposed to harsher realities.

Grounding the Self

The generation that witnessed this event and the subsequent undoing of our sense of safety must now make adjustments to the cultural course we are on. The threat of death must be reconciled with our desire to escape the limits of the body. We need a surer place to ground the self beyond our bodies. Driven to seek a relationship with something larger and beyond the feebleness of our flesh, we desire to touch God's attributes of transcendence. As opposed to us, trapped as we are by social and physical limits, God is self-sufficient, self-determined, and self-defining. As we find ourselves with overbooked schedules numbering our precious days, God is not limited by time but resides in the eternal now. Beyond the definitions of gender, race, and social context, God is an unobstructed pure Self. As we strive frantically to fulfill our desires, God, independent and wholly Other, is beyond need because God is the source of all that is good. As we attempt autonomy through radical individualism, the divine community continually calls us into relationship as the only viable grounding for the human self. A restored relationship with our Creator, the eternal I AM, provides the basis for personal identity, freeing us from seeking other harbors for the self. This redemptive relationship is the beginning of bringing the fragments of a disjointed body-self back into the whole. This is the God that Jesus came to reveal.

But we need more than the transcendence of a God beyond our human limitations. God must be immanent. We need a God who is near to us. The vulnerability of our bodies and the cultural weight our female bodies carry requires a spirituality that will be able to take us beyond our bodies and at the same time enable us to flourish within them. It must affirm and redeem the whole person. It must be able to release us from the fear of death that drives our flight from our bodies. It must release us from the need to offer up our bodies in acts of atonement, and it must allow us live fully in a redemptive community now. To live as full human beings requires that we bridge the gulf between our transitory body and a self that seeks permanence; otherwise disintegration becomes the primary feature of our lives.

The tension between the lost self seeking its moorings and the body's constant state of flux is at the center of our disintegrity. We swing between meanings: the body means either nothing or everything. This conflict drives the obsession with our bodies. It points to a perennial and deep-seated split in the intersubjective relationship of the body and the self. At war with ourselves, torn apart by our disoriented desires, cultural demands, the physical enemies of the body, and our misunderstanding of spirituality, we are in need of a different paradigm for thinking holistically about our nature and spirituality.

To begin the road toward a redemptive community we must understand how we got here. Several questions remain: How did we come to this place? What are the possible redemptive responses? Can the creation narrative of Genesis and the Jesus narrative lead us into an all-encompassing spirituality that takes seriously the entirety of the life that we live in the body? We are in need of redemptive narratives that will heal our fractured lives and allow us to face our human vulnerability.

6

Daughters of Eve

Our Creation and the Origins of Our Shame

But I think there is something else, too, an overlooked byproduct
of the hysteria to control and commodify an image of ideal beauty:
A crisis of the imagination, a dearth of stories, a shocking lack
of alternative narratives.

Rebecca Walker[1]

Jessica's dance students line up like broken toy soldiers. They wiggle and gyrate to the blaring of the Bee Gees' "Stayin' Alive," arms flailing and heads bobbing, attempting to match the tempo. All shapes, all sizes, these children were born with bodies that don't quite connect with their minds. Autism, cerebral palsy, and mental retardation create a scene where each child moves in her own unique and unself-conscious way. Cathy is an autistic girl who is completely nonverbal, and she is a lunger. Every time the music starts, her eyes light up with excitement and her face with a smile as her body eagerly and energetically lunges from side to side. In an attempt to communicate with this child, Jessica has incorporated Cathy's distinctive movement into the choreography of the annual school musical. The other children join the rhythmic lunging. When Cathy begins to recognize her body language in a bigger context, it begins to have meaning for her. Through lunging dance, her body-self connects to the world in ways that otherwise would not be possible. Through dance the humanity of these children is given poignant expression. Like voices, their body language develops its own cadence, allowing them to discover a physical place in the world.

These children's relationships with their bodies give us a poignant view of the dignity inherent in the human person. Lacking other accessible ways, through dance these children express their drive to engage in creative acts and to communicate in a relational way to the world. In their broken dance they reveal to us how they share in the *imago Dei* of humanity. This image is borne in a concrete and specific embodiment, continually reminding us of the creative works of God. Though present everywhere, God is revealed in the particularities of the world, including the peculiarities of Jessica's dance students. What is first glimpsed in any perception of the image of God is a body in physical and social space. Theologian Phyllis Trible has written, "To perceive the image of God is to glimpse the transcendence of God."[2]

Beginnings

The story of how humanity came to reflect the *imago Dei* is written in Genesis, the book of beginnings. Its first three chapters hold the key to understanding the entirety of the Bible. Genesis is also key to understanding the state of our lives and our relationship to God, humanity, and the earth. Like any overarching narrative, it has been interpreted and reinterpreted by an endless number of theologians, philosophers, and creative thinkers. If anything can be said about the first three chapters of Genesis, it has been already said. Every word has been examined, every implication explicated. With little elaboration, the narrator describes just enough of earth and human beginnings to inspire the imagination of artists and to provide the bedrock for the faith of countless Christians and Jews.

Genesis teaches the creation of all things by a powerful and personal God who is intimately involved. This was a creation *ex nihilo*, out of nothing except God's creative Word. Genesis also teaches that humanity's history and future are intertwined with both God and the rest of creation. But what might the Genesis story tell us about our bodies and lives as women? What might it tell us about the creation of the body-self and its relationship to the earth and others who live here with us? Genesis provides answers to these questions through two instructive ideas. First, it affirms that our bodies are of the earth and that the earth and everything in it is "very good." Genesis also affirms that we have been created in the image of God. These two ideas provide guideposts for proceeding to recover the body's meaning.

The first chapter of Genesis begins with the Spirit of God hovering over the primordial sea, a vast and shapeless chaos. This is a brooding and cherishing Spirit intent on a creative act. A period of six days follows when the Creator, in a great flurry of activity, goes about creating the sky, oceans, and land, then all manner of vegetation, birds, fish, and land animals. After God creates the earth with all its diversity of life, it is declared to be "good." It is so good, in fact, that God repeats this declaration at the end of every day of creation.

The Garden of Eden has captured the creative imagination for centuries. It is the subject of Milton's epic *Paradise Lost* and C. S. Lewis's novel *Perelandra*. Through art, literature, and our own imagination we envision Eden as a place of gentle and fragrant breezes, dew-dripped trees, luscious fruit, sparkling rivers teeming with life, a rainbow of flowers, trees, and lush plants. We imagine a place with creatures, great and small, living in a harmonious community. To think of Eden is to envision unlimited delights and startling abundance. But most of all Eden is *shalom*, a place of wholeness and peace. When we think of a place of peace, we think of belonging. I can always tell a great deal about a person if I get a chance to see where they live. It is not about its grandeur or humbleness, but the ambience, the *shalom* created by the placement of objects, aromas, and comfort both physical and emotional.

At the end of the sixth day, it is time to create the crowning glory of God's work: humanity. Out of a deep agreement in the entire divine community, God speaks: "'Let us make human beings in our image, according to our likeness; let them have dominion over the fish of the sea, over the birds the air, and over the livestock, over all the earth and over all the creatures that move on the ground.' So God created human beings in his own image; in the image of God he created them; male and female he created them" (Gen. 1:26–27 NIV). The words "Let us" speaks to us of God's community and God's desire that humanity also bear the image of the divine community. The narrative demonstrates both the unity and the diversity of humanity in man and woman, and it reflects our communal nature. This plural image of God in humanity, the *us* of God creating *them,* radically distinguishes the human creature from all other creatures. No other living creatures are said to be God's image bearers. Closely associated with this image bearing, at creation these are also the only creatures specifically signified as male and female.[3] Though we share procreation with other creatures, there is something distinctive about this male and female of humanity.[4] The Bible describes this mysterious nature of gender and sexuality as part of a harmonious union. Both the male and the female are necessary to fully manifest the image of God, and both carry the image of God. But the passage is also mysteriously silent on the content of maleness and femaleness. It fails to define specific roles or the nature of femininity and masculinity, allowing for great freedom in expression of individual uniqueness. What the passage does do is to put the male and female in sexual correspondence. Out of this sexual correspondence will emerge the social genders, grounded in our sexually differentiated bodies.

Each body-self participates in the divine image, showing humanity's uniqueness among other creatures in its spiritual, emotional, and intellectual aspects. Though the Creator has no body, the divine intent is that the human body be an active agent in communicating the image of God. Our bodies mediate personality, emotions, and creativity, all communicate attributes of God. Our bodies make us present even as God is present in a particular place of belonging. Every single human being reminds us of God's presence through the presence of his or her body. Our face-to-face way of relating makes us personal in all our dealings. Thus to have a body is to make ourselves known.[5]

The radical uniqueness of the body-self is furthered demonstrated by the Creator's first instructions to the man and woman: "Be fruitful and increase in number; fill the earth and subdue it." The Creator further distinguishes humans from other animals by addressing humanity directly, endowing them with speech. In language God shows that the plans for this human creature are loftier than for animals. Also, only the human creature has the cultural mandate to exercise dominion over the earth. This dominion involves care and service. As God's image bearer, humanity alone was created to participate with God in the rule of the earth. It was to be a communal effort in which man, woman, and God were to cooperate in cultivating the ground. In a place of prominence among the other creatures, humanity was created to be fruitful, increasing not only in number but in the works of God.[6]

I remember as a little girl accompanying my mother to *la feria* in Buenos Aires. This was an open-air farmers' market, a cornucopia of colors, sounds, and smells. My mother's selections of the freshest vegetables became part of a meal made completely from scratch in a tiny kitchen. This would take hours of stirring, simmering, and tasting. Today we are too busy to wait for the rewards of meals prepared in such a manner, or the reward of a profound communal connection. Our consumer mentality has caused us to lose the understanding that eating is an affirmation of life and an acknowledgment of our dependence on the earth and on those with whom we share our meals. Most of us don't grow even a fraction of our own food, and we have lost the pleasure of tending the earth, watching it bring forth its rewards. We have no idea how our food is produced or how it gets to our tables. Most of the winter we eat out-of-season fruit that has traveled expensive distances to get to us. Even shopping for our food at the local market, preparing it, and serving it has lost its holy significance. We engage in "industrial eating"—on the run, out of a box, or alone in front of the television—forgetting that there is a connection between eating and the land.[7] For many of us the act of eating has become a routine chore, food another object of desire simply to be consumed and forgotten. Our disordered way of eating, whether it is due to over- or undereating, reflects this severing of its meaning. Though we are physically satiated, we remain emotionally famished. Shouldn't eating from the earth every day produce in us a sense of reverence for what we do not have the power to provide for ourselves? For good or ill, the earth is subject to both our wisdom and our foolishness. To deny this power of humanity over the earth is to deny our responsibility. We have corresponding relationships of worship toward God, who has provided the breath of life, and of stewardship toward the dust of the earth, which provides food and from which we were created.

According to the second chapter of Genesis, the first man created by the hand of God from the dust of the ground was an act of self-revelation and self-manifestation. It was an intimate creation, this molding of man's body. God, as potter, creates a work of art in the first human. "The Lord God formed a man from the dust of the ground and breathed into his nostrils the breath of life, and man became a living being" (Gen. 2:7 NIV). Being brought forth from the clay of the earth places humanity in direct relationship to the earth. The dust of the earth and the breath of God together create the living being. If you ever become overly aware of your breath, anticipating each inhalation and exhalation, you may become frantic anticipating the next breath. With inhalations more than twenty-one thousand times per day, our breath is the life we share with all humanity.[8] On this breath we are utterly dependent. That we are the embodied breath of God mirrors the self-revelation of God.

But the earthiness of the first human creature also defines his limitations. In contrast to the boundlessness of God, we are of the earth, contained within its boundaries of space and time. Yet as bearer of the image of God, we differ from the animals. This first human creature was not a self-defined biological body without a culture. Once he had been created from the earth, "the Lord God took the man and put him in the Garden of Eden to work it and take care of it" (Gen. 2:15 NIV). The human is placed in Eden, a defined space, and in relationship to the rest of creation. There is no search for the self by this creature, because the self is in relationship to the Creator and grounded in the earth. The Creator assigns the meaning and definition of the body-self through placement in creation. No matter how much we talk about "going global," our day-to-day life is experienced in a particular place and our capacity to engage beyond our geography is limited. From the beginning, God and humanity have been in a relationship of cocreation through the work of building culture, thus marking history in time and space.

What Eden means is best understood against the description of the earth as barren in the beginning. In this barrenness God plants a garden. Eden is humanity's first home base, a protected place of belonging set aside. It is to be a temple where human beings will meet with God. And for the first human being, Eden provides the context of an immediate purpose; the work of keeping and maintaining the earth. Gardening is the work of taking bare soil and causing it to flourish. It requires planning, design, knowledge of the particular land, engineering, botany, horticulture, and seasons. The planting of a garden by God is a foreshadowing of the work humanity is to do; taking uncultivated land and tending it to bring out its full nature. Even as humanity needs the earth for food, the earth needs humanity to flourish. The Creator provides the blueprint, and from Eden humanity is to exercise stewardship over the rest of creation, a relationship of creature to creature. This cooperative effort of reworking the world is to occupy their days.[9]

The Embrace of Adam

We know from the rest of the Genesis narrative that for the first man, Adam, the work of caring for the earth is more than he can handle. Through a process of naming the animals, an act of relationship making and placing him over the animals, man becomes aware of his need for a suitable partner. The Creator recognizes the lack and makes the declaration "It is not good for the man to be alone. I will make a helper suitable for him" (Gen. 2:18 NIV). God then causes a deep sleep to fall upon the man and, like a surgeon, removes a rib from his side. From this rib God forms woman, a one-to-one corresponding being to join man in the work of the Garden.

When God brings his last creation, the woman, to Adam, Adam says, "This is now bone of my bones and flesh of my flesh; she shall be called 'woman,' for she was taken out of man" (Gen. 2:23 NIV). This emphatic description of the first woman by the first man expresses that in her he finds a reflection of his own humanity; this differentiated body-self is of and from him. Genesis states that both man and woman were naked and not ashamed. Embracing the brilliance of nakedness, they were in a state of complete vulnerability to one another, an unself-conscious presence. Unfettered in their body-self, they suffered no barrier of communication. There was no she-speak or he-speak. There were no hiding places within or without. They did not objectify their own or each other's body.

For this intimacy found in each other, God declares that man is to cleave to his wife and become "one flesh" with her. He is to leave his singularity for a community. In this moment the divine community, who has a vested interest in the marital bond as a one-flesh union of man and woman, witnesses the first marriage ceremony. This full embrace of the body-other establishes the uniqueness of human sexuality. His body is her body; her body is his body. In this first couple, the act of sex is the engagement of the whole person in a safe emotional and physical space. The body becomes the bridge between the self and the other, reenacting our entry into community. The human capacity to give the body-self to another reflects the self-giving of God to humanity. Out of an eternal love relationship within the divine community came the expressive works on earth of which humanity is benefactor. This self-giving by God is the pleasure of God.[10]

Bodily connection is the basis not only of marriage but of all our human relationships. We begin our lives and enter the community in the body of another, sharing in flesh and blood. Our earliest experiences as a human fetus are in and of the body of another. As women, we have the capacity to carry another within us, blurring the lines between the community and ourselves. As we image God in our sexuality, we experience our profound human capacity to enter into a variety of life-giving and life-receiving relationships,[11] but this deep, life-affirming connection extends to all human beings and is not expressed only in the act of sex. It is continually shared through the communal reworking of the earth and presence at a common table at which we give and receive nourishment. To reduce sexuality to the erotic would deny many human beings affirmation as full participants in the community.

The Gaze of Eve

Of all women, no woman has received more attention or been more maligned or layered with more social meaning than Eve. Eve carries the weight of the world's woes, the curse of woman, the supposed gullibility and inferiority of her gender. She has been viewed as a seductress and a subordinate. Histories and biographies have been written about her; theologians of every stripe have weighed in with assessments of her. She has been portrayed in art and described in poetry as a beautiful, long-locked, milky-white-skinned, tender creature.

There is no way to talk about women without talking about Eve. But many traditional descriptions of her sound like political moves to keep women in a certain social place. It is true that Eve and her legacy have been used as a cultural tool to control women and determine all of our futures. The challenge is to try to see this first woman as clearly as possible from what is present in the text, not what we bring to it. In order to do that, we need to do some recovery work.

God's motivation in creating the woman is that it is "not good" for man to dwell on the earth as a singular. God makes a plurality in humanity by creating a "suitable helper." This "helper" was no errand girl. The English word *helper* unfortunately does not do justice to the Hebrew *ezer*, which is a much more empowered word. This *ezer* was to be one who was equal to the task man had before him, a "helper" described by the same word often used for God in Hebrew Scripture (see Ps. 115:9–11), the helper who is God Almighty. Man and woman are to be a reminder of God's abundant provision for each other. In each other they will be reminded of God's pleasure in lavish self-giving.

The Garden of Eden is described as having "trees that were pleasing to the eye and good for food" (Gen. 2:9 NIV). However, there is one tree in the middle of the garden from which the first humans are not to eat, for God has said to them, "You must not eat from the tree of the knowledge of good and evil, for when you eat of it you will surely die" (Gen. 2:17 NIV). This particular tree was off-limits, indicating that humanity's stewardship over the earth was not an absolute authority but bounded within constraints. The freedom enjoyed by the first man and woman in the garden was not boundless even though it was abundant. If they ate from the tree of the knowledge of good and evil, they would experience evil at the expense of the good they already knew. They would personally experience and not just have intellectual knowledge of domination and death. God's direct warning was not to eat of this tree, for in the day that they ate they would die a spiritual death, bringing separation from God and the fruit of bodily death. Evil would be manifested on, and in, their bodies and the earth. Eating, which had been given as an act of life, would become an act of death.

Now, into the pristine setting of Eden enters the destroyer of human flourishing. The serpent, more cunning than all the rest of the creatures, approaches woman. In one of the most important dialogues in the history of humanity, the evil one, embodied as a serpent, begins a work of deception by enticing the woman to eat of the forbidden fruit: "You will not surely die. . . . God knows that when you eat of it your eyes will be opened, and you will be like God, knowing good and evil" (Gen. 3:5 NIV).

The serpent implies and elicits in woman a sense of lack where there is no lack. Woman, created without guile, begins to toy with the possibilities open to her. She begins to doubt God's expressed word. *Is God perhaps holding back a good thing?* she wonders. She gazes at the tree, beautiful to look at, laden with succulent fruit. *Is it possible that it can make one wise, like God?* Captivated by the tree's beauty, Eve's gaze ensnares her. Her natural appetite disoriented by a deception, she extends her hand, takes the fruit, and eats it.

The woman's unbelief in the Creator's words brought forth a work of rebellion in her body. Eating the forbidden fruit was an act of unrestrained self-determination because it was eating outside the boundaries God had assigned. It was eating to exercise power. Already satiated with the abundance of fruit and vegetables in the Garden of Eden, Eve, in effect, gorged by taking more. What had appeared as a luscious fruit quickly produced a bitter result.

This act of eating forbidden fruit has in recent years been seen as a ritual of empowerment within feminist theology. In this reinterpretation, the first woman is said to have been exercising power over her own life and challenging the existing order. Through ritual eating of an apple we follow the first woman in an act of subversion, encouraged to overthrow the oppressive patriarchal power that has dominated us.[12] One of the problems with this metaphor is that the first woman was not oppressed. She lived in an abundance of freedom and in the abundance of the earth. She clearly carried the image of God, reflected in her moral agency along with the freedom to exercise it. Her act was not a life-affirming ritual but an act of domination over creation and against God. She did not consult the man, and she was not dictated to by the man. She was not a victim. What she did with her God-given freedom is our legacy. Reenacting it becomes a celebration of death.

But Eve was not alone in the creation, and she was not alone in the fall from wholeness. The woman gave the fruit to Adam, who was with her, and he readily ate without a word. This silence of man was an acquiescence to what had just transpired. By joining her in eating the forbidden fruit, he became a coconspirator, without excuse. This was not seduction by the woman but free participation on the part of the man. Thus the fall was not only individual but communal. It carried both individual and communal consequences, and the social component of rebellion against God requires that we understand its systemic nature. Through a complex web of betrayals, codependencies, deceit, and injury we perpetrate rebellion against the Creator and oppression of each other and the earth. Made by God to be cocreators and free moral agents, we become consumers instead, slaves to our own desires.

The first three chapters of the Genesis narrative offer a profound paradigm for thinking about the nature of the pain we experience in our lives. The first effect of the fall was that, together, the eyes of man and woman were opened. They saw that they were naked, and in that instant shame entered the world and disintegrity invaded the body-self. The body and the self were alienated from each other, split apart, becoming a marred image of God. Once the couple became self-conscious, seeing themselves over and against their own bodies, their union with each other was severed. God calls to them in the garden: "Where are you?" Adam answers, "I heard you in the garden, and I was afraid because I was naked; so I hid" (Gen. 3:9-10 NIV).

The most severe consequence is that humankind is estranged from the Creator. Unable to endure the gaze of God, they seek protection from the earth. A series of four "I" statements reveals that man's previous wholeness as a body-self has been shattered, as well as his unity with Eve. The man first distances himself from the woman. The one he once called "bone of my bone, flesh of my flesh" he now blames for his own actions and as the cause of his shame. In effect, he blames God for giving him the woman—a ludicrous assertion, since she was given as a provision for his lack. Next, the woman blames the serpent. God curses the serpent for enticing the woman to eat, and condemns the serpent to crawl on the ground and eat dust.

But when God pronounces that the seed of the woman, her off-spring, will crush the serpent's head in the end, a bright spot appears on the horizon. It is a future promise for the woman, through whom the deceiver, the author of spiritual and physical death, will be con-quered and humanity redeemed.

God then speaks to the man and woman individually, and this is in itself evidence of the fractured union. Yet there are overlaps among the judgments. God doesn't curse the woman in judgment but describes the circumstances that will result from her abuse of her moral agency. The first is greatly increased sorrow and labor in childbearing. Not only does this have a bodily aspect, but the pain of motherhood also extends to emotional suffering associated with rearing children. The second consequence is woman's "desire" for her husband and his sub-sequent rule over her. Interestingly, God does not waste any time in the creation account giving us the reason for the gender dysfunction of the world. It is the result of a collaborative and codependent rela-tionship that has attempted to take power away from God. Man will seek to exercise power over woman—power that is reserved for God— by defining the boundaries of the woman's life. Expelled from Eden, Adam's first act, similar to the naming of the animals, is to name his wife Eve, "because she would become the mother of all the living" (Gen. 3:20 NIV). In this fallen way Adam begins his dysfunctional sub-ordination of woman.[13] The creature who was designed to work along-side him and to exercise care over the earth has been reduced to her reproductive role. It was not her created place as mother that was prob-lematic, but having her identity reduced to it, leaving a legacy by which helping and nurturing work came to be seen as the only "natural" place of women. Originally created a free moral creature to rule in an expan-sive way with man and together fill the earth and subdue it, woman now has the boundaries of her life limited by the man.

Yearning to recover the one-flesh union she had with man in Eden, woman will place man in the position reserved for God, looking to him for fulfillment. Instead of unity, woman will find that the man often becomes her emotional and physical master. Her exercise of power is centered on pleasing or manipulating the man (most readily evident in the use of sexuality), which in turn enslaves her more.

Even in advanced countries where women experience a great deal of social freedom and career success. many find their lives dominated by the expectations of a man or desire for the affection of a man. The legacy of maintaining relationships has fallen to women; we are the ones who seek out counselors, read books like *What Men Really Want*, and tune in to the Relationship Channel. Some, weary of the burden, choose to forgo relationships with men altogether. Such gender dysfunction is more elemental than either feminists or traditionalists care to admit. We've learned to live with gender dysfunction in the same way we've learned to live with disease, difficult work, and death. We have not, however, learned to mitigate its impact on our lives. According to Adrienne Rich, "the woman's body is the terrain on which patriarchy is erected."[14] But all is not lost, for remember, in woman's relational identity as the "mother of all living" there is hidden a promise for the redemption of the world.

To the man God describes a changed relationship with the earth. The whole earth is now in a state of alienation from humanity because of human disobedience. Man will struggle to bring forth food from it. It will abound with thorns and thistles and be unresponsive and hostile to him. Instead of pleasure in keeping and serving the earth, he will find toil and futility until he returns to the earth himself. The final declaration of judgment is "dust you are and to dust you will return" (Gen. 3:19 NIV). Since the cataclysmic fall, all of humanity is set against the earth. Our dominion of it becomes an attempt at domination. Instead of benevolent care, we exercise power over an objectified earth. This is part of the cultural legacy that has greatly accelerated under the oversight of the sciences and related technologies.

The mastery of nature through science was championed by seventeenth-century philosopher Sir Francis Bacon, who worked for the formation of organized scientific research. Bacon's inductive scientific

method has had an incalculable affect on our faith in science and technology to engage in the pursuit of "innocent" knowledge. In this way
we have strived to gain back our lost dominion over nature. Bacon
always presented the pursuit of mastery of nature in religious terms,
believing that the mastery of nature through science would allow
human beings to regain the position they lost on account of the fall.
According to researcher William Leiss, for Bacon "the victory over
death would be the sure 'sign' of innocence restored as a result of a
domination regained through science."[15]

When Bacon's questionable theology became completely secular-
ized, the promise of regaining paradise through technology was severed from any notion of the original reason for humanity's expulsion—
moral failure. Science and technology alone will not restore Eden,
because humanity will continue to find its way barred by a spiritual
lack. Even now we have more scientific knowledge than our moral
character can use responsibility. The attempted reentry into paradise
through the domination of nature has resulted in the abandonment of
humanity's original mandate to serve the earth in favor of plundering
the earth and alienating ourselves from nature. After the fall in Eden,
the domination of nature is parallel to the domination of woman, cen-
tering on her body.

God does not give up on humanity, however. Moved by compassion
to provide relief for the body-shame we experience, in a gracious act
God makes garments of skin to replace the hastily sewed fig-leaf garments. Here God offers the first sacrifice of an animal to atone for the
rebellion of humankind. Clothing now provides us with protection
from the harsh elements of the earth, covers our sense of shame, and
leads to the cultural art of personal adornment. As an art form it signals gender, connecting our sexed bodies with cultural signs. Clothing is highly contextual, so that what is appropriate in one scenario
and one geographical area is not in others. The cultural code is highly
nuanced, ever changing, and there is great variation from culture to
culture, but it is an important means of honest communication about
who we are. To obscure the nature of the sexed body through androgyny is to obscure the true nature of oneself. Historically there have
been many occasions when women went incognito as priests and war-

riors in order to escape their confinement to feminine roles. Joan of Arc is a notable example. In the twentieth century women in the United States were quick to adopt men's style of dressing in the process of emancipation. But men, except for drag queens engaging in the mocking of gender, have not followed suit in great numbers. Men are less likely to adopt social signals previously assigned to women, because to do so means identifying with woman's diminished social position.

Clothing plays another important role as a way to safeguard our social selves. It provides a means to keep ourselves to ourselves until a safe relational place is found. Numbed by the constant sight of skimpily clad people in the media and public places, we don't think about modesty much any more. For women, modesty can no longer be for modesty's sake, because modesty is a man's issue also. I once had an office that shared a garage elevator with a health club. On one occasion I found myself in the elevator alone with an attractive young man who was wearing only a skimpy pair of shorts. Little was left to the imagination; Calvin Klein would have been proud. It was a brief ride that felt too long, leaving me embarrassed for both of us. What stayed with me was the way this man gazed constantly and narcissistically at himself in the elevator's mirrored walls, then looked at me to see whether I was looking at him.

Modesty is an act of self-containment and a prelude to intimacy. Most of us experience problems with intimacy rooted in the dissonance of self-disclosure. We may be physically open up to a point yet emotionally impermeable. At times we may be emotionally available but find it hard to be physically open. Modesty allows physical self-disclosure to parallel emotional self-disclosure, moving toward integrity within the body-self.

Back to the Garden

What we see in the creation and fall narrative is a profound communal disintegration, splitting man from woman, the earth from humanity, the body from the self. On our bodies fall hard labor, disease, violence, and death; on the woman's body in particular fall painful childbearing, physical domination by men, and a quest for beauty motivated by desire for the man. On both man and woman falls alienation from the earth.

Driven from the Garden, humanity has tried to get back to it ever since. It is as though we have a collective memory of a place that we are seeking to recapture. Our imagination and intentional encounters with nature can inspire us with glimpses of the beauty that is possible. Whether it is in the form of grand utopian visions such as Thomas More's *Utopia* or myths of a matriarchal prehistory, or the more accessible acts of adorning personal environments, tending a small garden, or a caring for an animal, we sense a profound need to get back to the garden of human flourishing. Eden represents for us order, but not the order built by human organization and the exercising of power. It represents an order based on the wisdom of the true nature of things and establishment of beauty and justice.

As we continue to create a vision of Eden for ourselves, the cataclysmic effects of humanity's fall from original wholeness do not leave us without hope for ourselves or the world. First, we have the understanding that we have been created in the image of God and are intimately tied to the earth. This affirms both our uniqueness and our sense of place. Second, we have the promise that from the woman's body would come a redeemer. This is a hope of not only regaining a connection with our Creator but the room to regard our female bodies as instruments of divine expression, both as image bearers and as channels by which God is disclosed.

7

The Not-Always-
Virgin Mary

Our Bodies as Places of Redemption

The idea of maternal power has been domesticated. In transfiguring
and enslaving woman, the womb—the ultimate source of
this power—has been turned against us and itself made into
a source of powerlessness.

Adrienne Rich[1]

In *Grey Is the Color of Hope*, Ukrainian poet Irina Ratushinskaya recounts her memories of several years in the 1980s she spent as a prisoner in a Soviet labor camp. Her crime—poetry judged to be anti-Soviet. Her memoir tells of a group of women refuseniks who in harsh circumstances sought to maintain human dignity. The embodiment of this hope was a small patch of sandy Moldovian soil transformed with their bare hands and on their knees. In an otherwise gray environment, they cultivated a vegetable garden to supplement their meager rations—carrots, turnips, pumpkins, chives, and dill. Cut off from families and communities of origin, they created a new community. In a punitive action this attempt to rework the world was destroyed by their captors. But with a few hidden seeds, they found the resolve

143

to plant another garden. For a diverse group of women, a lowly vegetable garden provided a basis for building a common table and re-creating the world.[2]

Like these women and against all odds, our life is an attempt to re-create the world and to recapture the wholeness of Eden. Our search to heal the brokenness we experience arises from a spiritual need to deal with issues the body presents, both in life and death. If God is to redeem our whole humanity, there is cosmic necessity that God under-stand our embodied experience. Must not God identify with us and walk in our shoes, experiencing the mundane daily tasks of eating, work, and rest? Must not God also experience the rejection of the com-munity that each of us comes to know? To make a difference where it matters most, only a God near to us can provide the assurance that our flesh has meaning. Any spirituality we embrace must be one that has already embraced our bodies.

The spirituality that we embrace must resolve the often-contradictory social meanings of our female bodies. In my childhood world of a large extended Argentine community, three kinds of women were imprinted upon my emerging imagination, each image encompassing a host of bod-ily meanings. "Las buenas mujeres" were "good" women like my mother and aunts who were always busy in the kitchen, stirring, kneading, and trading female secrets such as homemade beauty remedies. "Mujeres rene-gadas" were embittered women; the Catholic nuns were their symbol, foreboding figures who walked down the streets in pairs wearing long black robes. In my Protestant community these women were considered troubled because they had denied their feminine nature by choosing not to marry and have children out of a misguided religiosity and Marian devotion. Then there were "mujeres pintadas" or "painted" women, who had shady pasts and questionable reputations—like my grandmother, a petite bleached blond who always wore bright red rouge, lipstick, and nail polish. Grandmother's past was shrouded in mystery because she had run off to who-knows-where, leaving my mother and her siblings to be raised by my great-grandmother. She was considered a shameful woman. Though my parents took me to visit my grandmother occa-sionally, it was clear she was not to be emulated. With these models of "good" and "bad" women, I was left to sort out the meaning of my female-ness and its implications on my personhood.

It has become clear to me that since our bodies carry the weight of the communal symbols and since our original state of wholeness was lost in Eden—in our bodies—so in our bodies redemption must take place. Our embodied experience, however, gives us no internal source from which this redemption can spring. As humans, we have no ability to re-create our lives from shattered fragments. Only a human being in the state of perfect integrity, a whole body-self, could attempt that. At the same time, only an infinite God not limited by cultural expectations or a body could redeem the whole creation. Because our bodies do limit us in cultural meaning, only a transcendent God who is beyond culture can release us from these definitions. But God must do it in place; that is, God must do it in a body.

Something about Mary

The recovery of the meaning of our bodies begins with the re-creation of the world promised in Genesis. The promise that the seed of the woman will crush the serpent's head places woman in the direct path of God's redemptive work. Even as Genesis is the story of creation, the Gospels are the story of God's re-creation of the world in and through Jesus. The narrative of Luke gives the account of the visitation of the angel Gabriel to a poor girl named Mary, living in the insignificant village of Nazareth. Gabriel pronounces this girl highly favored and blessed of God. She is told not to be afraid because she has been chosen to bear the Son of the Highest. So begins the fulfillment of the prophecy of Isaiah: "Look, the virgin is with child, and will give birth to a son whom they will call Immanuel, a name which means 'God-is-with-us'" (Matt. 1:23 NJB).

Mary is an unlikely candidate to be called "blessed," for she is an unremarkable young woman with a heritage so obscure we do not even know her parents' names. The Gospel of Matthew offers the legal lineage of Jesus, which includes the scandalous Tamar, who tricked her father-in-law into sleeping with her; Ruth, considered cut off from the

people of God due to her Moabite heritage; and Rahab, a lying prosti-
tute used by God to aid his people. Mary is simply a continuation of
God's use of unlikely women. Startled by the angel's proclamation,
Mary is told the Holy Spirit will come upon her and the power of the
Highest will overshadow her and she will conceive.

Mary responds with "You see before you the Lord's servant, let it
happen to me as you have said" (Luke 1:38 NJB). This active yes of
Mary provides an example of intentional cooperation with the divine
will. Mary's emphatic yes shows no passivity but instead a remarkable
openness to receive the divine into ordinary life. Given that she is a
betrothed woman, her response shows willingness to risk rejection in
a society in which virginity had a high value. She is willing to be considered a bad girl and to live the rest of her life under a cloud in order
to cooperate with God.

The consequences are immediate. Finding her pregnant, Joseph, the
man she is promised to marry, doubts her virtue. Like any man in his
culture and times, he is ready to call the whole thing off. But upon the
intervention of an angel, Joseph accepts Mary as his wife.

Mary of Nazareth is the Everywoman of history, ordinary and obscure. She represents what is possible for us as flesh-and-blood women
who yield ourselves to God. Mary recognizes her own powerlessness
and has no grand vision of herself as the model of virtue that she will
become. Limited by her gender and social placement, Mary has no
obvious hope for transcendence. Yet her yes provides hope that in our
bodies the works of God can be wrought. In her we find a sign of God's
willingness to use the insignificant, even the vulnerability and symbolic nature of our bodies. In a body that has been associated with
seduction and immanence and carries the communal relational load,
God pours out divine grace. Mary's prophetic song of God's redemption can become our song: "My spirit rejoices in God my Savior, for
he has been mindful of the humble state of his servant. From now on
all generations shall call me blessed, for the Mighty One has done great
things for me. . . . He has brought down rulers from their thrones but
has lifted up the humble" (Luke 1:47–49, 52 NIV; see Ps. 22:9; Isa. 44:2;
Jer. 1:5).

Throughout Hebrew Scripture we see God forming in the womb and calling forth from the womb, making it an instrument of the Creator. Parallel to creation of the earth out of nothing, so God brings forth the new creation, Jesus, out of virgin barrenness. Just as at the creation of the earth the Holy Spirit brooded over the surface of the primordial ocean, again the Holy Spirit as a nurturing power moves and overshadows the womb to bring forth new life. Without male seed and with Mary's cooperation, God enters the human community. In Mary's womb, Jesus becomes bone of bone, flesh of flesh with her and enters the human community in order to redeem it. In this way Mary makes a full contribution to the humanity of Jesus. This strikes at the heart of the Aristotelian idea that woman is basically infertile, deformed, and unable to bring forth seed: "In the very act of conception, it was the male seed that brought shape and solidity to the labile, unstructured emissions of the female."[3] In Jesus' conception the woman's body becomes an active agent and her full humanity is affirmed.

In Mary the womb also becomes full of the compassion of God—a continuation of God's ongoing involvement with woman. She who as Eve was called the "mother of all living" now as Mary becomes the mother of the "living one," and this Living One redeems woman's experience. Woman's life, having been reduced to the womb, is now freed from the definition of man by the intervention of God. The relationship between woman and God is now reestablished on God's original terms, redefining the borders of woman's life by embracing that which has been used to contain her.

This redefinition of woman's life as more than womb is seen throughout the work and teaching of Jesus. On one occasion when a woman encounters Jesus, shouting, "Blessed is the womb that bore you and the breast that nursed you!" Jesus responds, "More than that, blessed are those who hear the word of God and keep it!" (Luke 11:27–28 NJB). Mary and all women can become more than mothers or potential mothers. They can be true followers and agents of God's Word.

But after only a few scenes early in the Gospel narratives, the information about Mary becomes sketchy. We know little else about her. Nevertheless, as a symbol of womanhood Mary exceeds her biblical presence. Her legacy over the last two thousand years has been fertile ground for ideas about women to take root. Mary of Nazareth has not remained even close to the real-life women the rest of us are; in the centuries that followed her life many exalted her to the realm of the divine. Portrayed in art and music more than any other woman, she is an artistic subject of El Greco and Salvador Dali, who both painted the Annunciation. No one living in the Western part of the globe has escaped the resounding of the prayer "Hail Mary, full of grace, the Lord is with thee. Blessed are thou among women, and blessed is the fruit of thy womb, Jesus. Holy Mary, Mother of God, pray for us sinners, now and in the hour of our death. Amen." Repeated by millions each day,[4] this prayer to Mary is second only to the Lord's Prayer.

Mariology, a body of belief regarding a simple woman who was to be called "blessed," has unfortunately over the centuries reinforced the reduction of woman to a particular type of motherhood. Her story has grown much larger than what the biblical narrative provides. *Mater Dolorosa* became one of Mary's many names. It has defined woman-hood as passive motherhood, forever self-sacrificing, and a codependent responsibility for undoing the sins of the world. It has encased woman in the relational sphere, denying her contribution in other areas of life. Mary, as the God-bearer who became epic heroine, the Queen of the Heaven, becomes unrecognizable as a woman or a human.[5] As the Virgin Mother, Mary of church tradition remains a virgin forever, untouched by the passion of sex. In this way Mary remains sinless and set aside unto God. As a symbol of ideal womanhood she "establishes the child as the destiny of woman, but escapes the sexual intercourse necessary for all other women to fulfill this destiny."[6] This symbol of *perpetual* virginity points to the dangers of female sexuality. In fact, belief in the perpetual virginity of Mary includes the idea that even despite the birth of Jesus her virginity remained perfectly intact. There are various speculations about how Mary was able to maintain an unbroken hymen through the birth of Jesus, and these reflect a deep fear of woman's open and leaking body, suggesting that the female body must be forever contained and enshrined on the pedestal of virginity lest it wreak havoc on the world. Even as the birth of Jesus through the womb of Mary of Nazareth affirms the bodies of women as possible instruments of divine expression, the *perpetual* Virgin Mother of church tradition denies the reality of women's entire embodied life as good and spiritually significant.

The virgin birth, which was to be a sign of the supernatural nature of the conception and the divinity of Jesus, has been made into a sexual value statement about Mary. But the virginity of Mary is not and need not be perpetual, and the Gospel narratives do not convey in any sense the avoidance of "sexual pollution." There is no need to believe that after a supernatural conception the pregnancy of Mary and birth of Jesus were anything but physically ordinary. Thereafter the Gospel narratives plainly show that Jesus had other brothers and a sister. There is no reason to believe that Mary conceived these by anything other than ordinary means—sexual intercourse with her husband, Joseph. The idea of Mary's perpetual virginity has not served women well. It is an unfortunate disregard of the creation narrative establishing sexual union between man and woman as the Creator's design and has contributed to our ambivalence about our bodies.

In the creation of the perpetual virgin the spiritual significance of sexuality and chastity in the life of ordinary people has been marginalized. In an age of safe sex and disease-driven abstinence campaigns, the sexual ethic embodied in Mary has been widely rejected. The backlash against Mary has left no room for chastity as a worthy idea, neither in nor out of marriage. Today for single people over eighteen, chastity as sexual abstinence is considered as unrealistically quaint as the Madonna. Chastity brings to mind "puritanical values"—an association that is unfair to the Puritans—and nightmares of women held prisoner in chastity belts.

Actually chastity, equally applicable to men, is the practice of the principle that the body will not be turned over to serve what is not worthy of it. Chastity is when our bodily acts parallel our emotional and spiritual commitments, moving us toward living with integrity in our bodies and with others. Because there can be no self-giving without a foregoing self-containment, chastity is a significant precursor to the act of marriage. But chastity is not merely sexual self-denial. At the heart of chastity is self-containment unto God. First and always we reserve our deepest selves in devotion to our Creator. This provides

us an eternal anchor, allowing us a place from which to give ourselves
to others. Since God is the source of all that is good, we can give good
things to others only as we continually return to the Creator to fill our
lack. Our relationships with others must begin with our relationship
to God. Otherwise we ask others to provide something they are not
able to give, producing relational havoc. In its greatest integrity, chaste
singleness embodies this self-containment—a sign of great relational
wealth.

Going further, chastity as an idea that includes sexually active married people is practically nonexistent.[7] Exclusion of the married from
any remaining definition of chastity denies that a faithfully married
woman shares with celibate single women a certain bodily integrity
and therefore can be considered chaste. But even in marriage, a relationship that is defined by self-giving, each partner must reserve their
deepest self for God. The self-giving embodied in marriage can be trun-
cated, and marital sex can become unchaste. The introduction of
pornography to enhance sexual fantasies, the expectation that the other
partner must be available for any variety of sex, and denial of the emotional undercurrents of the relationship can render marital sex
unchaste. By refusing to use the partner as a mere sex object and by
establishing mutuality in regard to the marriage bed to reflect a shared
life, married people can embody sacrificial self-giving for the well-
being of the community.

Under the concept of chastity, marriage and singleness are not polar-
ities of experience but are profoundly intertwined. By moving both
married and single toward bodily integrity, chastity maintains the dignity of the single person and the one-flesh unity of a marriage. Singles
in their chastity remind the married of the need for the individual to
be self-contained unto God, while the married in their fidelity remind
the single of the need to be self-giving for the needs of the larger community. Both can come together to affirm the communal nature of their
bodies in a variety of life-affirming acts around a common table and
in shared work.

Unfortunately, our society lives in a state of disintegrity, with the
gulf that exists between our souls and our bodies illustrated by the
pursuit of sex without boundaries. The media's saturation with sexu-

ally driven content has accelerated from infamous "tease and please" articles in women's magazines to movies that eroticize every relationship. This cannot be better illustrated than with the popularity of the HBO comedy *Sex and the City*, where four thirtysomething women express an intimate bodily sexuality that is out of step with any corresponding emotional intimacy. The characters pursue sex as recreation, keeping score and acting out every sexual fantasy without regard for their own bodies or their partners'. Love, commitment, and faithfulness become four-letter words.

Sex, like other forms of pleasurable pursuit, has the ability to bring us into the immediacy of the body and give us momentary certainty. But that immediacy is complicated by the presence of another person. Because relationships can be painful, we are motivated to avoid intimacy by disassociating our bodies from our emotions. One way to avoid intimacy is to view the sexual partner as an object and to view our own body as a mere sexual apparatus. The more we practice out-of-context sexuality, the more we lose the ability to practice true intimacy, and the more sex becomes a performance. The gulf between the self and the body widens, and we continually seek to bridge that gap with pleasure in order to bring ourselves back into our body. It is a vicious cycle of drawing near and alienation, destroying the foundation of sexual desire—the need to give oneself fully to another person. More and more people are avoiding the other person altogether, at least in the flesh, and seeking both autonomous and anonymous sexual pleasure through pornography, phone sex, and the web. Disembodied sexuality further distances us from the responsibility of dealing with the demands of another person's presence, denying both intimacy and the body. The principle of chastity mitigates against this.

The disconnect sexuality we see in our society is the backhand of a long historical ambivalence about sexuality. The creation of the perpetual Virgin flowed from early church history, with its shameful and potent dose of asceticism and Gnostic influences. The Gnostics believed that the material world is evil and that only the spirit has a right to exist.[8] Women's bodies stand for "all that was open, aimless, lacking in shape and direction."[9] For the Gnostic, in order for woman to reach spiritual perfection she needs to escape her female identity, abolishing gender polarity. Early church fathers such as Origen, Ambrose, and Tertullian absorbed Stoic- and Platonist-inspired philosophies, practicing celibacy and seeing marriage as a lesser way of life. They came to accept an absolute division between the body and the spirit. Women, along with Eve, were regarded as sexually dangerous and described as the "devil's gateway."[10] Sex was a repugnant reminder of our earthiness, which Jerome described as "the vomit of marriage."[11] The result was that even in marriage sexual passion was to be highly regulated and must yield a stoic act for procreation alone.[12] Against this backdrop, church fathers encouraged vows of celibacy for both men and women, as a means to contain unruly flesh.[13]

As Mary became an imposing symbol of sexual renunciation in the Greco-Roman church and into the Middle Ages, women lost their voice unless they made vows to be consecrated virgins in the church.[14] As carnal daughters of Eve, women who wished to serve the church increasingly chose lifelong virginity. In this way they sought to abandon their unclean sexual nature and approximate a male life. Lifelong virginity had a secondary benefit as a way for women to escape from demands of marriage and motherhood and be rewarded with increased status in the church. For women this status afforded them opportunities to study, travel, and engage in a multitude of creative endeavors. During the Middle Ages, a time of high maternal death, frequent pregnancies, and no redemptive vision for marriage, marriage and motherhood must have seemed like a prison sentence to many. With the choice being between full personhood and diminished womanhood, for many the decision to lead a life as consecrated virgins was clear. Until the Protestant Reformation of the sixteenth century, marriage remained, after virginity and widowhood, a third estate and an inferior way of life.[15]

What Mary has come to represent is also inextricably linked to Eve, our first mother who has been viewed as the arch antitype of Mary. If Eve is the seductress and the cause of Adam's fall from innocence, then Mary is the perfect mother, unpolluted by sensuality and ready to intercede for the world. Neither of these stereotypes can be derived from the biblical text. Instead Mary of Nazareth is the true daughter of Eve who lives out God's promise to her mother by giving birth to her own

Redeemer. As Eve came from the first Adam, Jesus, who is called the second Adam, now comes from the woman. As humanity was created in the image of God, Jesus is said to be the image of the invisible God, the firstborn of the new creation (Col. 1:15).

The Virgin Mary of popular imagination is a complex mixture of ideas about womanhood, sexuality, and motherhood, eliciting both great reverence and great scorn. In an effort to reclaim Mary for all women, the virgin conception has been denied altogether by some, while others hope to find in her the feminine face of God they seek, the archetype of the Great Mother.[16] Although Mary of Nazareth as portrayed in the Gospel narratives is neither divine nor a perpetual virgin eternally set aside, we do need to recover both Mary as ordinarily human and the virgin conception as a supernatural intervention in order to regard Jesus as both human and divine. Recovering Mary of Nazareth from perpetual virginity and perfection will allow us to see the possibility that God can and does work through the ordinariness of our flesh. It can release us from regarding our sexual life as a hindrance to a spiritual life. We need the humanity of both Mary and Jesus to see the possibilities of God redeeming the world through a work in our bodies.

The Weakness of God

In Mary's experience we see the incarnation of God in Jesus, and in addition the ultimate claim against the idea that spirit and matter are irreconcilable. In our society the most common definition of spirituality is of the human spirit uniting with the Spirit of God. In other religious traditions, the suffering bound to the embodied experience has been considered unworthy of the divine nature. But in the incarnation the Spirit of God unites with flesh and enters the material world—a radical departure from the above. This goes smack against the notion that our body is a hindrance to our spiritual life and that true spirituality lies in escaping the body. It goes against the idea that God is too holy and too Other to ever be contained in a body of flesh. By God's taking on a body, the character of God is revealed in the particularities of flesh.

Of course the claim that God became flesh in Jesus is a startling statement, yet this is the exact claim of the Gospels. In Jesus we see full humanity and full divinity. A holy God enters the bloodiness of the womb, considered unclean under Jewish law, and makes it a temple. In the womb of a woman the eternal and transcendent Word by which the worlds were created becomes flesh: "Something which has existed since the beginning, which we have heard, which we have seen with our eyes, which we have watched and touched with our own hands, the Word of life" (1 John 1:1 NJB). The Word is God's self-revelation, disclosing what is in the mind of God, a personal communication with humanity. In Jesus the eternal I AM becomes subject to human limitations yet without sin.[17] In Jesus the infinite character of God meets the finiteness of our embodied experience: Creator and creature occupy the same space. In Jesus, the body-I AM, makes his residence among us, calling our entire body-self back into integrity.[18] This allows us to no longer separate our bodies from our spiritual search for redemption.

The inclusion of our bodies in redemption was seen firsthand by Mary of Nazareth. After a childbirth experience that was both humble and majestic, through Jesus she saw the reality of God's entanglement with ordinary life. The first thirty years of Jesus' life were probably ordinary and uneventful. The narrative tells us only that he "grew in stature and wisdom." We can imagine this God made flesh, the boy Jesus, learning to live in a growing and changing body. He came from the wrong side of the tracks; his hometown had inspired the saying "Can anything good come out of Nazareth?" Surely he experienced the limitations of race, gender, class, and the limits of a particular place.

Jesus' ministry began when he came to his prophetic forerunner, John the Baptist, an antagonistic wild man living in the wilderness preaching repentance. Jesus received John's baptism of repentance, and thus begins his public identification with ordinary people. John proclaims, "Look! the Lamb of God which takes away the sins of the world!" As Jesus comes up from the Jordan River, Luke reports, God speaks from heaven: "This is my Son, the Beloved; my favor rests on him" (Matt. 3:17 NJB). As the Son of God, Jesus has the right to call God "Father," using the Aramaic term of *Abba,* an endearing name expressing familial intimacy. To call God Father was for the religious of the time blasphemous, for it was considered to be a claim of equality with God. But Jesus went further; he taught that his followers could themselves unabashedly call God *Abba,* Father.

Immediately after baptism, the Holy Spirit drove Jesus into the wilderness (Mark 1:13). We are told that Jesus went without food for forty days, a fast to the point of starvation. Naturally we wonder whether such extreme fasting is an expression of self-hatred or holy anorexia, or suggests an ascetic trying to release his spiritual power from the trappings of the body. In light of the negative history of fasting and the deep suffering caused by anorexia, this is a legitimate question. But the fasting of Jesus during these forty days is not self-flagellation. I imagine Jesus overwhelmed by the pulling away of a curtain revealing to him the sins of the world for which he is to die. He is identifying with humanity and experiencing our lack in order to begin the work of redemption. Just as our spiritual distress readily shows up on our bodies, Jesus is God choosing to carry humanity's brokenness in his body, a necessary part of his ministry of compassion for the world. Through fasting Jesus lines up his whole body-I AM, both his humanity and his divine nature, with the suffering of the world. He who will later say "I am the bread of life" is now willing to go without bread to understand our lack.

After forty days, Jesus becomes hungry and the needs of his body begin to compete with the needs of the world. At this time of bodily and spiritual vulnerability Satan, the evil one, comes to tempt him just as he enticed our first parents in Eden. Unlike Eden, the temptation of Jesus is more aggressive because the stakes are higher. Satan seeks to disorient Jesus in his identity, his power, and the true meaning of his calling. Will Jesus be tempted to satisfy his hunger by turning stone into bread, asserting power over nature to prove himself? Will he be tempted to bow the knee to Satan in exchange for political power as a quicker way to world peace and personal glory? Will he be tempted to question God's love by throwing himself from the pinnacle to see if angels catch him? In all these temptations Jesus responds, "It is written . . ." appealing to the Word of God. Unlike our first parents, he refuses to offer his body for a lesser purpose than dying for the sins of the world. They had yielded their bodies for self-actualization, Jesus is yielding his body for the love of the world. Under physical duress he continues to orient his desires by his eternal "horizon of significance," his Father's will.

Both Jesus and our first parents were in a place of personal wholeness and perfection; but unlike Eden, in which man and woman found themselves in lush abundance, Jesus finds himself in a barren wasteland—and hungry. In Eden the man and woman had each other and God for companionship; Jesus finds himself alone. All are tempted to gain power outside their boundaries. All are tested in and on their bodies. In the wilderness, however, Jesus begins to undo the work of Satan in Eden.

Throughout the Gospel narratives we encounter Jesus experiencing human limits; hunger and exhaustion, grief and anger. Seven hundred years earlier the prophet Isaiah had predicted we would find him a man of sorrows who had no beauty that we should desire him; the religious and politically astute found him particularly offensive. He and his disciples were accused of politically sensitive missteps like breaking the Sabbath, failure to pay taxes, and eating with ceremonially unwashed hands. Jesus offended the religious by calling God his Father, claiming power to forgive sins, and joining the company of those who were on the outs of the social elite. His first miracle was turning water into wine at a wedding; later he was accused of being both a glutton and a drunk. Jesus understood the pain of those who were on the margins, socially and physically. Lacking charm, beauty, and political savvy, in our contemporary culture Jesus' unadorned persona would never inspire the cover of *GQ* or *Time*'s Person of the Year. God—emptied of his splendor—didn't look like the Savior of the world.

As a rabbi, Jesus did not introduce a systemic reform movement but came to proclaim the forgiveness of sins and the coming kingdom of God with its own distinctive politics. His work and teaching were grounded in the local, religious, and social power manifested in the daily lives of the people. He did not introduce a self-help program, positive thinking, or solutions to the current political power structure.

As a basis for a new religion, he left insufficient instructions for the building on an institution and left no singular successor. He had little regard for the conventional politics of the day or the prerogatives of wealth, two primary sources of systemic power; instead he taught that true power lies in becoming a servant to all. He questioned right practice with wrong motive, calling people to right practice with right motive. The coming kingdom was to be a radical revolution to begin in the hearts of his followers, calling for the devotion of the whole being, inside and out, heart and body, strength and mind. To this kingdom Jesus was devoted in his entirety, a kingdom to be sealed in and on Jesus' own crucified and resurrected body.

While we operate out of a sense of scarcity, Jesus called us to operate from God's abundance. He challenged his followers to sell all and give all to enter the kingdom of God. This radical who claimed to forgive sin and to be the "Way" to God called people to personal renunciation through acts of nonresistance to enemies, giving to those who take from us, and abandoning pursuit of positions of power. As a social or personal moral ethic, his teaching of the supremacy of the love of God and neighbor, including one's enemies, is virtually impossible for anyone to live up to. The only teaching his followers have found within their grasp is the grace of forgiveness and personal healing possible through faith in him. Only on this basis are the rest of his teachings made possible.

Because Jesus understood the nature of our embodied experience, his spiritual lessons used vivid language of the body: eating, drinking, work, and rest. He drew lessons from the earth, referring to sowing and harvest time, the lilies of the field and the birds of the air. His miracles were never flashy showmanship but remarkably grounded in the everyday lives of people. He showed his rule over nature through stilling a storm, walking on water, and producing an abundant catch of fish.

Our bodies, Jesus taught, are to be aligned with our hearts. Outward action is to be reflective of an inner attitude. His call to integrity in the visible body-self is a call to true holiness. All of Jesus' teaching was undergirded by his practical work of compassion manifested on people's bodies. He took care of hungry crowds by multiplication of meager amounts of food. He went through the countryside touching the blind, lame, deaf, mutes, and lepers. By his word alone deadly fevers were cured, demons driven out, and the dead brought back to life. The significance of this must be seen in light of the communal meaning of sickness and transgression in Jewish society. Jesus lived in a culture where physical wholeness and purity were considered necessary to spiritual holiness. Those considered "unclean" were ostracized from society, along with the sick and disabled. The social stigma of physical brokenness contributed to a profound sense of exclusion in Jewish society, just as today our age, gender, race, and lack of ideally defined beauty can be experienced as isolating. Pain and disease have their own isolating effect on the sufferer; the physically disabled are heavily dependent on others and in the time of Jesus were unable to fully participate in communal life. For an individual who had not been touched in years, the touch of Jesus' hands would have had a profound effect. It would restore not only the body but the person's relationship to God and community.

One of these miracles was the healing of a woman whose twelve-year bloody issue was not only a source of social disgrace but a sign of the curse of barrenness and physical powerlessness. Having used all her economic resources seeking a cure, and full of shame, she makes a bold move, pressing through a crowd to get to Jesus. Too embarrassed to ask for a miracle, she hopes to touch the hem of his garment, believing she will be healed.

Jesus immediately turns around, asking, "Who touched me?" His disciples are puzzled. So many people press against him that to identify any particular person would be impossible. But Jesus is calling the woman to disclose her faith and shed her shame within the community. As she makes herself known, he says, "Daughter, be of good cheer; your faith has made you well. Go in peace." In contrast to that society's belief, in every case where Jesus touched outcasts, instead of being defiled himself, their wholeness was restored (Luke 8:43–48). Redemption was to take place in our body-self and through the body of Jesus. It was a sign that the kingdom of God was among us.

In Jesus' ministry we see another new paradigm: In a society where pious Jews thanked God that they were not born women, Jesus' disciples included women; some of these women supported him financially out of their own means (Luke 8:2–3). In first-century Palestine women were considered unworthy and were not allowed to study the Hebrew Scriptures or speak in the synagogue. By calling a woman "daughter of Abraham," Jesus affirmed the full participation of all women in the sacred community (Luke 13:16). His friendships included Mary Magdalene, Mary of Bethany, and Martha. His teachings included feminine images, showing regard for women as representatives of the acts of God.[19] Jesus broke with tradition and included women among his theological students, refusing to reduce them to mothers, cooks, or seductresses. He was unconcerned that they would taint his reputation.

In a society ruled by males, women were highly affected by both the rules regarding uncleanness and those governing marriage and divorce. Women with their monthly discharges and pregnancies were often in the position of being unclean. Nevertheless, Jesus spoke to and touched women instead of regarding their bodies as a problem. In a time when women bore the brunt of sexual misconduct, Jesus also understood the nature of the double standard. As a pacifist and celibate man, he renounced two sources of male pride: aggression and sexual prowess. He pointed out unfair divorce and adultery rules allowing a man to do as he pleased while women were severely punished. He brought into question the viability of the "wired for lust" argument and the argument for the seducing nature of women. He set the sexual standard even higher, condemning the objectification of women. His relationships with women overthrew the gender power balance.

Jesus' understanding of the social meaning of women's bodies is reflected in one of the most sensual scenes in the Gospel. Jesus was known to dine with those of less than stellar reputations, but one dinner party was different. Invited by a religious leader (most likely out of curiosity) who was a Pharisee, Jesus was a guest at a spread that was most surely a Middle Eastern feast—lamb, barley bread, figs, olives, honey cakes, and wine. As a form of charity, the poor would be allowed to visit such a banquet, receive some of the leftovers, and listen to the conversation. It is easy to imagine a lamp-lit room, music, reclining guests at a sumptuous table, good conversation, and an uninvited woman in the crowd. This was no respectable woman, however. She was a woman known to have a questionable reputation, probably sexual in nature. She was known in the rumor mill, a local bad girl.

Unwelcome and obviously desperate to get to Jesus, this woman crashes the party. She goes to where Jesus is reclining and begins pouring costly perfumed oil from an alabaster jar onto his feet. Mingled with it are her own tears. In a scandalous act considered highly erotic, she loosens her long hair and begins to use it to wipe Jesus' feet. Showering his feet with kisses, a humiliating act, she places herself in a public position of emotional and physical vulnerability.

As the fragrance of the oil fills the room, the host thinks, *If Jesus were a prophet, surely he would reject the woman and turn her away.* Jesus knows the man's thoughts, however. In the ensuing conversation he compares the woman with someone who is in need of much forgiveness. He tells the host that because she has been forgiven much she loves much. And Jesus points out that the self-righteous host greeted him with no kiss, no oil for anointing the head, and no washing of his feet—all common acts of hospitality (Luke 7:36–50).

In this social setting, Jesus does not reduce the woman to her past or to her sex. Her reputation does not bring a rebuke from him. Instead he simply says, "Your sins are forgiven. . . . Your faith has saved you. Go in peace." He sees the entirety of her life. He offers embracing love in front of those who would exclude her. Because Jesus sees this otherwise invisible woman as more than her transgression, she is no longer trapped in her social experience. Jesus provides a way to escape the confinement of her reputation and a way back into the community. Through her acts of faith, she goes from being an outcast to experiencing the abundance of God's community, from a woman lacking integrity to a woman whose very acts reflect profound love.

Jesus understands not only the personal aspect but also the social nature of transgression and suffering. His work is not only to heal and forgive the individual but also to restore him or her to the community. Both the woman with the unclean issue of blood and the woman with the alabaster jar are social outcasts, but both take the initiative to move toward Jesus. Their embodied faith produces forgiveness and healing. They both make faith an act of resistance against the grip of personal brokenness and social exclusion, the power paradigms in which they find themselves. An unclean woman pressing through the crowd and a social outcast daring to enter where she is not welcome, through these acts of faith they break through the iron gates of exclusion and find themselves embraced by the love of God. To both Jesus says, "Go in peace," welcoming them into the *shalom* of God.

The incarnation of God in Jesus gives us a basis for including our bodies in the spiritual search. In Jesus we see God taking on the project of re-creating the world by becoming flesh and dwelling among us. God enters the ordinary of our lives to fully identify with us. We see the teachings of Jesus undergirded by a ministry of restoration in and on the bodies of his followers. The embodiment of God through the womb of a woman brings the spiritual search directly in and on the female body. We see God giving woman's bodily experience profound meaning. The entire Gospel narrative affirms our female bodies as a possible place for redemption to occur. As for many of the broken women and men Jesus encountered, our redemption begins with faith in his power to restore us to a renewed relationship with God. The source of redemption is the body-I AM, Jesus, from whom God mediates his grace to us. As for Mary of Nazareth, this grace embodied in us can make us active participants in God's divine plan of re-creating the world.

8

Made Flesh

How Jesus Takes Our Shame and Renews Our Imagination

I thank you, Lord, that you have permitted me, and wanted me
in the number of your women.

St. Catherine[1]

In Franz Kafka's short story "In the Penal Colony," a man is tried in a court where "guilt is never to be doubted." Through a violent and meticulous twelve-hour process, the condemned learns his crime as it is written on his naked body. The means is a sophisticated and elegant machine inscribing the words "Honor Thy Superiors." It is an apparatus of death, carefully designed for its exact purpose—the execution of judgment. As needles inscribe the name of the crime deeper and deeper into the flesh, the moment of truth and redemption comes around the sixth hour, when the accused finally deciphers his transgression. At this moment he experiences the peace of knowing why he is dying. Thus he is prepared to die by the machine of justice. But in an unexpected turn of events, the judge and executioner takes the place of the condemned. He has himself inscribed with the words "Be Just." In the process of his execution the machine is destroyed.[2]

In Kafka's story, only the judge and executioner has the power to release the condemned, to make the final atonement and destroy the machine. It is a useful illustration of our own battle with the social machine of false justice, which seeks to inscribe its demands on our bodies. Living in a society where we always fall short of the ideal, our "guilt is never to be doubted"; we are in need of freedom from the compulsion to adjust and readjust our entire body-self to meet impossible standards. To live in the world is to know without a doubt that we have fallen short and to experience continuous accusation. We are those who surrender to the scalpel, put ourselves under inflictive beauty regiments, and strive every day to meet the feminine ideal. We become slaves to the demands of conformity, acceptance, and inclusion. As we are always on the outside, desperately wanting in, our failure to meet the expectation brings upon us a sense of personal failure. In the process we objectify our own bodies and come to see them mechanistically and functionally, in the same way as the executioner. Always under the gaze of judgment, always under the cover of shame, we become a self-conscious distortion of ourselves.

Kafka's machine of justice represents for us who are confident that we are guilty the unrelenting demands of the world to atone in our bodies. But oppressive social demands play another role; their false guilt and shame mask the true guilt we bear as transgressors against God. The cultural systems that judge us against a distorted feminine ideal seem to provide a means to atone for our failures through consumption of cosmetics, diets, surgery, and self-help seminars. But the machine of false justice is never satisfied; it never says "enough." We never find ourselves good enough as women or as human beings. True justice and beauty are never served. We continually fall short and are caught in a process in which we become unjust ourselves, perpetuating injustice on others.

The New Community

Like the judge and executioner who takes the place of the condemned in Kafka's story, Jesus of Nazareth lived a life that was a preparation for his ultimate justice work on the cross. But if viewed merely as an example, the life of Jesus is not enough to provide a way for us to live in our bodies. It is not sufficient for him to give us a new moral ethic by which to live; he must show us how to face our own death. Because our flight from our bodies is motivated by a desire to escape death, how Jesus deals with this last enemy has a profound effect on how we live. It has the power to determine what kind of spirituality we will experience. On the cross the world attempts to make Jesus pay for a crime based on a distortion of the truth—a false justice based on false standards. By looking at the dying and death of Jesus we can find hope to escape the false justice of the world that continually reduces us to our bodies. Who we are can't be reduced to our body and its particularities, but on the cross we see the world's attempt to reduce a transcendent God to a crucified body. On the cross we also see the true justice of God satisfied as Jesus takes on our shame originating in our fall in Eden. The cross can become for us both the symbol of ultimate atonement and the place where we can come to be at peace with our own body.

From the time of his birth, death was in pursuit of Jesus. From the slaughter of the innocents (Matt. 2:16) to the numerous attempts by his enemies to kill him by stoning, death was always at his heels. Jesus had seen his forerunner John the Baptist beheaded for a much less disturbing message. In the brief three years with his closest disciples, he continually reminded them he came to suffer, die, and on the third day rise again. Because of his radical redefinition of love and justice, in the end his message would become intolerable to the hegemony of the day. In the end he would be killed by the political and religious system. Though he had shown his power over death through his miracles, now he would subject himself to suffering and death at the hands of his enemies. Only by facing death itself would Jesus demonstrate his ultimate authority over all the systems of the world. Only by triumphing over death would he be able to liberate those who due to their fear of death continue to seek escape from the limits of the body. A cross would reveal his depth of love for us.

But before Jesus' justice work is to have its culmination on the cross, he must establish a new redemptive community. In an upper room in Jerusalem, Jesus and his close disciples gather to celebrate the Jewish Passover. An unimpressive and common assortment, they are an unlikely group from which to establish God's kingdom. In preparation for the Passover, Jesus expresses his longing to share this familial meal with them, knowing it will be the last before his death. He understands that when his disciples no longer have his physical presence they will need a tangible reminder; a catalyst for a continual recalling of his presence. After the main meal, Jesus takes the bread and wine and gives them new meaning. Of the bread he says, "This is my body given for you; do this in remembrance of me" (Luke 22:19 njb). Then Jesus takes the wine and says; "This is my blood, the blood of the covenant, poured out for many" (Mark 14:24 njb). This redefined eating and drinking, which occurs after they have been satiated with the main meal, teaches them to look beyond the consumption of food. The bread and wine point them to a greater hunger and thirst. As they eat of the earth at this holy meal, Jesus himself becomes the inconsumable nourishment—the bread of life, broken. Later, the taking of wine and bread will serve as a recalling of his sacrifice for the forgiveness of sin. No longer trapped in the consumption of the earth, the bread and wine now fulfill their spiritual function, pointing us to what will satisfy our deepest lack.

In this last meal before his death, the body of Jesus is erected as the altar on which the new sacred community is built. The representational eating of his body and blood will serve to bind his followers together until he rejoins them in the future kingdom. In this sacramental meal they will share in each other's life. Through faith, becoming corporately more than a mere collection of individuals, his followers become the visible body of Jesus on earth. They are called to do the works of God in their own bodies. The fruit of the earth, bread and wine, becomes a means of grace foretelling the redemption of the whole creation, a creation eagerly waiting for the children of God to be revealed (Romans 8:19). In eating the bread and drinking the wine, we mediate the redemption of the earth and reenact the birth of a new community.

This holy Passover meal is bittersweet for Jesus. It is the beginning of the end in which he will be betrayed into the hands of the religious power structures. Seeking to catch him in blasphemy or to discredit him by implying he is a demon-possessed madman, they will finally find an unlikely ally within his inner circle. Jesus' betrayal will come from one who had listened to his teaching, seen his healing work, lodged and ate with him. Deeply saddened, Jesus tells the disciples, "In truth I tell you, one of you is about to betray me." Astonished, each asks, "Not me, surely?" Jesus responds, "It is one of the twelve, one who is dipping into the same dish with me" (Mark 14:18–20 NJB). Hastily, Judas Iscariot departs the gathering to betray him.

After this intimate meal in which Jesus demonstrates his love, he tells his incredulous disciples that even before morning they will all desert him. Vowing that it won't happen, after singing a hymn in unison, they depart to the olive garden, Gethsemane. In a familiar place for Jesus and his disciples, one last time Jesus comes face to face with his mission. Arriving late in the evening, he asks his weary disciples to maintain a vigil by watching and praying with him. Knowing the hour of his betrayal and death is near, he is extremely distressed. Falling on the ground, he prays, "Abba, Father! For you everything is possible. Take this cup away from me. But let it be as you, not I, would have it" (Mark 14:36 NJB). He tells his disciples that he feels as if he is dying, but instead of help, they show signs of abandonment. In one of Jesus' darkest hours the community fails him. Instead of providing comfort, they fall asleep.

Jesus continues to agonize over his impending betrayal, asking God to remove the cup of death from him if it is at all possible. He knows his will be a death of not only physical suffering but separation from God. Alone and anxious, he begins to sweat profusely; the drops "fell to the ground like great drops of blood" (Luke 22:44 NJB). Authentic in his humanity, his body takes on marks of emotional and spiritual distress.

Jesus eventually wakes his disciples. It's time to fulfill his mission by facing what is before him. Immediately Judas meets them, accompanied by a crowd armed with swords and clubs. Judas greets Jesus with a kiss, a prearranged signal to indicate that Jesus is the one his enemies are looking for. In a matter of hours the intimacy of the holy meal is forgotten, and an intimate sign of affection among friends becomes a sign of bitter betrayal. In that kiss, the mouth—a symbol of nourishment and self-disclosure—becomes the world's attempt to consume and silence the eternal Word.

Driven by political ambition, Judas has miscalculated the response of Jesus. He thinks that now, under threat of death, Jesus will be moved to use his power to seize political position. In the end a remorseful Judas hangs himself.

The Wounding of God

Jesus is bound and arrested. As he had foretold, his disciples, fearful for their own lives, scatter and abandon him. In the darkness of the early morning, Jesus endures a series of religious and civil trials on trumped-up charges of blasphemy and treason. In a power game among various competing factions, he becomes a scapegoat for an entire political and religious system. Envious of his influence with the people, the power systems seek to assert control over him by the violence of intimidation and force. The assertion of power is their currency, and they expect Jesus to respond in kind. In order to put him to death, the Sanhedrin, the Jewish supreme court, seeks witnesses against Jesus. What they came up with is a series of unclear and contradictory stories. Unable to find any collaborating testimony and with no evidence, they put him under oath and force him to answer, "Are you the Christ, the Son of the Blessed One?"

Jesus answers, "I am, . . . and you will see the Son of Man sitting at the right hand of the Mighty One and coming on the clouds of heaven" (Mark 14:61–62 NJB).

At hearing Jesus' claim to divinity, the high priest performs the required ritual tearing of his clothes. Jesus' claim to be the Son of God is considered blasphemy, sufficient grounds for a death sentence. Provoking rage among the court, Jesus is spat upon, slapped, and struck with fists. For the guardians of the Jewish law, the only alternative to violence would be to acknowledge him as their long-awaited redeemer. By six in the morning the Sanhedrin issues a scandalously rushed verdict of blasphemy, demanding death.

But there is a problem. The verdict of the Jewish court was subject to Roman law, and under Roman law blasphemy was not a punishable offense. Instead the court takes a charge of treason to Pilate, the Roman governor, accusing Jesus of making himself the king of the Jews. This makes Jesus a political threat to Rome, guilty of treason against Caesar.

Pilate is warned by his wife to be careful because she has dreamed that Jesus is an innocent man. But under extreme pressure to please the religious leaders and keep the people under control, Pilate finds it difficult to give Jesus a fair hearing. Fascinated by this so-called insurrectionist, Pilate asks Jesus directly whether he is the king of the Jews. Jesus answers, "It is you who say it" (Mark 15:2 NJB). Pilate repeatedly and desperately tries to get Jesus to defend himself. Finding no reason to condemn him, but with mounting outside pressure, Pilate is put into a political and moral bind by Jesus' silence. If he releases Jesus, the people will complain to the Roman emperor of Pilate's disloyalty. If he condemns Jesus, he will have innocent blood on his hands.

In an act of political expediency, Pilate delivers Jesus to be scourged, hoping to buy pity and justify his release. Scourging was a brutal beating in which the condemned was stripped, tied to a post, and beaten by several soldiers using short leader whips studded with sharp pieces of bone and metal that tore the flesh. Before a capital sentence, the beating itself could prove fatal.

Battered and bleeding, Jesus is made sport. Soldiers shout, "Hail, king of the Jews!" (Mark 15:19 NJB) and plunge a crown of thorns on his head. They cover him with a robe and ridicule him by placing a mock scepter in his hand.

The crowds that had once heard Jesus' teaching and seen his miracles now turn into a bloodthirsty mob. At the sight of a battered and bruised Jesus, stirred up by the religious leaders to the verge of a riot, they shout, "Crucify him! Crucify him!" (Luke 23:21 NJB). No one comes to defend Jesus or to testify of his healings and works of compassion. His closest disciples are nowhere to be found.

With no easy way to release him, Pilate, in a cowardly act, attempts to wash his hands of the blood of Jesus. At the suppression of justice, all that could be heard was the deafening cry "Crucify him!"

In all this Jesus remains silent. He who by his word alone healed many and calmed the storm refuses to use his power to call down a legion of angels to rescue him. He willfully gives up his voice that he might fulfill the prophecy of Isaiah, "Ill-treated and afflicted, he never opened his mouth, like a lamb led to the slaughter-house, like a sheep dumb before its shearers, he never opened his mouth" (Isa. 53:7 NJB). Jesus refused to respond in kind to the power systems falsely accusing him.

Overwhelmed from the scourging, unable to bear his own cross, Jesus is led outside the gates of the city to the hill of Golgotha, meaning the Place of the Skull. In a place of shame and exclusion, with condemned thieves, he joins the community of the transgressors to be "cut off from the land of the living." By nine o'clock in the morning Jesus has been stripped and laid on the ground with both arms outstretched as he is nailed to a crossbeam. The crossbeam is then attached to an upright beam in the ground, and his feet are nailed to that. In Roman crucifixion, death came painfully and slowly through exhaustion, thirst, and asphyxiation. On a machine of death, Jesus is crucified naked exposing his vulnerable body, open to the blows of the world.

Even though death on a Roman cross was painful, its primary function as a deterrent was public humiliation. The crucified died exposed in a bloody sweat and unable to control bodily excretions. It was a degrading and shameful death, devoid of human dignity. This form of execution was reserved for slaves, foreigners, and political troublemakers lacking status. For the Jews, to be hung on a tree was to be considered accursed of God. Actually innocent, Jesus becomes all that is base, despised in the world and accursed by God. Suspended in midair, he is rejected by the earth and barred from heaven. In this place between heaven and earth, Jesus takes on his own body humanity's sin and transgression against God. He absorbs both the false judgment of the world and the true judgment of God on our behalf. Though he has the power to come down from the cross, Jesus willfully remains the embodiment of love.

The pain and shame that we are unable to bear Jesus embraces to satisfy our need for a final atonement. On the cross Jesus receives on his body the painful inscription of the transgression of the whole world.

The intense pain that is inflicted on Jesus is intended to perform a specific task—to destroy his world. Elaine Scarry describes intense pain as "language-destroying: as the content of one's world disintegrates, so the content of one's language disintegrates; as the self disintegrates, so that which would express and project the self is robbed of its source and its subject."[3] Through torture, his enemies seek to destroy Jesus' intimate relationship with God his Father. But on the cross under extreme pain and suffering, Jesus the Eternal Word remains coherent, articulating profound love. Instead of lashing out against his enemies, his first words on the cross are "Father, forgive them, for they do not know what they are doing" (Luke 23:34 NJB). Jesus retains his integrity at a high price by not rendering eye for eye, remaining true to his teaching and faithful to God.

But the pain of Jesus is not only bodily, it is what Simone Weil would describe as "extreme affliction, which means physical pain, distress of soul and social degradation, all at the same time."[4] On the cross Jesus is spiritually bruised and crushed, taking on our transgression at the center of his being. His body merely bears the marks as evidence.

Fulfilling the prophecy "They will look to the one whom they have pierced" (Zech. 12:10, quoted in John 19:37 NJB), Jesus becomes on the cross an object of scorn, absorbing the contemptuous gaze of the world. He is mocked and taunted by his crucifiers, even those being crucified with him. They dare him to save himself and come down from the cross. The world's gaze seeks to control Jesus by nailing and reducing him to a cross. It seeks to define the terms of his life. But Jesus is God and can never be objectified or consumed. He can't be contained; instead through him eternally giving love is poured out. When we look at the cross we see not only an innocent man but Jesus reconciling the world to God by absorbing its sin and contemptuous gaze on our behalf.[5]

As he absorbs the gaze of the world, Jesus also experiences the withdrawal of God's gaze of love. At noon, darkness comes over the earth and Jesus cries out, "My God, my God, why have you forsaken me?" (Mark 15:34). Because God despises sin, God is not able to look on the Son. In order to avoid the look of contempt, in a moment God averts the gaze of love from Jesus. When we look at the crucified Jesus, what we experience is the vicarious absence of God's loving gaze. Those of us who have eyes to see, see our own lack reflected on the body of Jesus. We understand the nature of our separation from God—lost intimacy with the Creator.

Unable to bear watching his mangled body and humiliation, most of Jesus' followers have forsaken him. Those who had followed close now follow from afar, not wanting to risk being associated with a crucified Jesus. Hoping for a political victory establishing an earthly monarchy, they are now haunted by the reality of a seemingly powerless teacher. He had told his disciples that if he was lifted up from the earth he would draw all people to himself (John 12:32). But at Golgotha what remains is a small group of women, including Mary his mother, Mary Magdalene, and his disciple John, watching from a distance. The women's low status puts them in a position of having much less to lose in associating with the crucified Jesus. For Mary, his mother, the pain of bearing the Son of God is at its culmination.

For us who are conditioned by a culture of consumption to desire and appreciate what is slick and appealing to the eye, the cross with its debasement and bloodiness is an unlikely location to find beauty. But at this scandalous and wretched scene the women beckon us to join them. From the distance of time, what we see as we gaze toward the cross is the beauty of love spilled out. As Jesus hangs on the cross, a sword-pierced side gushing water mingled with blood reveals his internal wounds. Here the self-containment of God in human flesh becomes the self-giving of God for the sins of the people. This other-centered love, which is the pleasure of God, is the only beauty that can restore our imaginations. As the self-giving of God becomes the center, it displaces the observer from the center of things. It releases me from the shame and self-consciousness of my disintegrity, allowing me to self-forget. The perfect and holy Son of God becoming sin for me clarifies and reorients my gaze by restoring my sense of justice so I can see what is truly beautiful.

As we turn and fix our eyes on Jesus, we look away from false cultural idols, breaking our gaze, which is what gives cultural idols their power. As we relentlessly serve cultural idols, our chief offense is against God. With eyes on Jesus, we're free from the need to consume the false images of our imaginations. Simone Weil writes, "Sin is not a distance [from God], it is turning our gaze in the wrong direction."[6]

What cultural and media images have destroyed in our imagination the cross can restore. Under the continual assault of media images, cultural expectations, and our own disoriented desire, our imagination has died. We can't see beyond our social situation or picture how to live in our body with coherence and meaning. Through faith in the work of Jesus, however, we are able to see what is possible for our lives and to embrace authentic beauty in the world. As we regard our bodies free from false expectations, they can become temples of God's Spirit. Personal adornment becomes an act of affirmation and not an act of self-loathing. As we see its cruelty, violating our bodies through cosmetic surgery, excessive dieting, and bod-mod becomes repulsive to us. The renewal of the imagination made possible by the beauty of the cross has the power to release us from the constant pressure to compare ourselves to the false image. It allows us to look in the mirror without shame and to see others with new eyes. We will see beauty where we saw lack. We will see our naked faces reflecting the love of God. Because Jesus absorbs our shame, we will no longer feel compelled to offer up our body to the pursuit of inauthentic beauty devoid of true justice. We can see beauty in unexpected places and faces and join Jesus in embracing the untouchable, the marginal, and the broken. Because of the beauty of God's love poured out, our imagination can be infused with new life.

The justice work that Jesus does on the cross accomplishes a double purpose. By offering himself to the demands of true justice before God, Jesus destroys the false justice of the world. On the cross he identifies with us by bearing our true guilt and shame on his own body. Jesus, as the only righteous judge and executor of justice, takes the place of us the condemned. Writing in flesh and the ink of his own blood, he takes on our guilt, satisfying the justice of God and allowing us to shed our shame. Because Jesus is God, he is also able to absorb the false guilt of what we fail to do and the shame of what we are. For women, who often bear the brunt of physical and emotional abuse, Jesus, having taken the ultimate abuse in his whole being, silences the claims of the abuser. Claims that we are unworthy and devoid of dignity have been absorbed by Jesus through the wounds he suffered as

God. Women on whose bodies the dysfunction of the world is inscribed with violence no longer need to suspect that they somehow deserve the abuse. The work of Jesus as he identifies with our sin and alienation provides a powerful basis for the protest of our subordination in the world and a means to claim our human dignity.

Justice is satisfied. Now those who suffer from the urge to perform acts of atonement in their bodies are released. As we surrender to the faith protest of the cross, our identity is established in a new place. We no longer find ourselves needing to submit to reductionist social expectations of us as women or to use our body as ballast for the self. God's gaze of love covers our shame and becomes the only thing worthy of the service of our body. As we move in new and mindful ways in the world, in the midst of the disintegrity and suffering that we continue to experience, this new identity provides the freedom to be creatures who bear the *imago Dei*. In our specific embodiment we can be fully human, fully women, shedding the shame we acquired in Eden.

Even as in Eden the earth suffered due to our transgression, on the hill of Golgotha the entire creation bears witness to the work of Jesus to restore it. By three o'clock in the afternoon, having realized his mission and returned to intimacy with God, Jesus speaks his final words, "Father, into your hands I commit my spirit" (Luke 23:46 NJB). At the death of Jesus the whole earth enters into mourning. Amidst darkness and in the travail of an earthquake, creation gives witness to his sacrifice. Persuaded by the witness of the earth, those who have crucified him and watched this cosmic spectacle declare, "In truth this man was the son of God" (Matt. 27:54 NJB).

Death Destroyed

The women who had provided for Jesus' needs in life continue their provision for him in death. Joseph of Arimathea, a former secret disciple and a member of the Sanhedrin, claims the body of Jesus and washes and anoints it with one hundred pounds of myrrh, aloes, and spices, wrapping it in linen. The women who had not abandoned him at the cross provide the procession for his brutalized body as it is carried to a fresh rock-hewn tomb. To them a dead Jesus is not a mere body, an object, but *him,* their beloved teacher.[7] During the next day and a half they find themselves paralyzed by the Sabbath, unable to travel or purchase spices. Desirous to hold him in community and unwilling to let him go, early Sunday morning they rush to where he is buried, hoping to express their love by anointing his body, but perplexed in remembering Jesus' promise of a resurrection.

Their faithful perseverance pays off. Instead of seeing Jesus' body given up to death and swallowed by the earth, the women become the first witnesses to the resurrection. Coming to an open tomb, they are greeted by an angel asking, "Why look among the dead for someone who is alive? He is not here; he has risen" (Luke 24:5–6 NJB). They are instructed to go tell his disciples that he is alive.

Both terrified and ecstatic at the news, they run to tell the others. Coming to the disciples, what they find behind locked doors is a fearful group huddling in shock and humiliated by failure. Unprepared for the news, the male disciples are ready to dismiss the women's testimony as a nonsensical tale. Nevertheless, compelled by the women's fervent message, they dare to believe that Jesus has risen, fulfilling what he had promised.

The women run ahead of the others and back to the empty tomb, where the risen Jesus first reveals himself to Mary Magdalene by calling out her name. Falling to his feet in adoration, she and the other women become not only the first hearers and bearers of the good news but the first eyewitnesses to a risen Redeemer.

From this new beginning God continues the legacy of using women as instruments of grace. Instead of appearing to the powerful Pilate or the Sanhedrin, Jesus appears first to those of lowest status. Instead of calling a press conference, he sends discredited women as messengers into a culture that does not easily believe them. In this way Jesus continues to overturn the power paradigms of the world and establish his true justice.

From the women's first report to the despondent disciples, the news spreads quickly. During a period of forty days there are various visitations of the risen Jesus in which he eats, speaks, and talks with many. But not everyone is ready to believe based on second-hand information. Not willing to settle for disembodied faith or to hold on to a phantom, the disciple Thomas demands not only to see Jesus but to touch his wounds before he will believe. Thomas wants to experience the certainty and nowness of the body of Jesus. He is not willing to settle for faith in false hopes. He wants to see the historical markers of suffering on the One in whom he had placed his hope.

Jesus discloses himself to Thomas by inviting him to touch his nail-scarred hands and put his hand on his wounded side. This tangible evidence of the embodied Redeemer breaks through unbelief and allows Thomas to declare, "My Lord and my God!" (John 20:24–28). Thomas's statement reveals a profound spiritual awakening mediated by the visible and palpable signs on the body of Jesus.

Even though Jesus taught that those who believe without seeing are blessed, we have not been left without a physical manifestation of him. In the last Passover meal shared with his disciples Jesus established the communal meaning of his bodily sacrifice. As we join the community of followers of Jesus and participate in the holy meal, we bring to mind his body broken for us, continually reassuring us of the source of healing. The certainty of our senses as we take the bread and wine provides us with a means to apprehend what is not seen—the presence of Jesus. Even as each of us is broken in diverse ways, bearing marks of suffering as we come together as a sacred community, we embrace the broken body of Jesus in each other. This is not an ideal community of perfect people, because like his early disciples, his followers still forget his words, doubt his power, and find themselves returning again and again to him for healing. Living under spiritual assault and aware of our lack of wholeness, we continually need our faith to be embodied in tangible healing ways. In brokenness and faith around a common table, as sons and daughters of God, we remind each other of Jesus' healing presence breaking through our unbelief.

Eternal Bodies

The Gospel narratives make the incarnation of God in Jesus, his bodily suffering, and the resurrection central features of the faith of his followers. It is faith in a God who was wounded. The body of Jesus, with its eternal bodily scars, becomes the locus of our redemption, denying the finality of death. This victory allows Jesus to promise his disciples that death will not have power over them: "Whoever keeps my word will never know the taste of death" (John 8:52 NJB). Like all people, those who follow Jesus eventually die a physical death. But they die assured that their bodies will be restored to them in a future resurrection.

This is the uniqueness of the spirituality offered by Jesus of Nazareth that can profoundly change not only our spiritual viewpoint but our relationship to our bodies. Regardless of the efficacy of what he taught, only a spirituality that defeats death can allow us to embrace the life of the body. Now we can be free to accept our limitations and escape the fear of death. We no longer feel the need to control our body as a way to control our life. Otherwise we spend our spiritual energies trying to escape the body's claims or in nihilism embracing its tragedy. No longer subject to the fear of death that drives a flight from our body, we find that the cross, the symbol of tortured death, becomes the symbol of death defeated.

But the cross does more; on the cross the weakness of God supplants the oppressive systems of the world. Because our service to cultural idols is in and through our bodies, it was necessary for Jesus to provide redemption in and on his body by atoning to the one true God. Because Jesus experienced ultimate exclusion from the community, we can face the social exclusion we experience and overcome its power. Jesus freely chooses humiliation on the cross yet avoids its reduction of him to the cross by continuing to pour out divine love. Under the most extreme suffering Jesus overcomes the defining power of the world. This becomes the source of redemptive power for us. Allowed to live fully in the world, no longer compelled to offer up our body to cultural idols but free to give it on the altar of God, we participate in the life of God.

As for our first parents in Eden, acts emerging from unbelief still yield both spiritual and bodily death. Our bodies, which are perishing and returning to the earth, cannot contain that which is eternal. By dealing with the shame we bear before God and within ourselves, Jesus undoes the consequences of the fall, allowing faith to ultimately transform our decaying and wasting bodies into eternal bodies that will never die. This allows humanity the freedom to move toward integrity in the entire body-self and to recapture union with God. Such a hope in the redemption of our bodies changes even how we approach our life in the body today. As the cross reorients our gaze and desires, we can listen to the many ways our body points us to God through its hunger, need, and longing. As our body is reclaimed and is no longer an "unbearable weight," faith produces life-yielding works in and through our body. We become instruments of divine expression and agents of transformation in the world.

The redemptive work on the open, bleeding, and spilling body of Jesus destroys the works of the evil one and fulfills the promise given to woman. A promise that her offspring will crush the serpent's head, destroying the power of death, is Eve's revenge against the cruel oppressor. Even as we bring the human community into being through our bodies, Jesus brings forth redemptive community through his bodily sacrifice. Jesus, offspring of the cooperation of woman and God, becomes the Redeemer of the world.

From our ancient beginnings in Eden to the women we are now, we can join the women at the cross by looking toward the crucified. As we yield our bodies as instruments of divine grace, we can go from being mere jars of clay to becoming temples of God.

9

A Holy Kiss

Creating a Place for the Body

To attach oneself to place is to surrender to it and suffer with it.[1]

Kathleen Norris

I had not talked to Ellen for years. Victims of six job changes and three home moves between us, we'd lost touch. Buried in a sixty-hour-a-week job involving extensive travel, she was left with only enough energy to do her laundry and pack for the next trip. Then a downturn in the high-tech industry found her pounding the pavement with enough time on her hands to begin to feel human again—vulnerable and needy. She found herself spiritually thirsty, longing to return to her roots, and at the same time experiencing the intense sexual desire she'd long buried. As she was disconnected from familiar routine, her spiritual and sexual needs converged with the need to enter a relationship with both the divine and the human community.

Her sexual stirrings, as I saw them, were a bodily presentation of deeper needs, a connection I've noticed in many others. Sexuality is always socially and spiritually situated. Human needs for belonging, affirmation, and meaning that do not find satisfaction in a community will readily show up in sexual desire. But just as communal needs can't be reduced to sexuality, neither can sexuality be reduced to the erotic. What remains is a corresponding link between the two that should inform how we seek to satisfy both. There are multitudinous ways these needs can be satisfied while we remain true to the nature and depth of all our relationships.

Communal Yearnings

We learn to understand ourselves in context, and how we relate to our body is a response to our communal experience. I've already explored how a sense of disconnectedness from our authentic self and the community accounts for much of our bodily dysfunction—from eating disorders to sexual addictions to the simple sense of being unattractive. This disconnection from our true nature is supported by an interwoven system of unattainable social expectations and illegitimate authority seeking to do two things: suppress the truth about God and the truth about who we are. This system, along with our own internal scripts, denies our authentic humanity as men and women. It denies a humanity that is much more messy and needy than we would like it to be. Our lack is more profound than we will admit. With no other way to live, we readily accept the cultural narratives for our lives that have the power to become flesh in our bodies. False ideas about "good" women and "bad" women can powerfully shape our lives through the shame they produce. To escape, we must become aware of the multitude of scripts pressing in on our lives, particularly those with cultural legitimacy.

In community, across cultures, and through language, we create alternative diverse narratives by which to live. We define the world for each other. We name and give meaning to our experiences. Together we create stories by which we understand our lives, and we pass on the stories to subsequent generations. But in our assignment of meaning, we want more than an explanation of why things are the way they are. We want a narrative that embraces the life we live in the body—the mundanity of vulnerable flesh. For the followers of Jesus, the biblical narrative is a sacred text that defines the world, corresponding to what is true and real about the Creator and ourselves. This sacred text, the eternal Word, has become fully embodied in Jesus and is to be made flesh in us by faith. The only way for us to escape the world's oppressive paradigm is for God's self-revelation to become embodied in our everyday life. I believe the crux of the postmodern search for meaning is the need for the Word to be made flesh. It is the only way to escape the cultural dictates and to live a new story.

To move out of our life's current paradigm requires that we make an exodus to a new community. In the establishment of the community of his followers, Jesus addresses not only our need for permanence and deep roots of relationships but also our need to experience a spiritual resettlement. My own experience of leaving one geographical place, traveling across the globe, and finding myself in a new one has left an indelible mark. My immigration experience involved forsaking place and kin for the hope of entering another community with greater promise. Knowledge of what it means to be a stranger has provided me a living metaphor to make a more significant spiritual migration. All of us have a need to forsake the dictates of expectations and tradition, like the biblical Ruth who left her Moabite people and her familiar idols to join God's people. We also, as adopted sons and daughters, can make our way into the household of God and live as exiles in the world, for God's household is open to those beyond kinship. Instead of establishing gated communities that exclude, Jesus himself is the open gate allowing the stranger to enter and join the community established in his own body.

In the new sacred community, Jesus' abiding presence brings his followers together. While on earth, he promised to return and drink new wine with them in person at the full manifestation of his kingdom. Until that time he urged them to wait in Jerusalem for the promised Holy Spirit who would provide them power to become his witnesses. Following the example of the women at the garden tomb, Jesus' disciples went on to proclaim the eternal Word and embody the healing presence of Jesus in the world. The Holy Spirit would make his socially insignificant followers prophets in the world, giving them a voice to tell a new story.

At his ascension, Jesus told the disciples, "Look, I am with you always; yes, to the end of time" (Matt. 28:20 NJB). With the aid of the empowering Spirit of God, the reality of Jesus' presence becomes evident to us first through hearing. As followers of Jesus, we proclaim to each other the written and spoken Word. Before the eternal Word everything is open and naked; the Word uncovers our lack of wholeness, exposing our double life. It brings to light the battle manifested in our bodies, where we are creatures who are limited, vulnerable, and needy. Jesus, the self-revelation of God, accurately defines the boundaries of my life and the terms by which I am to live. In this way the Word gives me back myself. This is why the liturgy of speaking the Word is at the center of Christian worship. It is the presence of Jesus himself that reshapes our understanding of ourselves in a new narrative—the gospel we proclaim to each other.

The presence of the incarnate Word, Jesus, makes a claim on our lives above the demands of the world and its idols. Once surrendered to the crucified and resurrected Son of God, we begin to destroy the demands of cultural idols. Aided by the Spirit of Jesus, our imagination is renewed to see what is possible, "so that the life of Jesus, too, may be visible in our body" (2 Cor. 4:11 NJB). As together in worship we name the things in the world that exercise false claims on our lives, God's definition can be made flesh. This allows us to cooperate in the redemption of the world through the works done in our bodies.

By faith we identify with Jesus when we join the sacred community, receiving the Word being spoken in it. But the revealing Word that the followers of Jesus share with each other can't remain disembodied, merely an idea. That would deny God's taking on human flesh in Jesus. The Word must be made flesh also in me, but in order for that to happen I need to surrender to its definitions, its molding of me, and its demands on me. I need to find myself resurrected with Jesus, to identify with him as, crucified, he identified with me. The divine Word can make my body a meaningful conduit of God's self-revelation instead of my being merely pliable, dumb matter waiting for the world's inscription. We live as temples of God in which Jesus himself drives out the merchants that would trade in our flesh.

Through worship and rituals together as a sacred community, we begin to reclaim the body. Worship is an acknowledgment of that which has the power to define our lives, the most profound and human of religious responses. As we bring our bodies into worship, we will find like the psalmist that our bodies long for God and our spirits are thirsty for the Living One (Ps. 63:1; 95:6). Jesus taught that this worship must be in Spirit and in truth, and in a temple not made with hands—our own bodies. It must no longer be only empty outward rituals but must be done with integrity requiring our entire body-self—emotion, mind, and flesh.

Through faith in Jesus and acknowledging his claim, our work, our eating, our sleeping, our play become sacred acts, moments in which we commune with God. But there are times set aside in which we again remember the cross. We have an inherent need to mark hours and days and to regard certain spaces as sacred. Through reading Scripture, singing, and daily prayer on bended knee, we continually yield our body to God. Our body signals our allegiances. Religious communities have all but abandoned the practice of conducting prayer meetings kneeling. In an age of self-promotion, it tends to rub us the wrong way, associated with groveling. But according to one Anglican bishop, when kneeling is abandoned "something very important has been lost in our body language."[2] Another practice that has become obscure is the practice of Sabbath keeping. In a hurried age of consumerism, to enter into rest may be the spiritual discipline we need most, so that our reworking of the world does not become domination instead of dominion. In the cycle of work and rest, Sabbath allows us to return to our source, the Creator who makes human life possible. It serves as a periodic reminder of our dependency on God, the earth, and each other.

Worship cannot remain simply a solitary activity practiced in the privacy of our own homes. The presence of Jesus moves us to engage our bodies in communal rituals that allow us to remember and reenact God's works in each other's lives. Rituals provide rhythmic signification of our ongoing redemption. They make that which is transcendent near, and through them the followers of Jesus signify God's claim on one another's bodies. Rituals are more than acts of remembrance; they are means of grace, places and moments where by faith God meets us.

Through rituals done on the body, the community reaffirms the redemption of our entire body-self. Water baptism marks our initiation into the sacred community and our being reclaimed from the world by the Word as we identify with Jesus. The holy meal reminds us of our continual bond with the crucified as we return to bear witness in our bodies of his sacrifice. With the harvest of the earth on our tongues, the grace of God permeates our lives like the warm fragrance of wine, allowing us to become the *ecclesia,* a gathering of those called by God. Anointing with oil provides a means to restore the bodies of the sick and aid in their healing. The laying on of hands acknowledges God's setting aside of an individual and her separation from the world. These rituals allow us to signify the offering up of our bodies on the altar of God and provide us with a connection to our sacred history. In this way we build a common life.

Growing up, I was taught to regard all good works, including rituals, as suspect attempts to "earn salvation." I've begun, however, to have a fuller appreciation for our need of the ancient rituals that have been practiced by the followers of Jesus for two millennia. For me, the holy meal has changed from a familiar and often slighted ritual to a proclamation of the redemption of the community and the earth. I found myself unsatisfied with perfunctory and institutionalized offerings of the holy meal, along with the infrequency with which anointing with oil and laying on of hands had been practiced in my church experience. Such lack of ritual reflects a deep disregard for our embodied life. This disregard is rampant in most forms of contemporary spirituality, where the individual relationship with God takes precedence over the communal nature of that relationship. Spiritualities in which the transcendent truncates that which is near are inconsistent with how Jesus taught. Through his healing work and ministry on earth, he showed us that the entire body-self must be redeemed along with the community. The rituals of *ecclesia* established by Jesus and his early followers are, if nothing else, communal rituals. For better or worse, and even in the midst of a broken community, there is no more room for a spirituality of one.

This understanding of the embodied nature of my faith has increased my communal yearnings. Many times I have found myself driving by a locked church early in the morning or late at night wanting to stop, hungry to join the community in the holy meal. When I have been sick I have longed for the anointing with oil that would remind me of my bodily redemption. I have longed for laying on of hands that would set me aside unto God even in the smallest task. One Monday night as I passed by a dimly lit church building, I was reminded of our communal poverty, with efficiency driving out meaning and utility ousting community. The sign at the front of the church read, "Come on home, we have left the light on for you." Unfortunately, the church was probably locked, shut down in fear, proving spiritual metaphors of home to be empty.

The sacred community of Jesus established as his body on earth does not remain a community unto itself. It is a community that, like him, is to be ever sacrificing itself for the world, distinct individuals creating a unity of faith. Its purpose, its calling, is the reconciliation of the world to the love of God. From this sacred community we move to reclaim the entire human community in common work and vision.

The natural tendency in moves toward community is that the stranger is not welcome. When the followers of Jesus forget their calling to the world, they can become another self-interest group. Instead through faith the sacred community must remain open to the new immigrant with her bag of troubles. The only way we can embrace difference in each other is through the reconciliation work of Jesus, who calls out the *imago Dei* in each one of us.

Little Acts of Resistance

With the significance of the healing presence of Jesus we are left to determine how we are to live in the time between Jesus' resurrection and our own. How might we usher the kingdom of God into the everyday practicality of life? How might we put a down-to-earth face on our faith? In the midst of what remains—disease, decay, aging, media that won't shut up, friends who don't stay, food that is too rich—how do we live the full redemption of our bodies and community? How do we spread the communal vision of Jesus? Though he broke the power of the world's gaze on the cross, many of our lives continue to be defined by a masculinist perspective. SuperBowl cheerleaders are still smiling, promoting their bodies for consumption, while others are following a counter trend, attempting a return to modesty. Both are seeking to out-fox the gaze that continues to fall upon us. How do we cultivate the spiritual imagination when so much ammunition is aimed to shut it down? How do we live in our wasting bodies as if they are what they really are: temples of God? Are we doomed to be stuck in a limited sphere while we wait for the kingdom of God to be fully revealed? To live redemptively in the world will require that we engage in a life of both surrender to the crucified one and intentionality. To live a life of intentionality requires I know what I am moving toward.

I believe we move toward the establishment of the kingdom of God by intentionally building community. We do this by living little acts of resistance—everyday acts done in our bodies. If we believe we have been created in the image of God and that Jesus establishes true justice on the cross, then a certain type of life will follow. It will be a life engaged in redeeming and re-creating the world through a protest of faith in the knowledge that Jesus has torn down the "principalities and powers" over us (Col. 2:15). Our protest must be based on faith that an invisible kingdom is being made visible in the bodies of the men and women who actively follow the crucified and resurrected one. We women must participate actively in the community, refusing to use our sex as an excuse or a weapon. Instead we will honor the *imago Dei* in ourselves that allows us to speak up and build culture locally and globally. Our acts are means by which we extend the sacred community in concentric circles to the entire earth. By providing food for a local food bank I militate against hunger everywhere. In the words of Jesus, "In truth I tell you, in so far as you did this to one of the least of these brothers of mine, you did it to me" (Matt. 25:40 NJB). The smallest intentional movements reverberate throughout the interdependent human community against the tyranny that would reduce humanity to use or function. They are the extension of the Word, the eternal narrative, continually being made flesh.

We start moving toward a holistic social vision by seeking to answer the first question God asked our parents in Eden: "Where are you?" Since our expulsion from Eden, we are dislocated. We desperately need to know where we stand, where we belong, and what our boundaries are. When we venture beyond them, we need a place to return. Unsheltered in our globalized world, we speak of safe space, private space, or having no space. We want to go home, be home, and make a home. These are not merely metaphorical ways of speaking; they reflect our sense of bodily relationship to other people and the world.

I was surprised at how young my children were when they began expressing a need to physically pull away—a milestone that meant my sons were becoming independent human beings. But they came back time after time for the reassurance of a hug or a kiss to keep them connected. They needed a place to return. To make a home is to be with others in a deeply physical relationship, to share space, food, and bodies in a safe place. In our intentional acts to create safe places we cooperate with God to redeem the world.

Secluded in the writing process, I quickly identified with Kathleen Norris's *The Cloister Walk*. With my life set aside from the world in a kind of monastery, I wondered how I was going to live out the intention to move toward community. I decided to write a "Rule" like those of the monastic societies, tailored for new sensibilities. I wanted this Rule to honor my body as a sacred temple and to go beyond treating me as a product I must market to the world. I wanted it to take me beyond the utilitarian view of other people that focuses on what they can do for me and to see in them the image of God. I decided to talk less on the phone and instead get together with people in person, buy fewer clothes, and not rush through the moments of my life.

In the end I was often unable to meet my own expectations for myself. I failed to live up to my own Rule, revealing my disintegrity. At times I experienced joyous moments when my body-self seemed to dance, but at other times it seemed that grace had all but disappeared as I dragged my body around like a heavy weight. My actions have yet to catch up with my intentions, and thus my double-mindedness is revealed. But what remains is what is possible, that is, small movements done by God's grace moving me toward *shalom*.

We can begin these small intentional movements by admitting we need an immediate community: a household, neighborhood, or workplace that shares a common task and calling. This is our village, usually within several miles of where we live or any other place where we spend the bulk of our time. Frequenting the same places creates the opportunity for everyday inconsequential encounters to be repeated over and over. For those whose life passion and career are merged, the workplace can become a satisfying place of connectedness as we affect and transform the world by the work of our hands. However, for most people the American work environment is too hierarchical and rigid to allow the necessary messiness of community building. Others find their village vacant; the work of home and family life is too isolated from the larger world. Technology can be a source of disconnection, but perhaps the technological revolution may be applied to our jobs in ways that blur the edges between the workplace and home. Why not envision work that moves in step with the cycles of our bodies, allowing for the tending of our relationships—that offers mothers opportunities to make creative contributions to the world and fathers to nurture their children? Maybe we can begin to create more holistic ways of working and living that meet both our relational and creative needs.

In an attempt to build community, we must be guided by the understanding that physical presence increases commitment and commitment creates community. Spending an hour a week with a group of people does not build community, it only builds associations. In neighborhoods that allow us to avoid our neighbors and assume no local identity, we won't experience places of belonging. The myth of the self-sustaining nuclear family and the autonomous single makes for isolation and loneliness. Finding ourselves spiritually and physically scattered, we must intentionally gather in one or two places as our primary focus.

One way to enlarge and enrich one's immediate community is to extend one's household to include more than two generations or non-kin. No one should have to live or eat alone. I am raising children with my husband in a three-generational household, which includes my parents; this increases a sense of belonging in the present and connections to the past, while mitigating peer pressure. But some acts of community building happen unplanned: watching out for a neighbor's child, sharing an abundant harvest of backyard tomatoes, borrowing a cup of milk. By investing in a geographical place we understand ourselves in context and work against that state of affairs where we've learned to live as autonomous individuals.

We can work toward creating healing environments within sterile places such as drab offices, streets bare of trees, kitchens with never an intriguing aroma, churches in strip shopping centers. All these environments disregard our embodied humanity and how we experience the world. Instead of leaving, we can make small changes. Bring a friend's art into your office, plant a tree on your street, fill your home with the aroma of slow-simmering soup. Creating more human environments requires that we be present both physically and emotionally. When we invest in the people we are with and the places we are in, we create opportunities to offer, in the name of Jesus, a cold glass of water to world-weary souls. Soon, even in suburban America with fleeting visits to mega-malls, fragmented schedules, and rear-entry garages, we'll find ourselves sharing more than a backyard fence.

Another aspect of this intention to create healing environments involves recapturing the joy of working together in concrete, physical ways that engage our senses. In this information age, we spend so much time doing invisible mental work alone in front of a computer that we regularly need to get back to doing shared physical work. Physical work parallels our bodies. It takes up space like we do. It smells. It sweats.

Early in my career, after five years in a highly structured corporate job, I quit. I simply could not take the sterility of the mental work I was doing in isolation. I spent that summer at a camp for kids in the badlands of North Dakota, where I worked for room and board, cleaning floors and chopping onions, surrounded by people who shared the work with me. It provided a therapeutic way to clear my head and reground myself. Recently I've been exploring on the idea of starting a community garden with my neighbors. And when friends come for dinner, I've been known to tell a musician in the group to bring his or her instrument. When Andrew played his violin after our meal, he got an audience for his creative work and the rest of us got live music. There are many ways to create shared space that is more human and closer to our needs.

In a mobile society like ours, we make many choices over a lifetime about where to live and work. When presented with opportunities to improve our lifestyle, finances, or prestige we simply must consider whether we are giving up a sense of place in exchange for other less permanent benefits. Intentionally moving toward community means we don't move *away* from people but *toward* people. As we continually seek out greener pastures, we must ask, *Will these physical moves make a positive difference in the quality of our long-term relationships?* We need to be in the presence of others, especially at emotionally intense times, so we can find solace in times of grief and affirmation in times of joy. Disembodied communications don't feed our souls the way physical touch and proximity do. By intentionally choosing that which is most *present* over the more *absent*, we resist relational and communal poverty. By preferring meeting in person over technology-mediated communication, we build richer relationships and deeper community. Nothing clears the air in relationships like a face-to-face conversation. Nothing says you are important to me as much as honoring your physical presence. On a cultural level, the java-shop trend is one way we are dealing with increased disconnection. Providing a low-key gathering place, Starbucks understood our human need for shared space and opportunity to meet others—franchised it, and cashed in on community.

Another way we can contribute to a sense of place and belonging is by recovering the art of hospitality. Food and cooking have played an important role in my life, with milestones celebrated and personal hurts comforted around a table laden with homemade pasta. I can count on one hand the number of restaurant meals I ate with my family as a child, for they were considered of lesser quality, emotionally at least. Restaurant meals have been packaged and marketed to appeal to demand, and that produces an entirely different relational dynamic, making us all consumers. We learn to prefer going out so that everybody can get the kind of food they want, but when you are in someone's home and eat what is put before you, the host and you say to each other, "Your company is valued." Eating a home-cooked meal in each other's personal environment—and, even better, cooking together in our seldom-used gourmet kitchens—is an investment in a sense of belonging.

Small acts of resistance against the current power paradigm include caring for the weak, including the excluded, and loving the unlovely. Being with those who are ill, comforting the brokenhearted, and reaching out to the marginal are difficult. Often it is easier to care for those across the world than to care for those across the street. The person within touching distance will spill on you not only their soup but their troubles, insecurities, fears, and failures. Even when they say nothing, their presence screams, "I need." King Solomon, who said, "Better to go to the house of mourning than to the house of feasting" (Eccles. 7:2), understood the sobering effect of other people's pain. He recognized that seeing other people's vulnerability makes us aware of our own lack, and in the presence of brokenness we learn our own humanity.

A healthy communal experience yields various benefits. As a little girl surrounded by many aunts and female cousins, I never saw women agonize about their weight or spend endless hours on their appearance. When they were feeling a little down they would have *mate*, a tea drunk from a common cup, while knitting in a circle or bouncing one of many babies on their knee—a sort of group therapy. The community released them from self-consciousness and self-centeredness. Choosing to invest in community improvement instead of self-improvement is a powerful antidote to the vacant beauty culture and disconnectedness by which we're surrounded.

But achieving real belonging and connectedness is easier said than done. It does not show up at our doorstep ready to meet our needs. Other people don't always cooperate with our ideals; they grate on our nerves and ignore our needs. They wander in and out of our lives, don't show up when we need them, or betray us. Structural barriers that seem to have been built into our society—frequent job changes, long commutes, the radical separation of work and home—deny us what we most need. They take a toll on our ability to maintain even the most cursory of bonds. In addition, the automobile allows us to move from place to place unencumbered so we don't have to deal with the issues of a particular place. We can literally take flight. And in a culture of affluence I don't need you to make bread or soap for me because I can simply choose from hundreds of brands at my corporately owned megastore. I don't need you to play the piano, because my state-of-the-art stereo provides all the entertainment I need. So many available options make us feel we don't really make a difference in anyone's life. We don't expect people in our "community" to directly provide the basics of life. We are able to live as autonomous people wholly independent of others; then we wonder why we feel unfulfilled, unattractive, and disconnected.

I've often wondered: How many women with eating disorders are terminally lonely? How many eat their meager portions alone or gorge alone? How many women rushing to cosmetic surgery wouldn't bother if they felt they actually belonged to a community? How many casual campus sex hookups wouldn't happen if young people felt valued by somebody somewhere? These sad things are not simply just personal problems; they are failures of the community.

Thinking about this brings up the possibility that I have failed many of my friends who felt compelled to modify their bodies or rush from man to man. Could it be that by offering extra hugs, sitting through awkward silences, or looking more intently for the beauty in a friend, I could have created a redemptive situation for them? Maybe by practicing small acts of resistance and extending the embrace of Jesus I could have changed the way they view themselves and the world they live in. Maybe by embodying the eternal Word in concrete ways both of us could have been healed of our shame.

Intentional community building requires sacrifices and inconveniences and imposes limits on our freedom. It requires that we be willing to sit in its mess. But the satisfaction of our human need for a healing community begins in relationship with the divine community. God made flesh in Jesus has the power through his body, broken on the cross, to call us to wholeness on many levels, including our entire body-self. Our need for a sense of belonging is met not only in a geographic space but also in spiritual space, with women and men who share common vision and faith in the crucified. As I see myself in the faces of others who have chosen to live as spiritual exiles and participate in the sacred community, I can know that "in my flesh I shall see God" (Job 19:26 NKJV).

Epilogue

When I began to write this book, I had a sense the answer would be yes. Yes, the Jesus of Nazareth I'd followed since I was a girl would answer the questions about the body my friends and I were asking. But he would go beyond simply affirming our lives as women from a singular male point of view. In the battle between the world, the flesh, and the devil, it seemed the flesh—the part of us tending to go toward death—was now our greatest enemy. It was the flesh causing us the most problems, and I did not know where the process would lead me.

I needed to put flesh back on my faith, that is, if I was ever to offer it as my gift to the world. As I spoke with many women about issues of embodiment and spirituality, I heard two consistent longings: a longing for a faith that embraces the entire body-self and a longing for community. In the face of these two longings, we are, in the larger social context, settling for a spirituality largely disconnected from our bodies and their social meaning, yet on the other hand settling for a spirituality offering the immanent embrace of the goddess and a reduction of spirituality *to* our bodies. These two conflicting approaches express women's ambivalence about themselves and their approach to spirituality. But I knew this topic wasn't just about women. I knew men who suffered quietly in their need for community and to fully occupy their bodies. In their own search for transcendence, men had a desperate need to recover from viewing their bodies as mere instruments of achievement.

I was reminded of this need to put flesh on spirituality by feminist *thealogians* who expressed a rejection of the Judeo-Christian tradition due to what they perceived as its male-dominated anti-body message. A spirituality that is anti-body is by its very nature going to be antiwoman. And woman is what I am. In examining my faith, I knew I could not stop where the *thealogians* stop. Two millennia of church history have included otherworld fixations, misogynistic eruptions, and adoptions of Greek dualism with its denial of the significance of the embodied life. Church history has resulted in what is often a disembodied theology. Such a theology is composed of cosmic legal transactions more interested in the afterlife than in this life, more interested in our souls than in our bodies. This is a theology of transcendent ideals stripped of every vestige of blood, sweat, or tears. It is an "enlightenment" theology where truth is presented as a series of philosophical proofs while inadvertently forgetting that Jesus is the Truth *made flesh*. In the end, the God presented by this theology will not care what we do in our bodies. This God will not suffer with us. This could not be what I based my life on or offered the world.

Before writing this book, I knew many women had already left this disembodied theology for the arms of goddess spirituality, for it appeared to offer a more holistic affirmation of their lives. Other women were comforting themselves with a feel-good Christianity or the rhetoric of self-help that denies the social burden we woman all carry. Neither of these was an acceptable alternative for me. I was going to have to go further back, to our ancient beginnings and the root of my faith, Jesus of Nazareth. I was going to have to do recovery work to regain the full meaning of the Word made flesh for myself. No longer a tidy theological concept, the Word made flesh would have to suffer and die like flesh.

But I could not do this reclaiming work in a vacuum. My definitions and my perspective have been shaped by the multitude of my experiences from childhood until now. Guided by the witness of biblical writers, I would have to pull at the threads of my own tradition and my own life to weave a clearer vision of Jesus. Along the way, I've begun uncovering the bodily meaning of Jesus' work. Such a full significance not only retains his distinctiveness but provides for me the only viable way to affirm my own embodied life. It provides the defeat of death and redeems the meaning of my everyday acts. In this process I have recovered for myself the richness and present relevance of the Gospel stories. I have gained a fuller joy for my entire body-self.

As I began to write about the life we live in the body, there were several ideas I could not avoid no matter how unprepared I was to offer up new insight. People asked whether I was going to write about this or that—those sticky subjects that quickly deteriorate into dead-end rhetoric. At last I had to acknowledge many topics that were just there, like elephants in the middle of the room. I knew sexuality would come up, since in the contemporary mind the body equals sex. Our society is centered on either the containment of sex or reducing all needs to the erotic. But what I didn't know was that it would bring up a deep communal significance beyond the couple. I didn't know that people are looking not for a no-holds-bared sexuality but for sexuality to be defined more broadly than the erotic. The flagrant sexuality of MTV and sitcoms gives us a reduction of the expansive life-affirming motivation that our sexuality is. But people are longing for a broadening of what it means to be a sexual person. They want to understand how sexuality plays out in different scenarios and how it is expressed in a multitude of nonerotic ways for both single and married. I found that life-encompassing sexuality is addressed and expressed in the whole span of our life on earth, including God's own pleasure in self-giving both at creation and the cross.

There were other unexpected connections. I anticipated the topic of beauty; after all, that's the bottom line when it comes to our female bodies. We are not as beautiful as we wish to be. I knew the answer is not simply to tell women to cancel their *Cosmo* subscription, get a facial, and love themselves. This would be putting a Band-Aid on a deep wound. Neither could I tell women to look for the beauty that is within when we don't even know who we are. I didn't foresee our need to recover our spiritual imagination—the death of the spiritual imagination being at the root of our body issues. I expected bodily presence to be a theme, but not that the nowness of the body in pain and pleasure would be so instructive. It is always ready to remind us to pay attention to our spiritual needs. I anticipated that sensuality would come into play, but not that lack, desire, and self-giving would converge in our bodies and point us to God. I knew the topic of work would come up, but not that by being bearers of the divine image the sweat of our brow could become an act of reworking and redeeming the world. I knew women's greater vulnerability increases their exposure to abuse globally; I did not know that how a society treats the bodies of women could serve as a particular moral gauge. Distressed by the social meaning of woman's body that we carry as a burden, I found myself comforted by the parallel of the communal meaning of woman's body to the meaning of the body of Jesus. This, along with the active participation of women in God's redemptive plan, provides women with immeasurable God-given dignity.

Writing this book has given me opportunities to think about where my body is situated, the particular neighborhood I live in, how furniture in my house is arranged, even my sleeping position. A different type of self-consciousness has emerged, a willingness to become attentive to my body, embracing its pain and its pleasure. I've become conscious of my tears, my boisterous laugh, and the click of my shoes on the pavement. Writing a book is a largely mental process, but I found myself aware of hitting particular keys as I wore down the N and the D. When I was feeling under the weather, I was more sensitive to the ability of bodily discomfort to muddle my mind. I have taught myself to practice living in the moment and to fill the space I occupy today. Learning to more clearly define my physical place in the world, I am now more aware of cultural expectations about how I should look, act, and be—and more ready to disregard them. Never having worn much makeup, I find myself wearing even less and liking myself more. Freedom not to succumb to dictates of fashion allows the freedom for clothing to become an art form in itself. I still hope to find time for that while avoiding the prepackaged self sold at the mall.

Since we can't talk about the body without mentioning food, I figured food would show up in the text too. What showed up was the entire earth. There it was—linked to our bodies from the very beginning. Part of our community, the earth is our sister, joining us as witness to the redemptive work of Jesus. Who but he taught that lilies, grass, and birds are ready to instruct about process rather than production? Who but he taught that people and the earth are gifts, not utilitarian objects? By looking at eating disorders and the holy meal established by Jesus, I learned that eating (or *not* eating) is largely a social experience and should not be practiced alone. Taught to pray before meals in thankfulness to God, now at mealtimes I regard the entire earth as a gift. This makes rushing through a meal seem rude, and fast food an utter insult.

And then there is the bodily connection to the past. Generation to generation, a chain of genetic and familial history begun in Eden is brought to the present by a tide of bodily fluids. Unexpectedly my grandmother and great-grandmother showed up as I thought about the continual movement forward of the human community in birth and in death. My female ancestors' stories became the basis for my story, their pain and joy became my legacy. Now I look at my sons and see the future in their bodies.

Thinking about my body and the bodies of others has made me much more aware of other people's physical presence. I started a practice of looking for what is *there* instead of what is *not there* in everyone I meet. Plain people grew beautiful before my eyes. How people move in the space they take up, their dancing or sad eyes, the cadence and pitch of their voice impressed me. This is how Mary Magdalene finally recognized Jesus when he called her name at the garden tomb. Becoming more aware of other people's bodies as well as my own, I experienced an increased desire to hug people—and learned that people are remarkably huggable; very few refuse. Hugs exposed me to the solidness of some people and the marshmallow cushiness of others. Recovering the early childhood custom of greeting people with a kiss on the cheek as I had been taught in my native Argentina, I found emotional nourishment. People's warm bodily presence began to matter, and that meant I began to experience the coldness of the absence of certain people, separated from me by distances, circumstances, and time. I allowed myself to miss people, to feel the separation and experience the sadness of departures, for these are real losses we've become accustomed to deny.

Now at the end of this book, what I've gained in writing it is a profound appreciation for my own body and the presence of those who make up my everyday community. I now see my spiritual life in the context of my ordinary everyday life, which I experience in this imperfect yet wondrous body of flesh.

Notes

Chapter 1: *A Blank Canvas?*

1. Camille Paglia, *Vamps and Tramps: New Essays* (New York: Vintage, 1994), 30.

2. Elizabeth Wurtzel, *Bitch: In Praise of Difficult Women* (New York: Doubleday, 1998), 90.

3. Faith Popcorn, *EVEolution: Eight Truths of Marketing to Women* (New York: Hyperion, 2000).

4. Industry source at www.skininc.com, "The U.S. Antiaging Skin Care Market," 14 July 2001.

5. Patricia Hill Collins, *Black Feminist Thought: Knowledge, Consciousness, and the Politics of Empowerment,* rev. ed. (New York: Routledge, 2000), 70–72.

6. Eating Disorders Awareness and Prevention: www.edap.org.

7. *Slim Hopes,* video featuring Jean Kilbourne, producer/director Sut Jhally, Media Education Foundation, 1995.

8. Brenda Spitzer, "Gender Differences in Population versus Media Body Size," *Sex Roles: A Journal of Research,* April 1999, www.findarticles.com.

9. Eating Disorders Awareness and Prevention: www.edap.org.

10. J. D. Heyman, "Hollywood's Obsession with Weight," *US Weekly,* 19 March 2001, 53.

11. Spitzer, "Gender Differences in Population versus Media Body Sizes," reporting on Wilfley and Rodin's 1995 published research, www.findarticles.com.

12. Eating Disorders Awareness and Prevention: www.edap.org.

13. Statistics reported by the National Association of Anorexia Nervosa and Associated Disorders: www.anred.com.

14. Spitzer, "Gender Differences," www.findarticles.com.

15. National Association of Anorexia Nervosa and Associated Disorders: www.anred.com.

16. American Society of Plastic Surgeons: www.plasticsurgery.com.

17. Ibid.

18. Ibid.

19. Elizabeth Haiken, *Venus Envy: A History of Cosmetic Surgery* (Baltimore: John Hopkins University Press, 1997), 6.

20. "Attractiveness Still Key to Dating Activity," *USA Today,* January 1998, found at www.findarticles.com.

21. Naomi Wolf, *The Beauty Myth: How Images of Beauty Are Used against Women* (New York: William Morrow, 1991), 10.

22. Andrea Billups, "Hillary Reverses Cinderella Story," *Washington Times,* 2 February 2001, www.washingtontimes.com.

23. Betty Friedan, *The Feminine Mystique* (New York: W. W. Norton, 1963), 344.

24. Note that lesbianism is a complex system of thought and it is more than same-sex sex; therefore I have refrained from using this term.

25. Carrie Bradshaw character, *Sex in the City,* HBO, 1998.

26. Charles Taylor, *The Ethics of Authenticity* (Cambridge: Harvard University Press, 1991), 129.

27. *Babette's Feast,* produced by Just Betzer and Bo Christensen, Orion Classics, 1988.

28. Anne Marie Balsamo, *Technologies of the Gendered Body: Reading Cyborg Women* (Durham: Duke University Press, 1996), 27.

Chapter 2: *The Body Is My Altar*

1. Marilyn Bender in *The New Quotable Woman,* ed. Elaine Partnow (New York: Facts on File, Inc., 1992), 404.

2. Lynda Nead, *The Female Nude: Art, Obscenity, and Sexuality* (New York: Routledge, 1992).

3. See Mary Pipher, *Reviving Ophelia: Saving the Selves of Adolescent Girls* (New York: G. P. Putnam's Sons, 1994) for sources on the emotional lives of girls.

4. Madonna and Guy Sigsworth, "What It Feels Like for a Girl," *Music* (Maverick/Warner Brothers, 2000).

5. Andrea Dworkin, interview, *New Statesman and Society,* 21 April 1995, www.yelah.net.

6. Simone de Beauvoir, *The Second Sex,* trans. H. M. Parshley (New York: Alfred A. Knopf, 1953), 615.

7. William Wordsworth, "She Was a Phantom of Delight," Representative Poetry On-line, editor I. Lancashire, Web Development Group, University of Toronto, found at www.library.utoronto.ca.

8. Barbara Welter, *Dimity Convictions: The American Woman in the Nineteenth Century* (Athens: Ohio University Press, 1976), 21.

9. Patricia Hill Collins, *Black Feminist Thought: Knowledge, Consciousness, and the Politics of Empowerment,* rev. ed. (New York: Routledge, 2000), 47.

10. Joan Jacobs Brumberg, *The Body Project: An Intimate History of American Girls* (New York: Random House, 1997), xx.

11. Sut Jhally, producer/director, created by Jean Kilbourne, *Killing Us Softly* III, video, Media Education Foundation, 2000.

12. See the work of Jill Kilbourne, *Deadly Persuasion: Why Women and Girls Must Fight the Addictive Power of Advertising* (New York: Free Press, 1999).

13. Eating Disorders Awareness and Prevention: www.edap.org.

14. Ian Halperin, "Supermodel Beauty Myths," www.talksurgery.com, April 2001.

15. Neil Postman, *Amusing Ourselves to Death* (New York: Penguin, 1986), 71–75.

16. Michael Levine, "Why I Hate Beauty," *Psychology Today,* August 2001, 38.

17. Ariel Glucklich, "Self and Sacrifice: A Phenomenological Psychology of Pain," *Harvard Theological Review,* October 1999, www.findarticles.com.

18. Marilee Strong, *A Bright Red Scream* (New York: Penguin, 1998), 88.

19. Carl Elliot, "A New Way to Be Mad," *Atlantic Monthly,* December 2000, 73.

Chapter 3: *Body Bound*

1. Nawal al-Saʿdawi, "Growing Up Female in Egypt," *Women and the Family in the Middle East: New Voices of Change,* ed. Elizabeth Warnock Fernea (Austin: University of Texas Press, 1985), 111.

2. The existence of intersexed individuals brings forth a whole host of biological, cultural, and theological challenges. The struggle is between medical intervention with its multiple problems and cultural room for intersexed people. Otherwise a two-sex paradigm is by far the most pervasive experience, which is assumed here.

3. Gerry Goffin, Carole King, and Jerry Wexler, "(You Make Feel Like) a Natural Woman," 1971.

4. Natalie Angier, *Woman: An Intimate Geography* (New York: Houghton Mifflin Company, 1999), 73.

5. Miroslav Volf, *Exclusion and Embrace: A Theological Exploration of Identity, Otherness, and Reconciliation* (Nashville: Abingdon, 1996), 175.

6. Plato, quoted in Prudence Allen, *The Concept of Woman: The Aristotelian Revolution, 750 BC-AD 1250* (Grand Rapids: Eerdmans, 1997), 61.

7. Jean Bethke Elshtain, *Public Man, Private Woman: Women in Social and Political Thought* (Princeton: Princeton University Press, 1981), 37–39.

8. Allen, *Concept of Woman,* 57–74 on Plato.

9. Elshtain, *Public Man,* 37–39.

10. Allen, *Concept of Woman,* 121.

11. St. Augustine, *Basic Writings of Saint Augustine,* trans. Whitney Jennings Oats (Grand Rapids: Baker, 1992), II: 814.

12. Caroline Walker Bynum, *Fragmentation and Redemption: Essays on Gender and the Human Body in Medieval Religion* (New York: Zone, 1992), 131–34.

13. Allen, *Concept of Woman,* 60.

14. Charles Taylor, *Sources of the Self: The Making of Modern Identity,* (Cambridge: Harvard University Press, 1989), 145.

15. Susan Bordo, "The Flight from Objectivity," in *Feminist Interpretations of René Descartes,* ed. Susan Bordo (University Park: Pennsylvania State University Press, 1999), 50.

16. Susan Bordo, *Unbearable Weight: Feminism, Western Culture, and the Body* (Berkeley: University of California Press, 1999), 3.

17. Ibid, 5.

18. Ibid.

19. Camille Paglia, *Vamps and Tramps* (New York: Random House, 1994), 40.

20. Simone de Beauvoir, *The Second Sex,* trans. H. M. Parshley (New York: Alfred A. Knopf, 1953), xv.

21. Muriel Dimen, "Power, Sexuality and Intimacy" in *Gender, Body, Knowledge: Feminist Reconstructions of Being and Knowing,* Alison M. Jaggar and Susan R. Bordo, eds. (New Brunswick: Rutgers University Press, 1989), 41.

22. Elshtain, *Public Man,* 227.

23. Shulamite Firestone, *The Dialectics of Sex* (New York: Bantam Books, 1972), 206.

24. Elizabeth Taylor, "Harvard Study: Birth Control Use Linked to Increase in Women in Professional Roles," *University Wire,* 27 June 2001, www.ask.elibrary.com.

25. PBS Online, *Healthweek,* www.pbs.org/healthweek.

26. Kaiser Daily Reproductive Health Report, March 17, 2000, www.kff.org; reprint of Gladwell, "Birth Control Pill: The Downside of John Rocks's Invention," *New Yorker,* 13 March 2000.

27. In regard to fertility and contraception the issues brought by the intersection of race and class are numerous. Black and other minority women's experiences in the navigation of public and private spheres have particular nuances not experienced by white women. In contraception what is considered a privilege for white women—not reproducing—can

become a duty for black women. Thus discussion of contraception must take into account the racial and class dynamics in a society.

28. David Noonan and Karen Springen, "When Dad Is a Donor," *Newsweek,* 13 August 2001, 46.

29. Quoted by Yvonne Roberts, "Why Do Women Want Children?" *New Statesman,* 29 January 2001, www.findarticles.com.

30. Reported on www.childbirth.org.

31. Claudia Kalb, "Should You Have Your Baby Now?" *Newsweek,* 13 August 2001, 40.

32. Janice G. Raymond, *Women as Wombs: Reproductive Technologies and the Battle over Women's Freedom* (San Francisco: HarperSanFrancisco, 1993), 76, 96.

33. "Child of My Dreams Survey Draws Attention to 'Human' Side of Infertility," *PR Newswire,* 30 October 1998, www.findarticles.com.

34. U.S. Centers for Disease Control, "1999 Assisted Reproductive Technology Report," www.cdc.gov.

35. Frederic Golden, "Making Over Mom and Dad," *Psychology Today,* June 1999, www.ask.elibrary.com.

Chapter 4: *Es Una Nena!*

1. Charlene Spretnak, *The Resurgence of the Real: Body, Nature, and Place in a Hypermodern World* (Reading, Mass.: Addison-Wesley, 1997), 4.

2. Beauvoir, *The Second Sex,* 267.

3. Paula J. Caplan and Jeremy B. Caplan, *Thinking Critically about Research on Sex and Gender,* 2d ed. (New York: Longman, 1999), 98.

4. Royal Weld, "Vanishing Execs: Women," *Industry Week,* July 20, 1998, www.ask.elibrary.com.

5. Germaine Greer, *The Whole Woman* (New York: Alfred A. Knopf, 1999), 3.

6. Caplan and Caplan, *Thinking Critically,* 2–3.

7. Mary Stewart Van Leeuwen, *Gender and Grace: Love, Work, and Parenting in a Changing World* (Downers Grove, Ill.: InterVarsity Press, 1990), 73. See her discussion of sex differences, 54–71.

8. Lisa McLaughlin, "No Gender Gap," *Time,* 25 February 2002, www.time.com.

9. Dorothy L. Sayers, *Are Women Human?* (Grand Rapids: Eerdmans, 1971), 37.

10. Sandra Lipsitz Bem, "Gender Schema Theory," *Sign: Journal of Women in Culture and Society,* 8: 598–616.

11. Hagberg Consulting Group: www.leadership-development.com.

12. Ginia Bellafante, "It's All About Me," *Time,* 29 June 1998, 54. Also see www.catalystwomen.org regarding women trapped in mid-management.

13. Patricia Sellers, "These Women Rule," *Fortune,* 25 October 1999, 94.

14. Suze Orman, *The Courage to Be Rich* (New York: Riverhead, 1999).

15. Iyanla Vanzant, "How to Find the Joy," www.innervisionworldwide.com.

16. 2000 Catalyst Census of Women Corporate Officers and Top Earners, www.catalystwomen.org.

17. Matthew Valia, "Silicon Valley Women Still Hampered by Work/Life Challenges," www.diversityinc.com, 26 April 2001.

18. Patricia Sellers, "Secrets of the Fastest-Rising Stars," *Fortune,* 16 October 2000, www.fortune.com.

19. Quoted in Valia, "Silicon Valley Women."

20. Market Data Enterprises, "Market for Self-Improvement Products and Service," www.mkt-data.ent.com.

21. 2001 Women of Influence ad, *WE,* May 2001.

22. John Leland and Carla Power, "Spirituality for Sale," *Newsweek,* 20 October 1997, 53.

23. See www.salon.com/books.

24. "First Person," Lands End catalog, summer 2001.

25. Lise Funderburg, "I Don't have a Problem Representing Yoga," *Time,* 15 April 2001, www.time.com.

26. Ian I. Mitroff, "A Study of Spirituality in the Workplace," *Sloan Management Review,* Summer 1999, found on www.findarticles.com.

27. Michelle Conlin, "Religion in the Workplace," *Business Week,* 1 November 1999, www.businessweek.com.

28. Karen M.Thomas, "Healing Circle," *Dallas Morning News,* 8 January 2001.

29. Sharon Begley, "Religion and the Brain," *Newsweek,* 7 May 2000, www.msnbc.com.

30. "Cleveland Medical School Programs Incorporate Spirituality as a Prescription for Healing," *Jet,* 3 April 2000, www.findarticles.com.

31. Christiane Northrup, *Women's Bodies, Women's Wisdom: Creating Physical and Emotional Health and Healing* (New York: Bantam, 1994), 67.

32. George Gallup, "Spirituality in America," *Business Week,* 1 November 1999, www.businessweek.com.

33. Quoted in Damien Cave, "Got God," Salon.com, 27 January 2000.

34. Ray Kurzweil, "Live Forever," *Psychology Today,* January 2000, 66.

35. Neil Postman, *Amusing Ourselves to Death* (New York: Penguin, 1986), 114–20.

36. Brenda E. Brasher, *Give Me That Online Religion* (San Francisco: Jossey-Bass, 2001), 25.

37. Timothy Leary, "Using LSD to Imprint the Tibetan-Buddist Experience," www.erowid.org.

38. Jeffrey Kluger, "Mr. Natural," *Time*, 12 May 1997, www.time.com.

39. Robin Eisner, "Falling Off Prozac," www.ABCNews.com, 24 May 2001.

40. Mary Daly, *Quintessence: Realizing the Archaic Future* (Boston: Beacon, 1998), 5.

41. Charlene Spretnak, introduction to *The Politics of Women's Spirituality: Essays on the Rise of Spiritual Power within the Feminist Movement*, ed. Charlene Spretnak (Garden City, N.Y.: Anchor, 1982), xxiv.

42. See Cynthia Eller, *The Myth of Matriarchal Prehistory: Why an Invented Past Won't Give Women a Future* (Boston: Beacon, 2000), for a critique of this.

43. Judy Grahm, "From Sacred Blood to the Curse and Beyond," in *The Politics of Women's Spirituality: Essays on the Rise of Spiritual Power within the Feminist Movement*, ed. Charlene Spretnak (Garden City, N.Y.: Anchor, 1982), 265–79.

44. Carol P. Christ, "Why Women Need the Goddess," in *The Politics of Women's Spirituality: Essays on the Rise of Spiritual Power within the Feminist Movement*, ed. Charlene Spretnak (Garden City, N.Y.: Anchor, 1982), 75.

45. Ray Anderson, *On Being Human* (Pasadena: Fuller Seminary Press 1982), 210.

46. Camille Paglia, *Sexual Personae: Art and Decadence from Nefertiti to Emily Dickenson* (New York: Vintage, 1991), 3.

Chapter 5: *Jars of Clay*

1. Story and statistics provided by the Protection Project of the Foreign Policy Institute at John Hopkins University, Washington D.C.

2. Susan Brownmiller, *Against Our Wills: Men, Women and Rape* (New York: Simon and Schuster, 1975), 31. Quote from Patton's *War As I Knew It:* "I then told him that, in spite of my most diligent efforts, there would unquestionably be some raping, and that I should like to have the details as early as possible so that the offenders could be properly hanged."

3. See Brownmiller, *Against Our Wills,* for an extensive discussion about the use of rape throughout history.

4. Ibid, 266.

5. Mark Phillips, "Rape Now a War Crime," www.cbsnews.com, 22 February 2001.

6. Brenda Smiley "Rape Tore the Fabric of Bosnian Families," Women's E-news, www.womensenews.com, 11 August 2000.

7. World Health Organization, UNICEF data on www.uneca.org.

8. UNICEF, *Domestic Violence Against Women and Girls*, May 2000.

9. See Colette Dowling, *The Frailty Myth* (New York: Random House, 2000).

10. See ibid., 37. There is a great deal of individual variation regarding what a woman is able to do at any point in her life. Fit, athletic women have no problems with intense exercise well into the third trimester of pregnancy. Also see Natalie Angier, *Woman: An Intimate Geography* (Boston: Houghton Mifflin, 1999).

11. Robert Sullivan, "For Women, a Golden Age," *Time,* 3 September 2001, 62–3.

12. Jonathan Ganz, "US Soccer Stars Juggle Teamwork and Motherhood," www.cnnsi.com, June 22, 1999.

13. Simone Weil, *Waiting for God,* trans. Emma Craufurd, intro. Leslie A. Fiedler (New York: Harper & Row/Perennial Library, 1951), 118.

14. Elaine Scarry, *The Body in Pain: The Making and Unmaking of the World* (New York: Oxford University Press, 1985), 33.

15. Ibid., 13.

16. Weil, *Waiting for God,* 117.

17. Touch Research Institute, www.miami.edu/touch-research.

18. Natalie Merchant, "Trouble Me," *Blind Man's Zoo,* Ten Thousand Maniacs (Christian Burial Music, 1989).

19. William Raspberry, "What's Love Got to Do with It," *Washington Post,* 27 July 2001, www.ask.elibrary.com.

20. www.abcnews.com, 21 August 2001.

21. Alexander Schememann, *For the Life of the World* (Crestwood, N.Y.: St. Vladimir's Seminary Press, 1995), 95.

22. Peter Jennings, www.abcnews.com, 12 October 2001.

Chapter 6: *Daughters of Eve*

1. Ophira Edut, ed., *Body Outlaws: Young Women Write about Body Image and Identity* (Seattle: Seal, 1998). Forward by Rebecca Walker, xiv.

2. Phyllis Trible, *God and the Rhetoric of Sexuality* (Philadelphia: Fortress, 1978), 21.

3. Ray S. Anderson, *On Being Human* (Pasadena: Fuller Seminary Press, 1982), 105–6.

4. Trible, *God and the Rhetoric,* 79.

5. Mary Timothy Prokes, *Toward a Theology of the Body* (Grand Rapids: Eerdmans, 1996), 74.

6. Wendell Berry, *Sex, Economy, Freedom, and Community* (New York: Pantheon, 1993), 109.

7. Wendell Berry, "The Pleasures of Eating," in *What Are People For?* (New York: North Point, 1990), 147.

8. Body Wisdom Institute, www.body-wisdom.com.

9. Berry, *Sex, Economy,* 109.

10. Trible, *God and the Rhetoric,* 79.

11. Donna Hailson and Karelynne Gerber, "Cooking up Gotterdamerung: Radical Feminist Worship Substitutes Self for God," *Theology Matters,* July/August 1998, 1.

12. Charles Sherlock, *The Doctrine of Humanity,* Contours of Christian Theology (Downers Grove, Ill.: InterVarsity Press, 1996), 43.

13. Adrienne Rich, *Of Woman Born: Motherhood as Experience and Institution* (New York: W. W. Norton, 1986), 55.

14. William Leiss, *The Domination of Nature* (Montreal: McGill-Queen's University Press, 1994), 54.

Chapter 7: *The Not-Always-Virgin Mary*

1. Rich, *Of Woman Born,* 68.

2. Irina Ratushinskaya, *Grey Is the Color of Hope* (New York: Alfred A. Knopf, 1988), 105–13.

3. Peter Brown and Robert Lamont, *The Body and Society: Men, Women, and Sexual Renunciation in Early Christianity* (New York: Columbia University Press, 1988), 112. See Prudence Allen, *The Concept of Woman: The Aristotelian Revolution, 750 BC-AD 1250* (Grand Rapids: Eerdmans, 1997), 95.

4. Jaroslav Pelikan, *Mary Though the Centuries: Her Place in the History of Culture* (New Haven: Yale University Press, 1996), 2–3.

5. Elizabeth Abbott, *A History of Celibacy* (New York: Scribner, 1999), 60.

6. Marina Warner, *Alone of All Her Sex: The Myth and Cult of the Virgin Mary* (New York: Vintage, 1976), 336.

7. See Abbott, *History of Celibacy,* 17, and Brown and Lamont, *Body and Society,* 362.

8. See Brown and Lamont, *Body and Society,* 109.

9. Ibid., 111–12.

10. Ibid., 153.

11. Cunneen, *In Search of Mary,* 115, quoting Rosemary Radford Ruether, "Misogyny and Virginal Feminism in the Fathers of the Church."

12. Brown and Lamont, *Body and Society,* 149.

13. See also Rosemary Radford Ruether, *Sexism and God-Talk: Toward a Feminist Theology* (Boston: Beacon, 1983), chap. 6, discussion of Mariology as symbolic ecclesiology.

14. Cunneen, *In Search of Mary,* 77.

15. Brown and Lamont, *Body and Society,* 49.

16. Warner, *Alone of All Her Sex,* 336.

17. Phillip Edgcumbe Hughes, *The True Image: The Origin and Destiny of Man in Christ* (Eugene, Ore.: Wipf and Stock, 1989), 40.

18. To call Jesus the body-I AM is not to deny his full humanity beyond a physical body. See discussion of Apollinarianism and docetic perspective in Millard J. Erickson, *The Word Became Flesh: A Contemporary Incarnational Christology* (Grand Rapids: Baker, 2000), 60–61.

19. See ibid, 577–93.

Chapter 8: *Made Flesh*

1. Prudence Allen, *The Concept of Woman: The Aristotelian Revolution, 750 BC–AD 1250* (Grand Rapids: Eerdmans, 1997), 217.

2. Franz Kafka, *In the Penal Colony* (New York: Schocken, 1946).

3. Scarry, *The Body in Pain,* 35.

4. Weil, *Waiting for God,* 134.

5. See Jean-Luc Marion, *God Without Being,* trans. Thomas A. Carlson (Chicago: University of Chicago Press, 1991) for the relationship of the gaze and the idol.

6. Weil, *Waiting for God,* 124.

7. See Anderson, *On Being Human,* 144, for a discussion on death and dying.

Chapter 9: *A Holy Kiss*

1. Kathleen Norris, *The Cloister Walk* (New York: Riverhead, 1987), 244.

2. Wire report article, *Dallas Morning News,* January 2001.

Bibliography

Abbott, Elizabeth. *A History of Celibacy*. New York: Scribner, 1999.

Allen, Prudence. *The Concept of Woman: The Aristotelian Revolution, 750 BC–AD 1250*. Grand Rapids: Eerdmans, 1997.

Anderson, Ray. *On Being Human*. Pasadena: Fuller Seminary Press, 1982.

Angier, Natalie. *Woman: An Intimate Geography*. Boston: Houghton Mifflin Company, 1999.

Ashley, Benedict. *Theologies of the Body: Humanist and Christian*. Braintree, Mass.: Pope Center, 1995.

Balsamo, Anne Marie. *Technologies of the Gendered Body: Reading Cyborg Women*. Durham, N.C.: Duke University Press, 1996.

Beauvoir, Simone de. *The Ethics of Ambiguity*. 3d ed. New York: Carol Publishing Group, 1994.

―――. *The Second Sex*. Translated by H.M. Parshley. New York: Alfred A. Knopf, 1953.

Berkouwer, G. C. *Studies in Dogmatics: The Person of Christ*. Grand Rapids: Eerdmans, 1954.

Berry, Wendell. *Sex, Economy, Freedom, and Community*. New York: Pantheon, 1993.

―――. *The Unsettling of America*. San Francisco: Sierra Club Books, 1986.

―――. *What Are People For?* New York: North Point, 1990.

Birke, Lynda. *Feminism and the Biological Body*. New Brunswick: Rutgers University Press, 2000.

Bolen, Jean Shinoda. *Goddesses in Everywoman: A New Psychology of Women.* San Francisco: Harper & Row, 1984.

Bordo, Susan. *Unbearable Weight: Feminism, Western Culture, and the Body.* Berkeley: University of California Press, 1999.

———, ed. *Feminist Interpretations of René Descartes.* University Park: Pennsylvania State University Press, 1999.

Brand, Peg Zeglin, ed. *Beauty Matters.* Bloomington: Indiana University Press, 2000.

Brasher, Brenda E. *Give Me That Online Religion.* San Francisco: Jossey-Bass, 2001.

Brown, Peter, and Robert Lamont. *The Body and Society: Men, Women, and Sexual Renunciation in Early Christianity.* New York: Columbia University Press, 1988.

Brown, Warren S., Nancey C. Murphy, and H. Newton Malony. *Whatever Happened to the Soul? Scientific and Theological Portraits of Human Nature.* Minneapolis: Fortress, 1998.

Brownmiller, Susan. *Against Our Wills: Men, Women and Rape.* Simon New York: Simon and Schuster, 1975.

———. *Femininity.* New York: Linden, 1984.

Brumberg, Joan Jacobs *The Body Project: An Intimate History of American Girls.* New York: Random House, 1997.

———. *Fasting Girls: The History of Anorexia Nervosa.* New York: Plume, 1989.

Butler, Judith P. *Bodies That Matter: On the Discursive Limits of "Sex."* New York: Routledge, 1983.

Bynum, Caroline Walker. *Fragmentation and Redemption: Essays on Gender and the Human Body in Medieval Religion.* New York: Zone, 1992.

———. *The Resurrection of the Body.* New York: Columbia University Press, 1995.

Calvin, John. *Genesis,* ed. Alister McGrath and J. I. Packer. Wheaton, Ill.: Crossway, 2001.

Caplan, Paula J., and Jeremy B. Caplan. *Thinking Critically about Research on Sex and Gender.* 2d ed. New York: Longman, 1994.

Collins, Patricia Hill. *Black Feminist Thought: Knowledge, Consciousness, and the Politics of Empowerment.* Rev. ed. New York: Routledge, 2000.

Cooper, John W. *Body, Soul, and Life Everlasting: Biblical Anthropology and the Monism-Dualism Debate*. Vancouver, B.C.: Regent College Publishing, 1989.

Crow, Barbara A. *Radical Feminism: A Documentary Reader*. New York: New York University Press, 2000.

Cunneen, Sally. *In Search of Mary: The Woman and the Symbol*. New York: Ballantine Books, 1996.

Daly, Mary. *Gyn/Ecology: The Metaethics of Radical Feminism*. Boston: Beacon, 1990.

Descartes, René. *Meditations on First Philosophy*. Trans. Donald A. Cress. Indianapolis: Hackett, 1979.

Diamant, Anita. *The Red Tent*. New York: Picador USA, 1998.

Dowling, Colette. *The Frailty Myth*. New York: Random House, 2000.

Dworkin, Andrea. *Intercourse*. New York: Free Press, 1987.

Edut, Ophira, ed. *Adios Barbie: Young Women Write about Body Image and Identity*. Seattle: Seal, 1998.

———. *Body Outlaws: Young Women Write about Body Image and Identity*. Seattle: Seal, 1998.

Eller, Cynthia. *Living in the Lap of the Goddess: The Feminist Spirituality Movement in America*. New York: Crossroad, 1993.

———. *The Myth of Matriarchal Prehistory: Why an Invented Past Won't Give Women a Future*. Boston: Beacon, 2000.

Elshtain, Jean Bethke. *Public Man, Private Woman: Woman in Social and Political Thought*. Princeton: Princeton University Press, 1981.

Erickson, Millard. *The Word Became Flesh: A Contemporary Incarnational Christology*. Grand Rapids: Baker, 2000.

Faludi, Susan. *Backlash: The Undeclared War against American Women*. New York: Crown, 1991.

Fernea, Elizabeth Warnock, ed. *Women and the Family in the Middle East: New Voices of Change*. Austin: The University of Texas Press, 1985.

Firestone, Shulamite. *The Dialectics of Sex*. New York: Bantam Books, 1972.

Foster, Patricia, ed. *Minding the Body*. New York: Anchor, 1994.

Foucault, Michel. *The History of Sexuality: An Introduction*. Trans. Robert Hurley. 3 vols. New York: Vintage, 1976.

Freedman, Rita Jackaway. *Beauty Bound*. Lexington, Mass.: Lexington, 1986.

Friday, Nancy. *The Power of Beauty*. New York: HarperCollins, 1996.

Friedan, Betty. *The Feminine Mystique*. New York: W. W. Norton, 1963.

Goldberger, Nancy Rule. *Knowledge, Difference, and Power: Essays Inspired by Women's Ways of Knowing*. New York: BasicBooks, 1996.

Green, Joel B., and Mark D. Baker. *Recovering the Scandal of the Cross: Atonement in New Testament and Contemporary Contexts*. Downers Grove, Ill.: InterVarsity Press, 2000.

Greer, Germaine. *The Female Eunuch*. New York: McGraw-Hill, 1970.

————. *The Whole Woman*. New York: Alfred A. Knopf, 1999.

Grenz, Stanley J. *Sexual Ethics: An Evangelical Perspective*. 2d ed. Louisville: Westminster John Knox, 1997.

Grosz, Elizabeth. *Volatile Bodies: Toward a Corporeal Feminism*. Bloomington: Indiana University Press, 1994.

Gundry, Robert H. *"Soma" in Biblical Theology, with Emphasis on Pauline Anthropology*. 2d ed. Grand Rapids: Zondervan/Academie, 1987.

Hoekema, Anthony. *Created in God's Image*. Grand Rapids: Eerdmans, 1986.

Hughes, Philip Edgcumbe. *The True Image: The Origin and Destiny of Man in Christ*. Eugene, Ore.: Wipf and Stock, 1989.

Irigaray, Luce. *Speculum of the Other Woman*. Ithaca: Cornell University Press, 1985.

————. *This Sex Which Is Not One*. Ithaca: Cornell University Press, 1985.

Jaggar, Alison M., and Susan R. Bordo, eds. *Gender/Body/Knowledge: Feminist Reconstructions of Being and Knowing*. New Brunswick: Rutgers University Press, 1989.

John Paul II. *The Theology of the Body: Human Love in the Divine Plan*. Boston: Pauline Books and Media, 1997.

Kafka, Franz. *The Metamorphosis, In the Penal Colony, and Other Stories*. 3d ed. New York: Schocken, 1995.

Kidd, Sue Monk. *The Dance of the Dissident Daughter: A Woman's Journey from Christian Tradition to the Sacred Feminine*. San Francisco: HarperSanFrancisco, 1996.

Kilbourne, Jean. *Deadly Persuasion: Why Women and Girls Must Fight the Addictive Power of Advertising*. New York: Free Press, 1999.

Lehrman, Karen. *The Lipstick Proviso: Women, Sex, and Power in the Real World.* New York: Doubleday/Anchor, 1997.

Leiss, William. *The Domination of Nature.* 3d ed. Montreal: McGill-Queen's University Press, 1994.

Lloyd, Genevieve. *The Man of Reason: "Male" and "Female" in Western Philosophy.* Minneapolis: University of Minnesota Press, 1984.

Lorber, Judith. *Paradoxes of Gender.* New Haven: Yale University Press, 1994.

Mann, Judy. *The Difference: Growing Up Female in America.* New York: Warner, 1994.

Marion, Jean-Luc. *God Without Being.* Trans. Thomas A. Carlson. Chicago: University of Chicago Press, 1991.

Mason, Mike. *The Mystery of Marriage: Meditations on the Miracle.* Sisters, Ore.: Multnomah, 1996.

McNay, Lois. *Foucault and Feminism: Power, Gender, and the Self.* Boston: Northeastern University Press, 1993.

Moore, Thomas. *The Soul of Sex: Cultivating Life as an Act of Love.* New York: HarperCollins, 1998.

Moreland, J. P., and Scott B. Rae. *Body and Soul: Human Nature and the Crisis in Ethics.* Downers Grove, Ill.: InterVarsity Press, 2000.

Morris, Leon, *The Atonement: Its Meaning and Significance.* Downers Grove, Ill.: InterVarsity Press, 1983.

Nelson, James B., and Sandra P. Longfellow. *Sexuality and the Sacred: Sources for Theological Reflection.* Louisville: Westminster John Knox Press, 1994.

Norris, Kathleen. *The Cloister Walk.* New York: Riverhead, 1987.

Norris, Pamela. *Eve: A Biography.* Washington Square. New York: New York University Press, 1999.

Northrup, Christiane. *Women's Bodies, Women's Wisdom: Creating Physical and Emotional Health and Healing.* New York: Bantam, 1994.

Orenstein, Peggy. *Flux: Women on Sex, Work, Kids, Love, and Life in a Half-Changed World.* New York: Doubleday, 2000.

Pagels, Elaine. *Adam, Eve, and the Serpent.* New York: Vintage, 1989.

Paglia, Camille. *Sexual Personae: Art and Decadence from Nefertiti to Emily Dickinson.* New York: Vintage, 1991.

———. *Vamps and Tramps: New Essays.* New York: Vintage, 1994.

Peiss, Kathy Lee. *Hope in a Jar: The Making of America's Beauty Culture.* New York: Metropolitan, 1998.

Pelikan, Jaroslav. *Mary Through the Centuries: Her Place in the History of Culture.* New Haven: Yale University Press, 1996.

Pipher, Mary. *Reviving Ophelia: Saving the Selves of Adolescent Girls.* New York: G. P. Putnam's Sons, 1994.

Popcorn, Faith. *EVEolution: Eight Truths of Marketing to Women.* New York: Hyperion, 2000.

Postman, Neil. *Amusing Ourselves to Death.* New York: Penguin, 1986.

———. *Technopoly: The Surrender of Culture to Technology.* New York: Vintage, 1993.

Prokes, Mary Timothy. *Toward a Theology of the Body.* Grand Rapids: Eerdmans, 1996.

Ratushinskaya, Irina. *Grey Is the Color of Hope.* New York: Alfred A. Knopf, 1988.

Raymond, Janice G. *Women as Wombs: Reproductive Technologies and the Battle over Women's Freedom.* San Francisco: HarperSanFrancisco, 1993.

Rich, Adrienne C. *Of Women Born: Motherhood as Experience and Institution.* 10th ed. New York: W. W. Norton, 1986.

Roiphe, Katie. *The Morning After: Sex, Fear, and Feminism on Campus.* Boston: Little, Brown, 1993.

Rosen, Ruth. *The World Split Open: How the Modern Women's Movement Changed America.* New York: Viking, 2000.

Ruether, Rosemary Radford. *Sexism and God-Talk: Toward a Feminist Theology.* Boston: Beacon, 1983.

Sayers, Dorothy L. *Are Women Human?* Grand Rapids: Eerdmans, 1971.

Scarry, Elaine. *The Body in Pain: The Making and Unmaking of the World.* New York: Oxford University Press, 1985.

———. *On Beauty and Being Just.* Princeton: Princeton University Press, 1999.

Schememann, Alexander. *For the Life of the World.* Crestwood, N.Y.: St. Vladimir's Seminary Press, 1995.

Shalit, Wendy. *A Return to Modesty: Discovering the Lost Virtue.* New York: Free Press, 1999.

Sherlock, Charles. *The Doctrine of Humanity.* Contours of Christian Theology. Downers Grove, Ill.: InterVarsity Press, 1996.

Spencer, Aida Besançon. *The Goddess Revival.* Grand Rapids: Baker, 1995.

Spretnak, Charlene. *The Resurgence of the Real: Body, Nature, and Place in a Hypermodern World.* Reading, Mass.: Addison-Wesley, 1997.

———, ed. *The Politics of Women's Spirituality: Essays on the Rise of Spiritual Power within the Feminist Movement.* Garden City, N.Y.: Anchor, 1982.

Stan, Adele M. *Debating Sexual Correctness: Pornography, Sexual Harassment, Date Rape, and the Politics of Sexual Equality.* New York: Delta, 1995.

Stone, Linda, and Nancy McKee. *Gender and Culture in America.* Upper Saddle River, N.J.: Prentice-Hall, 1998.

Suleiman, Susan Rubin, ed. *The Female Body in Western Culture: Contemporary Perspectives.* Cambridge, Mass.: Harvard University Press, 1986.

Taylor, Charles. *The Ethics of Authenticity.* Cambridge, Mass.: Harvard University Press, 1991.

———. *Sources of the Self: The Making of the Modern Identity.* Cambridge, Mass: Harvard University Press, 1989.

Thesander, Marianne. *The Feminine Ideal: Picturing History.* London: Reaktion, 1997.

Tong, Rosemarie Putnam. *Feminist Thought: A More Comprehensive Introduction.* 2d ed. Boulder, Colo.: Westview, 1998.

Trible, Phyllis. *God and the Rhetoric of Sexuality.* Philadelphia: Fortress, 1978.

Turkle, Sherry. *Life on the Screen: Identity in the Age of the Internet.* New York: Simon & Schuster, 1995.

Van Leeuwen, Mary Stewart. *Gender and Grace: Love, Work, and Parenting in a Changing World.* Downers Grove, Ill.: InterVarsity Press, 1990.

Volf, Miroslav. *Exclusion and Embrace: A Theological Exploration of Identity, Otherness, and Reconciliation.* Nashville: Abingdon, 1996.

Waltke, Bruce K., with Cathi J. Fredricks. *Genesis: A Commentary.* Grand Rapids: Zondervan, 2001.

Warner, Marina. *Alone of All Her Sex: The Myth and Cult of the Virgin Mary.* New York: Vintage, 1976.

Warren, Karen J., ed. *Ecological Feminist Philosophies.* Bloomington: Indiana University Press, 1996.

Weil, Kari. *Androgyny and the Denial of Difference.* Charlottesville: University Press of Virginia, 1992.

Weil, Simone. *Waiting for God*. Trans. Emma Craufurd, intro. Leslie A. Fiedler. New York: Harper & Row/Perennial Library, 1951.

Welter, Barbara. *Dimity Convictions: The American Woman in the Nineteenth Century*. Athens: Ohio University Press, 1976.

Welton, Donn, ed. *The Body*. Malden, Mass: Blackwell, 1999.

Wolf, Naomi. *The Beauty Myth: How Images of Beauty Are Used against Women*. New York: William Morrow, 1991.

Wurtzel, Elizabeth. *Bitch: In Praise of Difficult Women*. New York: Doubleday, 1998.

Yalom, Marilyn. *A History of the Breast*. New York: Alfred A. Knopf, 1997.

Index

A.I. (film) 77
abortion 23, 25, 72, 73, 78, 109
Adam 133, 137–38, 152
adolescence 33, 337–38
adoption 181
adultery 159
advertising 14
affluence 118
aggression 159
aging 12
Aguilera, Christina 40
al-Saᶜdawi, Nawal 55
alienation 142
alternative medicine 95
Ambrose 152
American College of Obstetricians and
    Gynecologists 110
androgyny 25, 140–41
anointing with oil 184
anonymity 118
anorexia 19, 50, 78, 119, 155
anxiety 114
Aristotle 61, 147
asceticism 60, 151
atonement 48–50, 52, 165, 170
Augustine 61–62

autism 127
automobile 191
autonomy 122, 124, 188, 191

Babette's Feast (film) 29
Bacon, Francis 139–40
baptism 183
barrenness 158
Beatrice of Ornacieux 62
beauty 13, 15–16, 30, 41–46, 172, 195
inner and outer 34–35
beauty cult 15, 18–19, 21–24
Beauvoir, Simone de 41, 65–66, 81
Belief.net 95
belonging 129, 130, 133, 188, 190–92
Bem, Sandra 85
Bender, Marilyn 33
biochemistry 84
biological determinism 83–84
birth control pill 70–72
black slavery 107
black women 43
blasphemy 168–69
bod-mod 48, 51, 173
body:
    betrayals by 117

as canvas 51
denial of 24–25
dysfunction of 180
escape from 30, 124
and gender 72
and identity 55–56
limitations of 101–2, 106, 124
as machine 59, 64
meaning of 30–31, 52
as prison 64, 78
redemption of 145, 154, 161
and self 82, 90
and soul 26, 31, 57, 64–65, 113,
    114
and spirituality 9–10, 60–63
subjugation of 62
suffering of 114
as temple of God 178
vulnerability of 111–13, 117, 122,
    124, 146
war against 73
body piercing 48, 51
body-parts models 46
body-self 130, 132, 133–34, 137, 158,
    183–84
Bordo, Susan 64
Bosnian women 108, 118
Boys Don't Cry (film) 57
branding 51
breast 20
breastfeeding 76
breath 132
brokenness 114, 115, 116, 144, 158,
    160
Brown, Leslie 74
Brownmiller, Susan 107
Brumberg, Joan Jacobs 24, 43
bulimia 19, 50, 78
Bundchen, Gisele 45
businesses 94

calling 187
Campbell, Naomi 45
Catherine of Siena 62, 163
celibacy 152
certainty 113
cesarian births 76
chakras 95
character 43–44
chastity 26, 149
childbearing 74, 75–76, 87, 138
choice 89–90
Chopra, Deepak 92
Christ, Carol 99
Clark, Edward 110
Clinton, Hillary 23
cloning 77, 98
clothing 140–41
colonization 107, 110
commitment 26
community 26, 73–74, 75, 78, 97,
    106, 116, 118, 120–21, 134, 179,
    189–92, 193, 197
    see also new community
compassion 26
connectedness. *See* belonging
consumerism 22, 44, 48, 51, 93–95,
    131, 137, 172, 183, 190
contraception 23, 25, 72, 75, 78
cosmetic surgery 11, 19–21, 25, 45,
    49, 51, 78, 173, 192
cosmetics 14–15, 21, 164
Cosmo Girl 40
Crawford, Cindy 45
creation 128–33, 174
crucifixion 170–72
cultural mandate 131
culture 14, 31, 34, 102, 186
cyberspace 96–97

daily bread 102–3
Dalai Lama 94

Dali, Salvador 148
Daly, Mary 98
daycare 87
death 106, 114, 117, 120–22, 124,
    136, 177–78
depression 97, 114
Descartes, René 63
desire 28, 30, 137, 138–39, 142
    for God 27, 28–29
Destiny's Child 40
diaries 43–44
dieting 18–19, 21, 25, 161, 173
difference 82–88, 99
disease 113, 114, 120
divorce 159
domesticity 75, 87
dominion 131, 139
donor insemination 73, 76, 77
Dowling, Colette 110
drugs 97–98
dualism:
    Cartesian 64, 73, 90
    Greek 194
Dworkin, Andrea 39

eating 131
eating disorders 19, 180, 192, 196
ecclesia 184
ecofeminists 73
Eden 129, 132–33, 135–36, 142, 144,
    155–56, 174, 177, 186
El Greco 148
Eller, Cynthia 99
Elshtain, Jean Bethke 61
embryos, as property 77
Emily's List 14
Ensler, Eve 38
equality 83
essentialism 58, 100
Eve 134–38, 152–53

facelifts 20
faith 102, 160, 182, 183
fall 137, 139, 140, 142, 165
false justice 173
fashion magazines 14
fashion models 45
fast food 197
fasting 155
Favazza, Armando 50
Fawcett, Joy 111
female genital mutilation 109
femininity 15, 43, 46, 49, 110, 164
feminism 24–25, 57–58, 73, 88, 98,
    136
    backlash against 22
    second wave 68, 75
spirituality 98–101, 118
fertility 110
fidelity 26
Fiorini, Carly 88–89
Firestone, Shulamite 70
flesh 180, 193
food 30, 131, 196–97
forbidden fruit 135–36
forgiveness 160
freedom 27–28, 53, 78, 119, 122
Friedan, Betty 23, 68, 75
friendship 116
funerals 121

gaze 35–36, 39–40, 47, 186
gender 16, 25, 59–60, 72, 91, 130
gender differences 83, 87
gender dysfunction 139
Gilligan, Carol 88
Girl, Interrupted (film) 50
Gnosticism 151
God:
    abundance of 157
    compassion 147
    devotion to 149–50

as Father 155
immanence 124
self-giving 134, 135
transcendence 124, 128
weakness of 177
goddess spirituality 99–100, 194
Greer, Germaine 83
Grieco, Helen 91
grief 114, 121–22
guilt 164

Harris, Katherine 22–23
healing 160, 176
health clubs 21
Helen of Troy 42
helper 135
"heroin chic" 48
holy meal 166–67, 176, 184, 196
Holy Spirit 129, 147, 153, 181
horizon of significance, 26, 28, 156
hormonal therapies 71
hormones 84
hospitality 160, 190
household 187
Howell, Emily 86
hugs 197
human sacrifice 49
humanity:
authentic 180
unity and diversity 130

identity:
and body 55–56
as changeable 118
as free-floating 52
and gaze 40
see also self
idols 47–48, 49, 172–73, 182
Iliad 42
illness 26, 113

image of God 62, 128–30, 132, 136,
137, 142, 174, 185, 186
images 43–48, 53
imagination 42–43, 102, 173, 186,
195
in vitro fertilization 76–77
incarnation 102, 182
individualism 26, 118, 119, 124, 188
industrial eating 131
industrialization 67, 118
infancticide 109
infertility 74, 75, 76–77
integrative medicine 97
Internet 118
intimacy 115–16, 141, 151
isolation 188

Jerome 152
Jesus:
baptism 154–55
death 164–74
fasting 155
healing 157–58, 185
humanity 147, 153
incarnation 147, 153–61, 176–78,
194, 196
miracles 157–58
and new community 181–85
resurrection 174–76
sexual standard 159
spirituality 103
suffering 177
teachings 156–58, 161
temptation 155–56
virgin birth 148–49
and women 159–61
Joan of Arc 141
John the Baptist 154, 165
Joseph (husband of Mary) 146
Joseph of Arimathea 174
Judas Iscariot 167–68

Judeo-Christian tradition, as anti-
    body 193
justice 34–35, 41, 46, 142, 164, 173

Kafka, Franz 163–64
Kilbourne, Jean 18
Kilbourne, Jill 44
King, Billy Jean 86
King, Carole 58
kingdom of God 157, 158, 166,
    185–86
kinship 73–74, 118, 119
kneeling 183
Kurzweil, Ray 96

laying on of hands 184, 185
Leary, Timothy 97
Leiss, William 140
lesbianism 55–56
Lewis, C. S. 129
lifestyle 119
liposuction 20
Loncar, Mladen 108
loneliness 188, 192
Lopez, Jennifer 19
love 115

Madonna and Child 16, 17, 149
Madonna (pop star) 17, 37
Mariology 148
marriage 61–62, 71–72, 134, 149–50,
    152
Martha 159
Mary of Bethany 159
Mary Magdalene 159, 172, 175, 197
Mary of Nazareth 145–49, 153, 154,
    161, 172
    perpetual virginity 148–49
    as symbol of sexual renunciation
        152–53
Mary of Oignies 62

masculinization 110–11
Maslow, Abraham 93
matriarchy 99
meaning 180–81
media 19, 24, 40, 44–45, 46, 150
menstruation 37–38, 70–71, 98, 110
Merchant, Natalie 116
middle management 88
Milton, John 129
miracles of Jesus 157–58
miscarriages 76
Miss America constestants 19
mobility 118
modesty 141
monastic societies 187
More, Thomas 142
Mother Teresa 115
motherhood 17, 18, 70, 74, 75, 100,
    138, 148, 152
music videos 40
mutilation. See self-injury
mutuality 150

nanobots 96
narcissism 46
narratives 180
natural birth 75–76
natural family planning methods 72
necrotechnology 98
need 27–28
neighborhood 187
neurotheology 94–95
new community 165–66, 178,
    181–85, 186–88
new creation 147
Norris, Kathleen 179, 187
nurture 88
Nylen, Bob 95

"one flesh" 134
order 142
Origen 152

PMS 97
Paglia, Camille 11, 65, 102
pain 112–13, 117
Parker, Dorothy 21
Passover 165–66, 176
patriarchy 98–99
penance 62
perpetual virginity 151, 153
personhood 70
Pilate 169, 175
place 118, 119, 129, 181, 190
Plato 60–61, 63
Platonism 152
pleasure 27, 117
politics of difference 88
pornography 44, 109, 150
Post, Emily 121
postmodernism 181
power 89, 91, 98–99, 138
powerlessness 82, 86, 99, 102, 103,
   106, 118, 158
prayer 95
prayer meetings 183
pregnancy 70–72
presence, physical and emotional 116
Princess Diana 49
private and public spheres 68–69
procreation 70, 71
prostitution 105–6
Prozac 97
Puritans 149

race 16, 63
Rahab 146
rape 107–8, 118
Ratushinskaya, Irina 143
reconciliation 185
recreation 144, 145
redemption 49, 114, 124–25, 142,
   144–45, 158, 178
religion 93

Renoir, Auguste 36
reproduction 65, 70–71, 76, 84, 106,
   110
reproductive technologies 76–77
restaurant meals 190
resurrection 182
Rich, Adrienne 139
rituals 183–84
Roberts, Julia 45
Rubens 36
Ruth 145

Sabbath keeping 183
Sanhedrin 168, 175
Satan 155
Sayers, Dorothy 84
Scarry, Elaine 113, 171
science 139–40
self 57, 59, 191
   vs. body 20, 30–31, 52, 78, 82, 90
   in constant flux 119
   disconnect from community 180
   inner and outer 52
   unencumbered 16, 90, 191
   wandering 119
   see also body-self; identity
self-actualization 15, 51, 93, 156
self-consciousness 191
self-esteem 44, 89–90, 92
self-help 164, 194
self-improvement 92
self-injury 49–51, 117
self-inventory 90
sensuality 195
Serafem 97
serpent 136, 138
sex 30, 38–39, 116, 151–52
   disconnected from marriage 71–72
   without boundaries 150
Sex and the City (television series) 25,
   151

sex trafficking 105–6, 109
sexual abstinence 149
sexual addiction 180
sexual assault 40
sexual harassment 39
sexual orientation 56
sexual prowess 159
sexuality 26, 40–41, 59, 130, 134,
    139, 195
    as socially situated 179–80
    spiritual aspects 73
    and technology 72
    and virginity of Mary 148
shalom 129, 161
shame 164, 170, 172, 174, 177, 180
sickness 114
silicon implants 20
sin 173
singleness 150
social order 85
Sojourner Truth 43
Song of Songs 42
Southern belles 17–18
space 132, 192
spas 21
Spears, Britney 40
speech 131
spirit, and body 57, 96
spiritual needs 28
spirituality:
    as anti-body 9–10, 57, 79, 82, 153,
        194
    and consumerism 93–95
    power of 89
Spretnak, Charlene 81, 98
stalking 39–40
Stoicism 152
stories 180–81
strength 117
Strong, Marilee 50

subordination 16, 73, 107, 109, 138,
    174
suburban America 189
suffering 62, 106, 114, 115, 118, 120,
    158, 160
surgery 164
surrogacy 76

Tamar 145
taste 119
tattooing 49, 51
Taylor, Charles 26, 64
technology 27, 52, 139–40, 188
    and community 190
    as destroying women 98
    as escape from body 96–97
    and reproduction 76–78
    and sexuality 72
Tertullian 152
Thomas 176
Tiegs, Cheryl 76
time 132
touch 115–16
Touch Research Institute of Miami
    115
transcendence 13, 58, 63–65, 66, 70,
    74, 78, 124
transcendent beauty 34–35, 41
trauma 112
Trible, Phyllis 128
true beauty 142, 164, 173
truth 46
Turlington, Christy 93
"tyranny of pregnancy" 70

ugly 42
"unclean" 158
utopia 142

Vagina Monologues, The 38
Vanzant, Iyanla 90

Vashti, Queen 36
Vedas 95
victimization 107
Victorian America 110
village 188
violence 109
Virgin Suicides, The (film) 93
virginity 152
virtue 34–35, 41
"*Vogue* factor" 46
Volf, Miroslav 59
vulnerability 109, 123

"Wal-Mart effect" 119
Waldrop, Christiana 95
wedding ceremony 36
Weil, Andrew 97
Weil, Simone 113, 114, 171, 173
Western art 36
western expansion 107, 110
western philosophy 60–62, 63
Wolf, Naomi 21, 22, 24
womanhood 43, 58, 70

womb, earlier too 24, 26, 59, 147, 154
women:
    cultural expectations 110–11
    as disciples of Jesus 159
    in home 65–67
    as instruments of grace 175
    as objects of consumption 17
    vulnerability 106–11
women's magazines 19
women's sports 111
Word of God 181, 182, 194
Wordsworth, William 42
work 68–69, 188, 195
    physical 189
    specialization of 119
World Trade Center attacks 122–23
worship 182–84
Wurtzel, Elizabeth 13

Xena (television series) 99

youth culture 48